More Advance Praise for *The Language of the Game*:

"Laurent Dubois weaves together fantastic stories and eloquent insights from the game's poets to form a beautiful, communal love letter to football. *The Language of the Game* offers fresh awe and understanding for any fan and manages to put into words just what is so bafflingly magical about the act of kicking a ball."

—Gwendolyn Oxenham, author of *Under the Lights and In the Dark*

THE LANGUAGE
OF THE GAME

THE LANGUAGE
OF THE GAME

How to Understand Soccer

LAURENT DUBOIS

BASIC BOOKS
New York

Basic Books
Hachette Book Group
1290 Avenue of the Americas, New York, NY 10104
www.basicbooks.com

Printed in the United States of America

First Edition: March 2018

Published by Basic Books, an imprint of Perseus Books, LLC, a subsidiary of Hachette Book Group, Inc.

The publisher is not responsible for websites (or their content) that are not owned by the publisher.

Print book interior design by Jeff Williams.

The Library of Congress has cataloged the hardcover edition as follows:
Names: Dubois, Laurent, 1971 author.
Title: The language of the game : how to understand soccer / Laurent Dubois.
Description: First Edition. | New York : Basic Books, [2018] | Includes bibliographical references and index.
Identifiers: LCCN 2017044787 (print) | LCCN 2017050879 (ebook) | ISBN 9780465094493 (ebook) | ISBN 9780465094486 (hardcover)
Subjects: LCSH: Soccer. | Soccer—Handbooks, manuals, etc.
Classification: LCC GV943 (ebook) | LCC GV943 .D87 2018 (print) | DDC 796.334—dc23
LC record available at https://lccn.loc.gov/2017044787

ISBNs: 978-0-465-09448-6 (hardcover), 978-0-465-09449-3 (ebook)

LSC-C

10 9 8 7 6 5 4 3 2 1

*To all those who love soccer
and to those who don't
but love someone who does*

CONTENTS

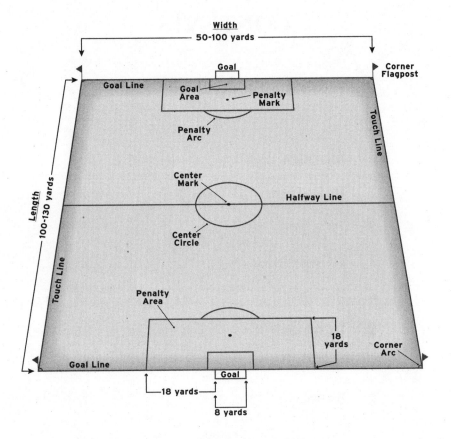

THE PITCH

INTRODUCTION

What is soccer?

It is a game you play on a rectangle of ground bracketed by two goals, one at either end. That shape is everywhere. Fly into almost any city in the world and look down, and you will see it—probably with people running back and forth, whether it is morning, midday, or night.

Many other soccer games are played in improvised spaces: a bit of grass in a park in Brooklyn or Rome, a courtyard in a housing project, a stretch of rocky dirt in a shantytown in Buenos Aires or Kinshasa, a rooftop in Tokyo, a black sand beach at the end of the road in Grand'Rivière, Martinique.

Soccer is possibility. In Chile there is an expression, *rayando la cancha*, which means "marking the field." It is what you do to transform a place into a soccer pitch, an action so common in Chile that the expression can be used to describe any kind of beginning.[1]

All you need is a ball. If you don't have one, you can make one. And even if you don't have one, you can play. That is what a group of boys do in the film *Timbuktu*, by Mauritanian director Abderrahmane Sissako, when the Islamist group that has taken over their town bans the sport and takes away their ball. In one of the most beautiful sequences I have seen in any film, the boys play the game anyway. They dribble and tackle. Take a penalty kick. Score a goal. Celebrate.

The ball is unnecessary, in the end, because soccer, more than anything, is an idea.

Soccer is life. In her account of traveling the world looking for pickup soccer games to join, former US collegiate soccer star and filmmaker Gwendolyn Oxenham writes of visiting a park in Rio de Janeiro. There, waiters gather after their restaurants close. They start playing at midnight and often keep going until dawn, delighting in the movement and creativity that defines Brazilian *futebol*. "I wash the dishes, I sweep the floors, I put the chairs up on the table," one player tells her, "and then I come here to play, to live." Oxenham understands. "For as long as I can remember," she writes, "*futebol* has been how I come all the way alive."[2]

Soccer comes from a specific place and time: the schools and universities of nineteenth-century Great Britain. The Laws of the Game, which still govern how soccer is played, were first set down in 1863. Because of the country's dominant global presence—not only through the British Empire but also through the British merchants and companies based outside the colonies—the game was soon on the move. It spread quickly. By the end of the nineteenth century, it was being played in Europe, Latin America, Southeast Asia, and throughout much of Africa, even in areas outside the British Empire's sphere of influence. The game has shown a remarkable capacity to flourish nearly everywhere it has taken root. Played in Senegal, it seems as completely Senegalese as any other form of local culture. Soccer is absolutely German. It is absolutely Argentinean. It is absolutely Haitian. And, of course, it is perhaps above all absolutely Brazilian. In fact, the English often have to remind the rest of us that they were the ones who invented it. As perpetually beleaguered English fans know, at least when it comes to global competition, having invented the game hasn't given them much of an advantage.

There are good reasons for soccer's universal appeal. It is a simple game, easy to learn and grasp. A few instructions, a finger pointed at the goal, and off you go. It is democratic in this sense, and also in the way that it accommodates all kinds of body shapes and sizes. In fact many great soccer players are of slight or short physique. "I love the way that small men can destroy big men," writes the novelist Nick Hornby, an ardent fan of the English club Arsenal. "Strength and intelligence have to combine" to make a great player.[3]

There are a surprising number of small goalies, for instance. Their ability to see and move, and the size of their personalities, is more important than their physical size. If you put Lionel Messi, often considered the best forward in the world, in a suit, he'd look at home in a cubicle in some office park working as an accountant. One of the greatest strikers of all time, the Brazilian Manuel Francisco dos Santos, known as Garrincha, had bowed legs—an inheritance from disease and hunger suffered in his youth. As a result, he moved, and dribbled, in an unusual way. That was part of his brilliance, enabling him to constantly outsmart defenders. In his autobiography, the great Argentinean player Diego Maradona recalls how the president of the Italian soccer club Juventus once declared that with his physique he'd never go anywhere in the sport. "Football is so beautiful," Maradona writes, "so unlike anything else, that it finds a way to fit everyone in. Even dwarves like me."[4]

There is one major check on this openness to diverse body types. Soccer's global institutions, along with the soccer industry and media, are dominated by men. Sexism shapes the practice and representation of soccer everywhere, and in turn soccer's gender divisions often play into and confirm stereotypes. Women's soccer struggles to gain equal recognition and financial support. The policies and practices that have excluded women depend on the idea that soccer is fundamentally male and that women are interlopers, or at least newcomers, in the sport.

This is an illusion. In fact, women have played soccer as long as men. In the early twentieth century, women's soccer was hugely successful in England, drawing massive crowds to stadiums. Then, in 1921, the English Football Association banned women from using its fields and stadiums, essentially driving women's soccer underground. There were similar decisions made in other countries. But, in the face of concerted opposition, women never stopped playing. In 1970, the first Women's World Cup was organized independently in Italy. The next year, the Women's World Cup was played in Mexico City, in the Azteca stadium, where Brazil had famously won the men's World Cup the year before. Footage and photographs from the women's games show a packed stadium. The 1971 Women's World Cup has been almost totally forgotten, even though the crowd appears to have been larger than that at the 1999 Women's World Cup final at the Rose Bowl in Pasadena, California—usually cited as the women's soccer game that drew the largest live crowd in history. These are reminders, however, that soccer is—and has always been—a women's sport.

Soccer is a language, probably the most universal language on the planet. It is spoken more widely than English, Arabic, or Chinese and practiced more widely than any religion. In 1954, the French soccer journalist Jean Eskenazi wrote an essay on the "universality" of the game. It is, he declared, "the only denominator common to all people, the only universal Esperanto . . . a world language, whose grammar is unchanging from the North Pole to the Equator." Although mutually intelligible everywhere it is played, it is still delightfully varied, "spoken in each corner of the globe with a particular accent." The Swedish writer Fredrik Ekelund similarly calls the game the "Esperanto of the feet." The novelist Karl Ove Knausgaard, who wrote a book of letters about the 2014 men's World Cup with Ekelund, offers a vivid example of how this language works. Picked up once by a German truck driver while he was hitchhiking, Knausgaard found he had no common language with which to pass the time during the long ride. Then, he began saying the names of soccer players. He started with a Norwegian footballer, Rune Bratseth, and the German recognized him, "brightening up and repeating it several times." Knausgaard continues, "Then he said a name, so I said Ja! Ja!" These names, keys to a broader set of shared memories and experiences and feelings, were a thread of connection.[5]

Every soccer game is a story. But it is not easy to capture it in words. Why, wonders the Mexican novelist and journalist Juan Villoro, has there never been "a great football novel"? The answer, he suggests, may be that every game is already "its own epic, its own tragedy, its own comedy," all at once. The works of literature that do try to narrate soccer, including many remark-able short stories, often do so by piecing together fragments of story, attempting to capture the way moments on the pitch some-how condense the drama of life. Knausgaard imagines a piece of writing about just one game, one that would concentrate "on only these ninety minutes, chart all the incidents, all the moves, also all the names and not just follow them on the pitch but in life, their stories before the game, parents, grandparents, brothers and sisters, friends, what happened after the game, the follow-ing years, the career that finished, life in a satellite town outside some Colombian or Iranian city." In any given game, he suggests, is a whole world. The ninety minutes are "inexhaustible." Perhaps David Kilpatrick had the right idea when he decided he would write a short poem in response to every game in the 2014 men's World Cup, considering "each game itself a text to be read." He sat in front of his television, pen in hand, producing sixty-four poems, at turns humorous, tragic, elegiac.[6]

Soccer never stops. The clock never stops ticking, for any rea-son—there are no time-outs, no pauses. There is just halftime, and then a break before and between overtime periods, if they occur. The only concession to the fact that time may have been lost because of injury or intentional time wasting on the part of a team is the referee's right to add time to the end of the game, but it is almost never more than five minutes. Soccer time is very different from what we experience in basketball or American football—where the clock starts and stops constantly, making the actual time it takes to watch any game unpredictable—as well as from baseball, which has no clock at all. This is one of the de-fining features of the game. Although you never know what will happen in a soccer match, you can be sure about how long it will take: ninety minutes, usually a little more, or 120 if things go into overtime, and a little longer if there is a penalty kick shoot-out.

Soccer's rules have changed little since they were set down in the nineteenth century. It's true that a few people have offered intriguing alternatives to the way it is structured. In the 1960s Asger Jorn, a Danish Situationist artist inspired by Marxist ideas, decided there was no reason to limit soccer games to only two teams in perpetual opposition. Why not open things up a bit? He created "three-sided football," sometimes more pointedly called "Anarchist Football." It is played on a hexagon with three teams and three goals. There is no referee—no state to legislate what happens—and the game turns into a complex swirl of temporary alliances and understandings. Two teams can go against one, collaborating at least for a time, but also change tactics and friends as the situation warrants. And the winner of the game is not the team that scores the most goals, but the one that, through collaboration and alliance with other teams, manages to suffer the fewest goals against them. The game has a regular following in Europe, with matches organized in England and France, and a nascent set of leagues in the United States too.

For now, though, soccer remains a dialectic, never-ending struggle between two teams. "In a football match," the philosopher Jean-Paul Sartre writes—with delicious understatement— "everything is complicated by the presence of the opposite team." Imagine how wonderful it would be if there weren't any defense: so much easier to dribble a ball gracefully across the pitch, pass to your teammates, and score a beautiful goal. There also, of course, would be no drama—and therefore no point. It is the back-and-forth between offense and defense, which generations of players and coaches have tried to figure out how to control, that makes soccer beautifully unpredictable and therefore endlessly fascinating.[7]

Soccer is, as we often hear, the "beautiful game." What makes it so? A "beautiful play," writes literary theorist Hans Ulrich Gumbrecht, "is an epiphany of form" that happens through the "sudden, surprising convergence of several athletes' bodies" in a particular place, at a particular moment. Such moments are delightful precisely because they are unpredicted and unknown even for the "players who perform them, because they must be achieved against the unpredictable resistance of the other team's defense." The fact that such a play has to overcome intense and carefully deployed opposition, whose goal is to "destroy the emerging form and precipitate chaos," is what makes it feel like a kind of miracle. "There are few experiences," admits Gumbrecht, "that make my heart beat faster than a beautiful play." It is also evanescent, as is the feeling it produces. Although you can watch a replay of an amazing moment in soccer, that never really captures the epiphany and awe that accompany its first unfolding. That is one of the reasons we return again and again to the game, hoping to catch a glimpse of beauty that we never can predict, or even imagine, before it happens.[8]

Soccer is sensual. It is about the pleasure of watching athletes' bodies, their faces, their motion, admiring and commenting on their hairstyles and tattoos. When we talk and write about soccer, we evoke—more often unconsciously than consciously— its sensuality, its role as a source of pleasure. "The goal is soccer's orgasm," notes the Uruguayan writer Eduardo Galeano, probably the sport's most eloquent and poetic chronicler. The ball goes into the goal, inciting shouts of ecstatic joy. The sexual metaphor is, on one level, obvious: it is about male penetration. Yet what this metaphor actually means to those who play and those who watch is anything but simple. And goals, in any case, are very rare, a fleeting exception within the game. Soccer may be the most tantric of sports. Some of the greatest and most riveting games end o–o. Perhaps what is truly sensual about soccer is that it is about interplay, relationships, motion between people, all tied up with our deepest and most mysterious emotions.[9]

In soccer, there are simply no guarantees. A team can seem to be doing everything right—have a coach nicknamed "the Professor" who recruits the best players in the world, approach their training scientifically, mobilize the best doctors and studies, analyze and perfect tactics endlessly, bring in team psychologists, energize a devoted fan base in a beautiful stadium at the heart of a global capital—and still never quite live up to expectations. Even after all that, on a bad day, the team can seem like a collection of players who have no idea what they are doing on the pitch.

Soccer is corrupt. There is money to be made, and prestige to be had, being associated with the sport. Its governing institutions the world over have attracted people who are cynical and morally bankrupt, who have found ways to profit through backroom deals and payoffs between soccer federations and media conglomerates. Soccer is also, increasingly, a world of deep inequality. Most professional players, particularly women, are paid very little. Young players, notably those from Africa and Latin America, are often deeply exploited by unscrupulous youth academies, agents, and teams. The most visible players, those who make huge fortunes, are a tiny minority, though their success is a magnet for all others who put everything on the line to succeed.

The citizens of the global country that is soccer, fans and players, have little sway over the administrative and financial institutions that increasingly control the game. Those institutions trap us, in a way, because they know we will keep coming back, drawn by the sport we love. There are forms of resistance against the federations and leagues, and some efforts to create alternative structures for the game, freed from greed and corruption. Yet for now we largely surrender, perhaps unaware of our power and what we stand to lose if we don't ultimately find a way to keep control of the game.

Soccer is a good place for thinking. "You run but the ball is nowhere near you," writes Juan Villoro. "You stop, you do up your bootlaces, you shout things no one hears, you spit on the ground, you exchange a harsh look with an opposing player, you remember you forgot to lock the terrace door." In fact, he continues, for the "majority of the game"—and, by extension, the majority of a life in the sport—"the football player is no more than the *possibility of a footballer*," spending "long stretches in this strange state, being-nowhere-near-the-ball."[10]

Soccer is boring. Sometimes, more often than many of us will admit, you will watch a game and it is simply awful. The team is out of sync with itself, the referee is making bad calls, people are arguing stupidly, nothing is happening. The game stretches out, a desert devoid of interest. You wonder why you are wasting your time when you could be doing any number of more reasonable things—spending time with non–soccer loving family and friends, baking, learning to juggle or ride a unicycle, taking a stroll through the woods. And then, a surprise! A player suddenly awakens, moves, alights. You sit up. Is something beautiful or interesting going to happen? Too often, the moment passes. Often enough, though, the context changes, the feel changes, and suddenly the game becomes what it can be: beautiful and riveting. The interplay between the boring and the fascinating is, among many other things, what makes soccer so much like life.

Soccer is powerful. Whether in the form of an impromptu pickup game in a local park or a World Cup game watched by hundreds of millions across the globe, soccer can have something of the miraculous about it. It creates strong solidarities and produces memories—of exhilaration in victory or trauma in defeat—that sear themselves into our minds. Recalling his experiences playing on teams that brought together different ethnic groups in Zanzibar in the 1940s, one player explained what it meant to have Arabs, Africans, and migrants from the nearby Comoros islands all together: "You can't hate me while I'm playing with you in the same club. You love me because I'm playing with you. You learn to appreciate me like a broth " Multiplied exponentially, and across the globe, these types of experiences have made it so that ball games—soccer most of all—are now, as Gumbrecht writes, "the central sports fascination of our time—a fascination so existentially important for many of us that we have a hard time imagining our world without it."[11]

In the United States, soccer is suburban. On any given Saturday, minivans and SUVs crisscross the arteries of suburbs across the country, ferrying boys and girls to youth leagues, depositing them on the pitch, and leaving the soccer moms and dads on the sidelines to chat or yell at their confused kids about tactics and the importance of passing the ball. I was one of those kids, growing up in Bethesda, Maryland, a suburb of Washington, DC, in the 1970s. Like many other children, I loved soccer. My family had emigrated to the United States from Belgium, and we spoke French at home. Like other immigrant children, part of my job was to figure out and navigate American culture. On the field, I made friends—some of them immigrants like me. I remember the occasional victories that I celebrated wildly and also moments of peace on the field. After practice or a game, I would come home dusty, tired, and a little elated.

For most of the kids who play this way, including me, soccer is mainly a youthful pastime that gives way to informal play in amateur leagues or pickup games later in life. The best players to come out of these youth leagues can be recruited into selective club teams that offer higher-level training and more intense competition. The most talented go to college on athletic scholarships and, in some cases, are recruited to play in national training academies that feed the US national team.

The Bethesda Soccer Club, in the area where I grew up, was founded in 1979 to train talented local players and put them in competition with other high-level teams in the region. In 2017 alone, thirty-five players who had come through its program were heading off to play at colleges and universities on athletic scholarships. One member of the Bethesda Soccer Club was Lizandro Claros Saravia, who had arrived in the United States from El Salvador as a child in 2009. His immigration status had been unclear for much of his life. He had been categorized as a refugee, and though technically vulnerable to deportation, had been allowed to remain in the country with the understanding that he would make scheduled visits to Immigration and Customs Enforcement officials. Playing with Bethesda, he earned a scholarship to attend Louisburg College in North Carolina. However, in August 2017, he reported to Immigration and Customs Enforcement that he was planning to attend college and he was immediately arrested by officials operating under new guidelines from the Trump administration. He was deported a few days later. The move infuriated his former Bethesda teammates, who rallied with his family in front of the headquarters of the Department of Homeland Security. "We're disgusted with the government," one declared. "This is about so much more than soccer now," another explained. "We want our friend back."[12]

Soccer is an immigrant. It is Nadia Nadim, whose family fled Afghanistan when her father was killed by the Taliban. After a harrowing ride in the back of a truck across Europe she ended up in rural Denmark. Next door to the center for refugees where she grew up was a soccer training complex, with more green fields than she had ever seen before. As she and her friends watched the games from the nearby woods, they discovered something: there were soccer balls stuck in many of the trees, lobbed up there from errant passes. If you shook the trees, the balls fell down. Nadim and her friends, writes Oxenham, ran around the woods "shaking the trees, a fantastic gleeful scavenger hunt." They threw the newer balls back over the fence onto the fields, but Nadim kept several of the deflated, older ones, filled them with air, and every morning took the kids from the center and went out to the fields to play. They got good at juggling the balls: Nadim set a record of fifty-eight times one day. Her mother found her an old, used pair of cleats in a local store.

To soften their stiff leather, Nadim slept with them and soaked them in water. Nadim eventually worked up the courage to ask one of the Danish coaches next door if she could play too. The coach put the unknown player in as a defender, but during her first game she kept running up the field and scored three goals. Today, she is the star forward of the Danish national team, playing in international competitions for her country and professionally in the United States and England.[13]

Soccer is Joe Gaetjens, the Haitian who scored one of the most famous international goals in US soccer history. In 1950, the US Soccer Federation scrambled to put together a team to participate in the World Cup to be held that year in Brazil. The core of the team was players from St. Louis along with a star from Pennsylvania, Walter Bahr, but the US Federation felt the team needed a few additional players. Scouts found two recruits playing in professional clubs in Brooklyn. One, Joseph Andre Maca, had played professionally in Belgium before World War II, then joined the resistance to the German occupation and, after US troops liberated his country, migrated to New York. There he had found a home on a team called Brooklyn Hispano. The local rival team, Brookhattan, included Gaetjens, whose Belgian father lived in Haiti and who was studying accounting part-time at Columbia University, washing dishes, and playing soccer as often as he could. He had played professionally and on the national team in Haiti before coming to the United States. At the time, Fédération Internationale de Football Association (FIFA) regulations concerning the nationality of players were relatively flexible. As long as a player declared they intended to become a US citizen, they could play on the US team. Maca and Gaetjens both declared they wanted to be Americans and were immediately sent to Brazil to play for the United States. They faced off against England, one of the greatest teams in the world, in the Brazilian town of Belo Horizonte. In what remains the greatest soccer upset in US history, they defeated the kings of soccer 1–0. The winning goal was a header scored by Gaetjens. He was carried off the pitch on the shoulders of jubilant Brazilian fans.[14]

Almost seven decades later, the US men's national team features the Haitian American Jozy Altidore, who grew up in New Jersey. He plays alongside Clint Dempsey, who grew up in Nacogdoches, Texas, playing with many Mexican and Mexican American teammates at school and in a local adult league, as well as the young star Christian Pulisic, who grew up in Hershey, Pennsylvania, but moved to Germany as a teenager to train in a soccer academy there. At the 2014 men's World Cup, the German Jurgen Klinnsmann coached the US team, and in searching for talent he drew upon the unique US diaspora that results from a global network of military bases. He recruited five players to the team who were the children of African American servicemen stationed in Germany, and who had therefore been trained in that country's excellent soccer academy system. It was these players, along with Dempsey, who scored all the goals for the team during their run in the 2014 tournament. Three years later, the US failed to qualify for the 2018 men's World Cup, a devastating setback that has the US Soccer Federation, and many fans, reeling and wondering how and why this has happened, and what it portends for the future of the sport in the country.[15]

Soccer is still struggling to find its place in US sporting culture. It seems to be always arriving yet never fully at home. This is so even after decades of exponential growth in soccer, which might just be played recreationally today by more people than any other sport in the US.

There is a persistent yearning among many who love the game to earn soccer the same media attention—and investment—as American football, basketball, and baseball. People have tried to do this for decades. In the 1970s, a group of investors created the North American Soccer League with the goal of expanding professional soccer in this country. The most remarkable team in the league was the New York Cosmos, which recruited foreign stars such as Pelé and Franz Beckenbauer and for a time filled Giants Stadium for league games and exhibition matches. The Cosmos folded in 1985, and the story of the team's rise and fall is told in the 2006 documentary *Once in a Lifetime*. The film highlights the fact that money, big stadiums, and foreign stars—a recipe still being pursued by Major League Soccer (MLS), the premier professional men's league in the United States, today— still may not be enough to guarantee soccer a place in US mainstream sports culture. Over the past decade, professional soccer has expanded steadily in this country, with certain MLS teams— notably in Portland and Seattle—garnering massive and enthusiastic fan bases that would be the envy of many teams in Europe or Latin America. The United States is also one of the centers of professional women's soccer, with the National Women's Soccer League (NWSL) hosting some of the best players from around the world and building up a good fan base in many parts of the country.[16]

Many American fans believe that the United States needs soccer, now more than ever. But what kind of soccer do we want?

The fact that US soccer culture has in many ways lived, and thrived, on the margins of mainstream sports is part of what has made it a vector for different ways of thinking about what this country is and can be, and what role sports can play in that. Megan Rapinoe, a star of the women's national team, was the first white professional athlete in any sport in the United States to kneel during the national anthem in solidarity with NFL quarterback Colin Kaepernick's protest against racism and police violence. She did so not during a professional game but an international one, where she was playing as a representative of the United States—making the protest in some sense even stronger. She was criticized by the US Soccer Federation for doing so, and they passed a rule outlawing such protests in the future. Yet here the federation is probably at odds with the political currents shaping the culture of soccer fandom in the United States. In the past few years, fans of MLS teams have waved "Refugees Welcome" banners, inspired by teams that did so in Germany, and there are always some rainbow flags in the stands, too, announcing support for LGBT rights. Some supporters of the US national teams sometimes fly a boldly modified US flag, where the red and white stripes are replaced by the colors of the rainbow. And there is also an explicit effort to celebrate the global quality of US soccer. In both the MLS and the NWSL, fans welcome players from around the world playing on US teams by flying their national flags, so that alongside the pitch, side by side, are the colors of the United States, Colombia, Ghana, Mexico. Most soccer lovers in the United States, meanwhile, religiously watch the games of the professional European leagues in England, Germany, and Spain. They proudly wear the jerseys of European professional teams like Manchester City, Bayern Munich, and Barcelona. These teams are themselves collectives of athletes from all over the world—Senegalese and Spanish, Portuguese and Brazilian, Bosnian and Belgian, Russian and Japanese, with an occasional American player too—playing together. In the United States, soccer is a way of feeling connected to many places at once and offers different ways of imagining ourselves within the world.[17]

My own life as soccer fan is an example of this. I am a devoted fan of the French national team. Though I grew up speaking French and have lived in the country, this is not about nationality. It is, rather, a result of the symbolism I have found embodied in the French team. My work as a historian has focused on how France's colonial history, particularly in the Caribbean, has shaped its present. In the summer of 1998, I had just finished my dissertation, and as I watched that year's men's World Cup felt as if everything I was arguing about the presence of the colonial past was playing out, in riveting and incontrovertible fashion, on the soccer pitch. A French team made up of players with backgrounds from all over the world—Algeria, Armenia, Guadeloupe, New Caledonia—won the World Cup for France for the first time, defeating Brazil in the final game in Paris. The country erupted in days of celebration that commentators could only compare to the liberation of Paris in 1944. In the next years, I became particularly taken by the story of the defender Lilian Thuram. Born in Guadeloupe, he had grown up in a housing project south of Paris. After becoming a national icon thanks to his performance in the 1998 World Cup, he began to speak out politically on behalf of marginalized communities in France, eloquently evoking the histories of slavery and immigration.

I had watched France win in 1998 from afar, so when the team went on a surprising run in the 2006 men's World Cup—once again led by Thuram and Zinedine Zidane—I flew to Paris so I could celebrate their second World Cup victory in style. Instead, I watched as Zidane head-butted an Italian player, Marco Materazzi, and was sent off the field. France was defeated in penalty kicks. The defeat hit me so hard that I wrote an entire book: *Soccer Empire*, published in 2010, tells the story of Thuram's life and activism, Zidane's head-butt and what it meant, and more broadly how soccer has shaped society, and society has shaped soccer, in France and its empire throughout the twentieth century.

In 2010, I flew to South Africa for the men's World Cup, one of the many US fans who made up the largest contingent of foreigners to travel to the tournament. Before leaving Durham, I'd watched the US pull out an amazing last-minute victory against Algeria at my favorite pub, Dain's Place, leaping up and hugging a sweaty mass of friends and strangers in celebration. I arrived' in Johannesburg in time to watch Ghana defeat the US, eliminating them from the competition. I knew what I had to do, of course: along with seemingly everyone else, I became a Ghana fan, bought a scarf with the national flag on it, and went to watch the team play Uruguay in the Soccer City stadium. What I witnessed there was one of the most heartrending matches in World Cup history, ending in Ghana's defeat in penalty kicks.

I was lucky to be able to process that night with the other members of what we dubbed our roving World Cup seminar— Paul Gilroy, Achille Mbembe, Sarah Nuttall, Vron Ware,—all scholars who, like me, share a passion for understanding the cultures of soccer. During those days in South Africa, we practiced our vuvuzela skills together, enjoyed the late-night suppers Achille prepared for us after matches, and talked constantly about what soccer is and could be. I took some satisfaction in watching the Netherlands defeat Uruguay in Cape Town a few days later, and I finally made the right choice by rooting for Spain in the final game. Before it began, I watched as Nelson Mandela was driven out on the pitch and waved at us, an event that on its own would have been life changing. Yet it was later, watching Andrés Iniesta score for Spain, just in front of where I sat in the stadium, and then standing around in a dazed glow as the team celebrated, I understood that—for an instant—I was at the center of the world.

Over the past decade, soccer has been increasingly woven into my life as a writer and teacher. At Duke University, where I teach, I developed a class called Soccer Politics, where I've explored the history and topics I write about in this book, always learning as much from the insights and research of my students as I teach them. While my book *Soccer Empire* was a love letter to the French team, this book is my love letter to soccer. It is a way of sharing what draws me to the sport: that it seems to me to be a vital—and increasingly necessary—place for imagining different kinds of futures for ourselves, our community, and our world.

Soccer is sanctuary. On November 13, 2015, the Stade de France—where France had won the World Cup in 1998—was one of the targets of a string of terrorist attacks in Paris. There were sixty-five thousand people in the stadium watching a game between France and Germany, including the French president François Hollande. The plan was for three suicide bombers to enter the stadium and set off their bombs in the stands at the same time that gunmen attacked the Bataclan nightclub and other targets elsewhere in Paris. Fifteen minutes into the game, one of the attackers was entering through a tunnel into the stadium when a security guard frisking him noticed he was carrying explosives. The man backed away and set off the bomb in the tunnel. The sound echoed through the stadium, and for a moment the French player Patrice Evra, who was dribbling with the ball, stopped. Yet it wasn't clear what the sound was—it sounded distant; it could have been a firework or a flare. And so he kept playing, and the crowd kept watching, unaware of what was happening outside the stadium.[18]

The security team of the Stade de France decided it was best not to stop the game, concerned about the panic that this would cause and unsure whether additional attackers were waiting outside to target exiting fans. The president was quietly escorted out, but the players weren't told what was going on. Two of those playing that night would later find out they had relatives who were victims of the attacks. It was only near the end of the second half of the game that news of what had happened elsewhere in the city spread into the stadium. The players finished the ninety minutes and went into their locker rooms, and an announcement was made asking fans to stay in the stadium for a while so that security could organize an orderly exit. The stands didn't feel safe, however, and so tens of thousands walked down onto the pitch, finding a sense of security out on the grass, talking quietly, together. When they ultimately left the stadium, some fans burst into the national anthem, La Marseillaise, as they walked through the tunnels and out into the city. The stadium had remained, through it all, a kind of refuge.

Soccer is about much more than winning. If it weren't, it is unlikely so many of us would follow it so closely and passionately. There has been a strong tradition among players, journalists, coaches, and fans of emphasizing that what is truly important about this game is the beauty it creates, the moments of communion and joy it generates not because of its outcome but because of the intricacies of the process of getting there. Victories are wonderful, but the greatest victories—a World Cup or a Champions League trophy, for instance—are incredibly rare. In every tournament, every team but one ends up losing at some point along the way. Defeat and loss are fundamental to the experience of following the game. And the games, in any case, are endless: win one and soon you'll lose one, lose one and maybe you'll win one next time. What would be the point of all of this, if the game were not ultimately the source of something beautiful, of something joyous and meaningful?

Soccer is, most of all, human. If, as Franklin Foer wrote memorably, "soccer explains the world," it is also true that the world explains soccer. The currents that connect the sport with the human life that surrounds it, and infuses it with meaning, go both ways. Given that it is probably the most widely shared form of culture on the planet, soccer must have something to teach us about being human. My hope here is that better knowing the sport—its history, its form, its mythologies, its spiral of stories—will make watching it a more beautiful, pleasurable, and rich experience. This book, then, is an offering to soccer, to all that it gives us. It is an invitation to speak its language and to make of it what you will.[19]

1

THE GOALKEEPER

"**I** was twelve when I turned my back on you," Gianluigi Buffon —one of the great goalkeepers of all time—wrote in a 2016 love letter addressed to his goal. As a child growing up in Italy, Buffon had learned that the glory of the game was in attacking the goal, trying to score against it. But then he made a fateful decision, going with his "heart" and "instinct." He put behind him his past as a regular player in order to guarantee the goal "a secure future." It was, he admits, a strange choice, a kind of curse. "The day I stopped looking at you in the face is also the day that I started to love you," Buffon writes. "To protect you. To be your first and last line of defense."[1]

It was not that he never looked at the goal. It was just that, when he did, it was because he had failed to defend it and thus had to fish the ball out of the back of the net. He had to promise the goal "that I would do everything not to see your face." After all, he writes, it was "painful every time I did, turning around and realizing I had disappointed you. Again. And again." This only deepened the "vow" that defines his life as a player: to protect the goal and act as "a shield" against all its enemies, even if that means putting its welfare above his own. Buffon presents himself as the gallant hero in a tragic, if slightly absurd, romance. "We have always been opposites yet we are complementary, like the sun and the moon. Forced to live side by side without being able to touch. Teammates for life, a life in which we are denied all contact." Buffon ends his letter articulating his commitment. "I was twelve when I turned my back on my goal. And I will keep doing it as long as my legs, my head and my heart will allow."

The goalie, writes philosopher Edward Winters, is often seen as "the guardian of honor. . . . The keeper's job is to frustrate." Goalies are there to stop the goals, to prevent the celebration. From the perspective of the opposing team and its fans, and maybe from the perspective of soccer itself, goalkeepers can be seen as the enemy of joy, the very antithesis of the game. Even Francis Hodgson, an amateur goalie who has written a spirited defense of the position, admits that the player is there precisely to "prevent the very thing that everybody present wants to occur. . . . At root, he is an anti-footballer. By being devoted to the prevention of goals he is set against the core of football." In his history of the goalie, Jonathan Wilson offers an even more dramatic depiction. Soccer is rooted in old, sacred traditions in which games were part of fertility rites and harvest festivals, with the scoring of a goal auguring well for births and crops. Therefore, the goalkeeper is not just a "symbolic prophylactic" but "the destroyer of harvests, the bringer of famine."[2]

What, then, goes on in the mind of the goalie? Buffon explains his existence by depicting himself as a tragic, chivalric hero. He stops players from scoring because he loves the goal, so much so that he is willing to spend his life next to it while making the ultimate sacrifice: turning his back, never looking, protecting it because that is the only way to truly show his love. Perhaps what stands out most about Buffon's letter, though, is the loneliness it describes. This is the soulful truth of the position. Isolated from the game, the goalie hears the crowd roar behind him. The flowing pattern of the game unfolds ahead, the action going on—at least if he is lucky enough to have a good team—far in the distance, past the halfway line. Juan Villoro notes that as "the great loner" in the world of soccer, the goalie has also "more time than anyone to reflect." That is why, he writes, "thinkers and eccentrics gravitate to the position. . . . All keepers know the rich interior life their profession entails." The goalie must, Villoro suggests, learn to be particularly philosophical, living out a kind of "symposia" on the turf.[3]

Goalies mostly patrol what is known as the penalty box. It is an area around the goal, marked off by lines. Forty-four yards across and eighteen yards deep, the penalty box is slightly larger than a basketball court. Within it, the goalie can use her hands to catch and pick up the ball, and penalties committed within the box lead to a direct penalty kick on goal. The two penalty boxes at each end make up a significant part of the soccer pitch. The size of the field varies; the Laws of the Game stipulate it can be anywhere between 100 and 130 yards long and between 50 and 100 yards across, though the range is smaller for international matches. Most pitches in stadiums are around 100 yards long and 60 yards across. Still, in a game defined by constant movement of players up and down the pitch, the goalie is the most immobile, only rarely venturing outside the borders of the penalty box and almost never as far as the middle of the pitch. He spends his time in front of goal that, compared to him, is frighteningly large, usually twenty-four feet across and eight feet high. In front of the vast, yawning goal, the goalie faces an onrushing team. He can only cover the space by making just the right moves at just the right time.[4]

I was the goalie for my suburban American youth team, and there was a beautiful kind of peace to the role. I watched, from a quiet distance, as the pattern of the game played out in front of me, at ease when the ball was far off, gradually more and more alert as it approached. Then, of course, my defenders would screw up, the ball would come streaking toward me, and, in a gesture of complete irrationality and abandon, I would throw myself in its path. Then, often enough, after all that, as my face smashed into the dirt, the ball went into the net anyway. And it was all my fault.

I was spared this experience much of the time only because an Icelandic wunderkind named Yakko had miraculously descended into the precincts of Bethesda, and, even more incredibly, ended up on our second-rate team. My job mostly consisted of watching him leave a trail of opposing players lying on the ground; he would score one goal after another, then run back to us, all smiles and high-fiving me as if I had contributed somehow by standing inert in goal.

I do remember well, though, the brief period when my Bolivian coach (who, he always reminded us, had once "played with Pelé") decided I should be a striker. I'd apparently dribbled better than anyone (save Yakko) during a drill. Plus, I was Belgian, which I think he hoped conferred on me some special skill in the midst of the desert of talent that was late 1970s suburban Maryland. My career as a striker was relatively short, but I do recall the incredible freedom I felt, the lightness of trying to score rather than attempting to stop others from doing so. It was sometimes my fault if we didn't win. But it was never my fault if we lost, the way it was when I was a goalie.

Years later, in 2010, I was in South Africa for the men's World Cup and watched a game alongside the retired Cameroonian goalie Joseph-Antoine Bell. For years, he played for Olympique de Marseille, where he became a favorite of many of the team's fans of immigrant background, and he also played internationally for Cameroon. That night, we watched an exciting German team trounce England, 4–1, giving Bell ample opportunity to comment on the failures of the English goalie David James. After one goal, Bell noted that if James had just stayed in position, closing down the angles of the onrushing German forward, he would have blocked the ball. Instead, James had tried for a more dramatic save and in the process left part of the goal unguarded. "The problem is that human beings are programmed to try and be heroes," Bell told me with a smiling wisdom that I sensed had been earned through many mistakes. For goalies, he went on, this is dangerous, because in many cases the dramatic diving save is less effective than just moving incrementally to be in the right place at all times. The latter, of course, is much less likely to be noticed and celebrated. But to be a real hero as a goalie, Bell suggested, may mean not being recognized as such.[5]

Winters notes that the most celebrated move for a goalie is "the fingertip save," when a goalie stretches out, flying, and manages to keep the ball out of the net with the very tips of his extended fingers. "The fingertip save," Winters writes, "is the utmost frustration, as it prevents the anticipated climax of the game: a spectacular goal." And yet, like a goal, it "makes the game more beautiful." The goalie, Winters notes, has perhaps the most "dangerous job" on the field, since the goalie places his body in the way of the "raw, unbridled ambition of the goal-hungry striker who slides in stretching his foot out, studs first." There is some consolation in the fact that goalies are, among all the players, the most likely to talk with their team's fans, who traditionally gather behind the goal on one end of the field. When the goalie is in front of his team's supporters, he will sometimes engage in friendly banter with them, and as a result "there grows an unparalleled affection between the keeper and the fans." On the other hand, of course, when the goalie is positioned in front of opposing fans, he is more vulnerable than any other player to a constant barrage of insults, not to mention the occasional bottle or rock or coin thrown from the stands.[6]

The loneliness of the goalie is perhaps most poignantly captured in an anecdote from Christmas 1937. About half an hour into a game between the English teams Charlton Athletic and Chelsea, a fog descended onto the pitch so thick that it was impossible to keep playing. The two managers walked onto the field and told their players the game would have to be abandoned, and the crowd of forty thousand dispersed. The goalie for Charlton, Sam Bartram, couldn't see any of it through the fog. He stayed on the pitch. As he later recounted, while he stood there alone, he thought "smugly" that his team must be giving Chelsea "quite the hammer" at the other end of the field. But clearly they had not scored, for no players were coming back to the halfway line to restart the game. "Time passed, and I made several advances towards the edge of the penalty area, peering through the murk," he recalled. "Still I could see nothing. The Chelsea defense was clearly being run off its feet. After a long time a figure loomed out of the curtain of fog in front of me. It was a policeman, and he gaped at me incredulously. 'What on earth are you doing here?' he gasped. 'The game was stopped a quarter of an hour ago. The field's completely empty.'" When Bartram finally got to the dressing room, the rest of his team, "already out of the bath, were convulsed with laughter."[7]

The policeman's question—"What on earth are you doing here?"—has gone through many goalies' heads at one time or another, as they stand alone in the box, wondering what is to come from out of the fog of the game. Yet the goalie is vitally important to any team: the last line of defense, often the only hope for a team at those moments when everything might go wrong. Never at the center of the pitch, the goalie is still often at the center of the most pivotal moments of the game. At her best, of course, the goalie can actually form the root of a team, serving as the foundation for plays, passing the ball forward in the hope that others will score, setting the game in motion again and again, hectoring and encouraging the players who, unlike her, get to streak forward toward the other end of the pitch. That is why the most important quality of a goalie is not her physical size, but the size of her personality, her ability to inspire confidence and strength in her teammates, even when they have their backs turned, as they often do, focused entirely on the other goal far across the pitch.

The solitary goalkeeper was a relatively late development in the game. In the old English folk games that helped inspire modern soccer, hundreds of villagers divided into two teams and tried to get the ball to one goal or another—sometimes separated by miles. In these messy, chaotic events there could be lots of goalies, often a string of younger kids, not tough enough to survive the brutal fray but a little helpful if they lined up in a last-ditch effort to stop the onrushing attackers.[8]

Because so many different styles of ball games had developed, schools and universities in England decided in the mid-nineteenth century to come up with shared sets of rules to make it easier to play against each other. This was not always easy, so, at what turned out to be an epochal meeting in 1863, a group of captains from various teams in and around London met at London's Freemasons' Tavern. They were alumni of different schools and universities, with different traditions of play, but they managed to hammer out a shared set of rules. They called them, ponderously and ambitiously, the Laws of the Game. And they went further, deciding to create an organization: the English Football Association, which would become the model for the associations that now exist in every country in the world and a few places that aren't countries too.[9]

Because the rules of the game spread outward from England, these original "laws" established the most important features of soccer as it is still played today. The most important of these laws was that players were not allowed to use their hands or carry the ball. This set the game apart from what came to be known as rugby, as well as from Gaelic football, Australian Rules football, and American football. The game was officially known as association football, because it was governed by the rules of the Football Association. This gave rise to the term "soccer," a colloquialism

probably developed by English university students, who shortened "association" to "soc-er." That term became standard in the
United States because it distinguished the sport from American
football, but it was also still used regularly in England as late as
the 1960s. In most of the world, the game is known through local
versions of the word "football"—*fútbol* in Spanish, *futebol* in Portuguese, *fußball* in German.[10]

The game conquered the world more rapidly than any other
cultural form in human history. By the late nineteenth century,
it was being played all over the world, with clubs and competitions proliferating on six continents. In contrast to American
football and basketball, which have both seen many significant
rule changes since the nineteenth century, soccer's Laws of the
Game have been remarkably stable. In the decades after 1863,
the Laws of the Game were expanded and cemented. Since then,
there has been some tinkering here and there, but the core has
never changed. In a sense, it is the most conservative of sports;
those who govern the game and many fans and players have consistently resisted any major changes to the rules. While there are
occasional suggestions in the United States that the rules should
be changed to make the sport more appealing to audiences used
to the high-scoring games of basketball and American football, in
most of the world, people seem pretty happy with soccer as it is.
Why, after all, change something that is so beloved in so many
different places and cultures? What is there to be improved,
when it is already the most popular form of leisure and spectacle
on the planet?

There were a few refinements made to the goal in the years
after 1863. The original laws had set the breadth of the goal at

twenty-four feet across, but it had no top. The ball simply had to pass "over the space between the goal-posts," as high as you wanted. A player could kick the ball high, the way a kicker does for a field goal in American football. This made stopping the ball from going over the goal line difficult. Three years later, the goal got an upper limit eight feet high. This was marked at first by string or tape, and soon after by sturdier crossbars. By the end of the 1860s, then, the standing rectangle that is the goal—a shape that populates the entire world—was set.[11]

It took a bit longer for the position of goalie to come into existence. In early versions of the game, the final defender just did what he could to stop the ball from going in, using his feet or body. In 1871, the Football Association updated the rules and allowed for a team to have a player who "shall be at liberty to use his hands for the protection of his goal." This player could use his hands anywhere on the field. The position, then, was a sort of one-player relic from the earlier versions of the game that allowed players to carry the ball, as rugby and American football continued to do. In 1887, the rules were changed so that the goal-keeper was limited to using his hands only in his team's half of the field. In 1912, the goalkeeper was limited to doing so only in his own box. From then on, the penalty box became what Wilson calls a "virtual cell for the keeper," and their role in the game became "psychologically circumscribed." The goalie's advantage over other players only exists in this limited space, which makes venturing outside it potentially dangerous.[12]

The goalie's formal role—in all its loneliness and occasional glory—was essentially established by the early twentieth century. The only other significant change in rules about the goalie came many decades later in 1990. The modification was made after a European Cup that was widely criticized for its defensive, and often boring, style of play. In that tournament, teams who were ahead and wanted to run out the clock repeatedly used the technique of passing the ball back to their own goalie, who would then hold on to it—in one case for a full six minutes. So, a new back pass rule was promulgated: if a defender passes the ball back to their own goalie, the hands cannot be used, thus forcing a more rapid return to play. This change had a significant impact on the game, making it easier for the offense to pressure the other team because a defender no longer has the option to simply pass the ball back to the safety of the goalie's arms. It has also meant that goalies have had to get better at handling the ball with their feet when facing opposing forwards after receiving a back pass.[13]

There are different names for the position—goalkeeper, goalie, keeper—that are all basically interchangeable. Yet goalies themselves have widely different personalities and styles of play. One of the most influential early goalies was an Englishman named Leigh Richmond Roose. A Welsh preacher's son, Roose was born in 1877 and started playing in goal when he was studying medicine. Goalies, Roose explained, didn't need to play the position according to the "stereotype" and could "cultivate originality." He stood out from other goalies at the time because of his willingness to wander far away from the goal, sometimes even bouncing the ball all the way up to the middle of the field. This was not an easy task. At the time, referees allowed players to tackle one another much more violently than they do today. Roose had to dodge around defenders who were intent on knocking him down hard enough to make him drop the ball. His ability to hold on to the ball with his hands throughout his team's half of the field was frustrating to other teams, and directly inspired the Football Association's 1912 rule limiting the keeper's use of his hands to the penalty box. Roose left his mark on the game in another way, however, because he was a master at setting up his team's attacks. He was extremely good at "clearing" the ball: kicking it far up field from the goal so that his players could rapidly move toward the opposing goal. A goalie, Roose explained, had to be creative and unpredictable, using "a variety of methods in his clearances" in order to "confound and puzzle attacking forwards." A failed clearance that gave the attackers the ball, of course, could be a disaster for a goalie, noted Roose. A strong clearance that passed the ball ahead to attacking players, however, could lead to a goal for his team. Roose's playing style was successful and popular among the crowds, helping him redefine the position. Roose joined the British army at the outbreak of World War I in 1914. He was decorated with the Military Cross in 1916 after continuing to fight even after having been badly burned with a flamethrower, but died a few months later at the Somme. His playing style, however, had transformed the position of goalie. One of his Sunderland teammates claimed that he was the "mould from which all others were created."[14]

In part thanks to Roose's influence, the goalie became an object of fascination and, sometimes, adulation in the early twentieth century. "God himself stood in goal," one newspaper declared in 1929, celebrating the success of the German keeper Heinrich Stuhlfauth in a game against Italy. Stuhlfauth became a star in the 1920s, playing on the Nuremberg professional team and on the German national team. He perfected ways of patrolling and defending the goal from within the penalty box. Stuhlfauth had a powerful presence, and he emphasized the importance of timing and placement to success in the position. "A good goalkeeper does not throw himself about," he claimed. "Crash landings and panther-like jumps" were only necessary when he had not calculated things correctly. Part of the key was knowing how to "leave the goal at the right moment." Stuhlfauth knew that, from the stands, it often seemed like he wasn't going to make it to the ball when he ran out toward an approaching attacker. He noted, however, that the goalie had a crucial advantage, as he could "get to the ball more quickly because the ball comes towards the goalkeeper while the opponent has to run after it." By running out from goal, he could almost always "nullify the attack." He was good at this partly because, before being a goalie, he had played for many years in an attacking position. This experience gave Stuhlfauth a better sense of the precise timing and speed of an attack.[15]

He wasn't the only goalie compared to a divinity during this period. The Spanish keeper Ricardo Zamora was known as "The Divine One" and became one of the early soccer celebrities: a teammate called him "more famous than [Greta] Garbo and better looking." He was the first great star of the Spanish professional team Real Madrid. In one game against archrival Barcelona, Zamora dived to stop a ball and created a great cloud of dust. Many in the stadium assumed that the opposing side had scored, but "as the dust cleared, Zamora emerged, standing impassively with the ball in his arms." According to Wilson, it was "probably the most famous save in Spanish history." Zamora's fame traveled far. When a man named Niceto Alcalá Zamora became president of Spain, Stalin apparently assumed he was the soccer player, saying: "Ah, that goalkeeper!" Zamora's presence and stature, according to Eduardo Galeano, "sowed panic among strikers." Galeano imagines how the daunting goalkeeper made attacking players feel: "If they looked his way, they were lost: with Zamora in goal, the net would shrink and the posts would lose themselves in the distance." He "hypnotized anyone who set foot in the box." Even a star like Zamora, however, had his lows. At one point, as the keeper for Spain, he allowed seven goals by the English team and was widely ridiculed in the British press.[16]

Though he became famous as a novelist rather than a soccer player, the Russian writer Vladimir Nabokov played as a goalie during the same period, leaving us a beautiful depiction of how the world looks from the position. He started in the position as a boy attending Tenishev School in Russia, where the head-master wondered suspiciously why Nabokov liked this position rather than "running about with the other players." Later, as a student at the University of Cambridge in the wake of World War I, Nabokov played on a university team. In his autobiogra-phy, *Speak, Memory*, he writes luminously of soccer games as the "windswept clearing in the middle of a rather muddled period" in his life. Some games were played on "bright, bracing days—the good smell of the turf, that famous inter-Varsity forward, dribbling closer and closer to me with the new tawny ball on his twinkling toe, then the stinging shot, the lucky save, it's protracted tingle." But there were other, "more esoteric days, under dismal skies, with the goal area a mass of black mud, the ball as greasy as a plum-pudding." He writes, "I would fumble badly—and retrieve the ball from the net." Then, "mercifully," the game would move away from him, to the "other end of the sodden field. . . . Mists would gather. Now the game would be a vague bobbing of heads near the remote goal," he recalled. "The far, blurred sounds, a cry, a whistle, the thud of a kick, all that was perfectly unimportant and had no connection to me." He would sometimes lean "back against the left goalpost," closing his eyes, listening "to my heart knocking and feel the blind drizzle on my face and hear, in the distance, the broken sounds of the game." He was so isolated that he felt like "less the keeper of a soccer goal than the keeper of a secret." To be a goalie, he suggests, is to know a certain secret that only others who have occupied the role can understand.[17]

In those quiet moments by the goal, he felt like "a fabulous exotic being in an English footballer's disguise," and he returned to Russia in his mind, composing poems "in a tongue nobody understood about a remote country nobody knew." Among the differences between England and Russia he'd noticed was the way the English thought about the game, and specifically about the goalie. In England, goalies got little attention because there was a "national dread of showing off and a too grim preoccupation with solid teamwork." As a result, the English just couldn't understand the beauty of the "goalie's eccentric art." However, among Russians and Latin Americans, Nabokov writes, protecting the goal was considered a "gallant art," and the goalie was therefore "surrounded by a halo of singular glamour." He continues, "Aloof, solitary, impassive, the crack goalie is followed in the streets by entranced small boys," as much "an object of thrilled adulation" as a "matador" or a "flying ace." Photographers, "reverently bending on one knee," might capture him "making a spectacular dive" as the "stadium roars in approval," then he "remains for a moment or two lying full length where he fell, his goal still intact." Nabokov depicted the goalie dramatically as "the lone eagle, the man of mystery, the last defender."[18]

The writer and philosopher Albert Camus was also a goalie. One might even attribute the entire structure of his existentialist thought to this fact. In his memories of his time playing soccer, Camus hinted that the sport was central to the way he came to see life and his relationship with others. Camus was the son of a French man and a woman of Spanish descent who were part of the European settler community in the French colony of Algeria. Camus was born in 1913, and the next year his father died fighting in World War I. He was raised by his mother. She could neither read nor write, and, because of a hearing impediment, she had to read lips to understand what others were saying. Growing up poor in the working-class neighborhood of Belcourt, Camus played soccer in the streets and at age fifteen joined the team at his local high school, wearing an "odious" uniform of purple and red.[19]

By that time, soccer was well established throughout Algeria, with several clubs in the capital city of Algiers. Camus joined one of them, the Racing Universitaire d'Alger (RUA), which was affiliated with the university. Because it was considered representative of the "high-class elites" of Algiers, the team was on the receiving end of fairly intense hazing: bottles were thrown at the players from the stands, and opposing players were intent on inflicting maximum physical pain on them. Camus was actually quite poor—Galeano suggests he had first taken up the position of goalie because there "your shoes don't wear out as fast"—but he still didn't escape the abuse. He long remembered his "bulldozing centre-half," Raymond Couard, who protected him as best he could. "But it was never enough."[20]

Camus later recalled the experience of confronting one particularly rough forward nicknamed "Pastèque"—watermelon—over and over again. "He commanded all his weight against my kidneys. I also received a shin massage from his rough boots, some shirt-grabbing, occasional knees in the noble regions, and sandwiches in the post." But, Camus went on, he came to understand that even the relentless Pastèque had "good in him" and should be respected as a player. "The world has taught me much, but what I retain on morals and the obligation of man, I owe to sport, and it's at RUA that I learned it."[21]

What had he learned, precisely? In his novel *The Stranger*, Camus famously wrote from the perspective of a narrator who, when he learns he is going to be executed, reminds himself that "it's common knowledge that life isn't worth living anyhow." As he puts it, "Whether I died now or forty years hence, this business of dying had to be got through, inevitably." Maybe it was the goalie in Camus—drawing on the intimate understanding of futility that comes from having to pull the ball out of the net, again and again—who created a character who understood that, in "the wide view," it really makes no difference when one dies because "other men and women will continue living, the world will go as before."[22]

Existentialist philosophy, at its core, is about accepting the inevitability of death and the concomitant absurdity of life. But it is also, at least in its slightly more optimistic variants, about using that knowledge to find a way to live in the world, to keep going, knowing that while we can make choices about how we live each day, we can't ultimately control the outcome. More than any other player in soccer, the goalie is always reminded of this. However hard she tries and whatever effort she makes, the goalie will often be powerless in the face of fate, the ball endlessly slipping past her into the net. And yet, somewhat miraculously—but also absurdly—the goalie keeps trying anyway. Even if her team is down by many goals and is clearly going to lose, the goalie—knowing there is really no point—still dives courageously, bashing into the ground, trying to stop one more goal from going in.

Many goalies find themselves buffeted by the ups and downs of soccer. "It's always the keeper's fault," writes Galeano, "and if it isn't, he still gets blamed." Goalies do not have the chances that other players have to erase the memory of a mistake. Defenders can experience the deep shame of scoring an own goal—sending the ball into their net by accident when they are trying to stop it from going in—but they can then at least hope to reverse the impact of this by scoring a goal themselves, restoring the balance of a game. Other players can "blow it once in a while" but then "redeem themselves with a spectacular dribble" or a "masterful pass," as Galeano notes. But years of brilliant saves sometimes don't make up for a crucial save missed. The rage directed at goalies by fans, who sometimes never forgive, is matched only by the rage they direct at referees. "The crowd," Galeano notes, "never forgives the keeper."[23]

This also means that the fortunes of goalies can go up and down with remarkable intensity and unpredictability. The legendary Russian goalie Lev Yashin experienced this over the course of his storied career, alternately heralded as a national hero and virulently attacked as the cause of his team's downfall. Yashin,

Galeano writes, stopped over a hundred penalty shots in his career and "who knows-how-many-goals. . . . He could deflect the ball with a glance." Yashin profoundly shaped how the position is played today because he performed on an expanding international stage that had not existed in Roose's time. Like Roose before him, he "saw the value in commanding his box and the space beyond" and frequently left his box to clear the ball. Yashin was "noted both for his physical courage and his heading ability." That didn't keep from being a scapegoat. In 1955, he was blamed for a loss by his professional team, Dynamo Moscow, in the Soviet Cup final. A cartoon showed him wearing boxing gloves instead of those of a goalie and announced, "The Cup would undoubtedly have been ours . . . but for Comrade Yashin." Five years later, he was celebrated as "the best goal-keeper in the world" after his performance for the USSR in the 1960 European Championship. Yet in 1962, he was again blamed by many for the poor showing of the USSR in the men's World Cup. His wife remembers that upon his return, based on one ill-informed account of the game from the official news agency, everyone claimed, "Yashin lost the World Cup." By the 1966 World Cup, he was once again celebrated for his feats on the field. As he grew older, however, he suffered from the physical toll of being a goalie, which can be extremely hard on the shoulders and hips. The constant diving and hitting the ground, over and over again in practices and in games, can cause serious injuries and also wear down the bones, cartilage, and ligaments over time. Along with the physical suffering, of course, was added the psychic cost for Yashin of never being sure if he would leave a game considered the cause of a nation's downfall or a shining hero.[24]

Sometimes a goalie makes a save that is long remembered for its pure improbability: when everything seemed lost, he produced a miracle. This was the case in the 1970 men's World Cup, when the English keeper Gordon Banks faced off against Brazil, perhaps the most brilliant attacking team ever assembled for the tournament. In the tenth minute, the forward Jairzinho sent a beautiful cross toward the goal. Banks read its arc and moved to cover it. The ball was heading toward Pelé, who, as the Scottish sports journalist Hugh McIlvanney wrote at the time, rushed toward the goal, "reading the situation flawlessly and moving as perhaps only he could," and rose "in an elastic leap, arching his back and neck to get behind and above the ball. . . . The header was smashed downward with vicious certainty," aimed at an opening that Banks had left exposed. Pelé was so sure the ball was going in the net that he shouted "goal" as he headed it. The heavily pro-Brazilian crowd jumped, ready to celebrate. "But Banks, hurling himself back across the goal at a speed that will never cease to awe those who were there or the millions who watched on television, was already twisting into range as the ball met the ground two or three feet from his line." As it rose he flicked it upward with his right hand—and over the crossbar. He later thought the ball had been at shoulder height when he reached it. In fact, however, the ball was just a foot or so off the ground. He had moved so quickly that he didn't even remember precisely how extraordinary his motion had been. "This is without question the greatest save I have ever seen," said his teammate Bobby Charlton.[25]

Goalies can sometimes play absolutely extraordinary games, only to be remembered for a single failure at the very end. During the 2010 men's World Cup, when Algeria played the US in the final match of group play—with the winner guaranteed to win a slot among the final sixteen in the tournament—the backup goalie for Algeria, Raïs M'Bolhi, took to the pitch after an injury to the starting goalie in the previous match. He was brilliant, stopping strike after strike from the US and basically keeping his team in the game. In the final minutes of the game, in extra time, Landon Donovan outwitted the Algerian defenders, rushed forward, and scored a brilliant goal. M'Bolhi's team was out of the World Cup.

The US goalie that day was Tim Howard, who made history at the 2014 men's World Cup in Brazil when he stopped a record sixteen shots that came at him from a brilliant Belgian team. His exploits earned him the ultimate form of contemporary celebrity: a meme called #ThingsTimHowardCouldSave. In the images that flowed across the Internet, he had stopped any number of things from happening, including the 9/11 terror attacks. Someone edited the Wikipedia page for the US Secretary of Defense and, briefly, gave him the position. Of course, rather than seeing Howard as an endlessly heroic goalie, one might instead argue that the US defense was just terrible, forcing the goalie into situations he never should have been in. And, in the end, the sixteen saves weren't what mattered: instead, the two goals he ultimately let in, late in the game, were what counted against him. The goalie, writes Wilson, "will have the least to do when his side has played best and will be at his best only when the rest of the team has in some way failed. He is like a lifeguard or a fireman, to be thanked in times of crisis even as everybody wonders why the crisis arose in the first place." For all Howard's heroism, he still couldn't save his team, which lost 2–1 to Belgium, eliminating them from the World Cup.[26]

The best goalies have a powerful presence in goal, and their confidence extends outward to their defenders and the rest of the team. This is the case of the American goalie Hope Solo, who is riveting to watch as much for the brilliant, acrobatic saves she makes as for the psychological intensity with which she confronts opposing forwards. Like many other goalies, she didn't start out in the position, and she learned to play by scoring goals, not stopping them. As a girl, she was a strong forward, constantly scoring goals. As she recalls it, "No coach would have ever dreamed of taking me off the field and sticking me in goal." She found solace from a difficult life on the football pitch. "I knew how soccer made me feel," she writes, "and I knew I wanted to hold onto that feeling for the rest of my life." She continues, "Life was calm and ordered on the soccer field," where she felt "free and unburdened."[27]

"Goal-keeping isn't glamorous," Solo writes. "It's tough and stressful and thankless." Because youth soccer coaches often put less athletic kids in goal, there's also a "stigma about goalkeeping." When Solo was recruited into an Olympic Development Program (ODP) in Washington state, she started playing the position regularly. During her first game with the ODP team, the starting goalkeeper suffered a concussion after colliding with another player in the net. The coach, perhaps sensing something about Solo that would make her a good goalie, asked her to take over for the injured player. She did well and began playing occasionally in the position. Though Solo kept playing forward on her club and high school teams, she found that her knowledge of "how a forward attacks" allowed her to better position herself in goal and know when to run out and break up plays. Anchored in two roles, with a "double identity," she learned how to think like a goalkeeper and a forward at the same time, closely watching attackers so she could position herself to stop them from scoring.[28]

In 2000, she got her first invitation to train with the US Women's National Team, then coached by April Heinrichs. The team was fresh off their epochal victory in the 1999 Women's World Cup, which had drawn record crowds. Solo was a young and untested player, and she found "the skill and confidence level" of the veteran players "daunting." She found herself in goal behind the legendary defender Brandi Chastain, who had scored the winning penalty kick against China in the 1999 tournament final. Chastain had become an icon not only because of her goal, but because the image of her celebration—in which she had ripped off her shirt, revealing her sports bra—was on the cover of *Sports Illustrated* and heralded by many as a symbol of the bold strength and success of female athletes. For the young Solo, it was terrifying to be on the field with the famous player. At one point, Chastain turned around to the young goalkeeper and "barked: 'That's your ball.'" Solo recalls, "*Oh fuck*, I thought. *Brandi Chastain is yelling at me.*" In another practice, Solo maladroitly punted the ball up into the air, and the striker Mia Hamm stopped short, looked at her, and said, "Do you want me to fucking head the ball? Then you need to fucking learn how to drop-kick it." Solo was mortified: "*Oh, God,* I thought. *Now Mia Hamm is yelling at me.*"[29]

A goalie's size is important. Being tall, and having long arms, is an obvious advantage when trying to protect the goal. Yet perhaps even more important is the size of a goalie's personality. A successful goalie projects authority, commanding and controlling her defenders. She arranges them to defend the goal on free kicks and corner kicks, calculating angles and interpreting the positioning and movement of the opposing players. The confidence of defenders depends on the strength of the goalie—knowing that the goalie has things covered in front of the goal enables them to stand firm, as well as take risks when necessary. When a team has confidence in a goalie, the defenders can move more freely up the field toward the opposing goal, putting more strength in the attack and pressuring the other team. In this sense, the goalie, though invisible in the attack, plays a crucial role in giving the rest of the team the space and inspiration to move forward quickly and aggressively.

Solo learned about the importance of authority the hard way. She first played for the US Women's National Team in a game against Iceland in April 2000, and she was chosen again to play archrival Mexico on Cinco de Mayo in Portland. The US dominated the game, winning 4–0. At one point, with Mexico on the attack, Chastain let a ball through and Solo had to dive to make a save. Solo writes, "Brandi turned around and yelled at me— 'Come on, Hope!'—blaming me for not coming out for the ball." Solo knew it was actually Chastain who had made the mistake, but—too respectful of the authority of the veteran player—she didn't respond. "That was my mistake," Solo admits. Afterward, Heinrich spoke to Solo about that incident on the field and her interaction with Chastain. "'That tells me you're not ready, Hope,' she said. 'We all knew Brandi made a mistake. Yet you didn't have the courage to call her out and yell back at her. You're not ready to lead the defense.'"[30]

In time, of course, Solo would be ready. Though she missed the 2000 Olympics, she played on the under-twenty-one team, and Heinrichs soon brought her back onto the roster of the national team. She attributes much of her improvement to a goalkeeping coach at the University of Washington, Amy Griffin. Soon after Solo starting playing for Washington, Griffin handed her a note that said, "A goalkeeper cannot win a game. A goalkeeper saves it." What Griffin taught Solo was ultimately the key to goalkeeping: the "intellectual side" of the position, the endless work of observation, of calibration, of constantly adjusting one's position, and of readiness in relationship to the flow of the game. Before training with Griffin, Solo writes, she had taken a relatively direct approach to guarding the net, waiting in goal and using her size and reflexes to stop what came at her. She learned that the key to goalkeeping at the highest level was to think tactically, remaining a few steps ahead. That meant taking charge of positioning defenders, reading the runs of opposing players as they moved across the field, and understanding "how to anticipate and predict what was happening in front of me." The key to this was figuring out where the opposing players would likely move and shoot from, and calculating the angles so that she could position herself most effectively. Goalies constantly have to make critical decisions about where to place themselves, and Solo learned how to know when to leave the goal line to confront an onrushing player and when to stay back. All this new awareness made the position "much more interesting." Rather than "ninety minutes of waiting for my defense to make a mistake," it became "ninety minutes of tactics and strategy."[31]

One of the highlights of Solo's career came during the 2011 Women's World Cup when the US faced off against Brazil in a riveting game. In the second half of the game, with the US leading 1–0, the referee gave a red card to US defender Rachel Buehler when she tangled with Brazilian striker Marta Vieira da Silva, known as Marta, in front of the goal. That call was controversial, but it was only the first of a bizarre string of refereeing decisions. The Brazilian player Cristiane Rozeira stepped up to take the penalty kick, and Solo made a brilliant diving save. The referee, however, immediately called for the penalty kick to be retaken. It wasn't clear why at the time, although it was later understood that the call was for encroachment—one of the US players had started to run into the penalty area before the ball was kicked, which is indeed technically a foul, although quite rarely called. Solo argued with the referee and got a yellow card. Then Marta walked up to take the second penalty kick and struck it fast into the net. Solo was beaten this time. The sequence was enough to drive any goalkeeper mad. Solo kept her composure, though, throughout the rest of the game, even making key saves. In the shoot-out, Solo blocked one crucial penalty kick, winning the game for the US.

In the 2015 World Cup, Solo's goalkeeping was once again critical to the US success. Against a powerhouse German team in the semifinal, Solo saved the game early on when the referee granted a penalty kick. German star striker Célia Šašić stepped up to take it. I was there in the stadium that day, and I could barely watch, sure that Šašić would make it. Solo did something odd, clearly aiming to psych out the German striker. She started to sort of stroll away from the goal. It almost looked, for a moment, like she had just decided that she was done, that she was leaving for good. As Carli Lloyd remembers, "It was a very leisurely stroll. If there were flowers nearby, she would've stopped to pick them." It was a dangerous move: the referee could have given her a yellow card for it. Just in time, Solo turned back, came into goal, and stared down Šašić who, very uncharacteristically, sent the ball wide to the left of the goal. We went crazy in the stadium. "Sometimes," Lloyd recalls, "even in the heat of a big game, you can feel the momentum shift on the spot." That moment was "one of those times," and the US went on to defeat Germany, and then win against Japan in the final.[32]

All goalies live with the knowledge that, in one instant, they can make a mistake that they will never live down. Certainly, the goalie who has been treated the most cruelly in history—and who is perhaps most deserving of his own existentialist novel or philosophical treatise—is the Brazilian Moacir Barbosa Nascimento. He was in goal during the 1950 World Cup final that pitted Brazil against Uruguay in the Maracanã stadium, which had been built for the tournament. There was an aura of inevitability about Brazilian victory: the tournament was on home soil, the people were confident that they played the best soccer on the planet, and all that was needed to take home the trophy was a draw in the final game. Barbosa was one of the great goalies of his generation. His "calm self-assurance," writes Galeano, "filled the entire team with confidence." And yet—with an estimated two hundred thousand spectators looking on—two defenders lost track of the Uruguayan player Alcides Ghiggia, and Barbosa dove the wrong way. His fingers grazed the ball, and when he got up he thought he'd knocked it safely outside the post. But when he turned around, there it was—in the net. The stadium was taken over by the "the most raucous silence in the history of soccer." When the game ended, Jules Rimet, the French founder of the World Cup, had to wander about the pitch as devastated Brazilian players and fans milled about. He finally found the Uruguayan captain and shoved the trophy into his arms, then shook his hand silently. He had a prepared speech congratulating the Brazilians in his pocket, but had nothing to say about what had just happened. Tens of thousands of devastated fans spent the entire night in the stadium in silent mourning, unwilling to leave, perhaps hoping that they would somehow wake up from a nightmare.[33]

Brazilians experienced the loss as a massive national trauma. The game even has its own name, the Maracanazo. A Brazilian midfielder described the moment in simple terms: "The world collapsed on me." The playwright Nelson Rodrigues went so far, stunningly, as to dub the moment "our Hiroshima." He was not the only one to think of the event as a wartime defeat: a nine-year-old kid named Edson Arantes do Nascimento—who would later be better known by his nickname, Pelé—sat by the family radio and, as he later recalled, felt an "immense sadness." He experienced the defeat as "the end of a war, with Brazil the loser and many people killed." In 1986, Paulo Perdigão—a journalist, film critic, and specialist on existentialist philosophy who translated Jean-Paul Sartre's *Being and Nothingness* into Portuguese—published a book called *Anatomy of a Defeat*. As Wilson notes, he reprints the entire radio commentary from the game—which he describes as both a "Waterloo of the tropics" and the Brazilian equivalent of a Wagner opera—"using it as the basis for his analysis of the game almost as though he were delivering exegesis on a biblical text."[34]

Barbosa's entire life after that was defined by that one instant—his slight miscalculation of angles and velocity, momentum and friction. As Wilson describes it, he seems to have known, right then, what had happened: this was his "assassination," and that "his life as a normal citizen was over. The video of the game shows him down on one knee after the goal, slowly, sadly raising his powerful body as though he knew already the burden he would carry for the rest of his life."[35]

The failure, of course, was not just his. Every player on the Brazilian team that day contributed to the loss. Why not blame the forwards who failed to score, rather than the goalie who had let the ball in? But that is not how it works. The visibility and concreteness of the failure of the goalie makes him the perfect scapegoat for what seems like an impossible and unexplainable loss. The team's two defenders—who, like him, were Afro-Brazilian— were also singled out as culprits in the loss. The criticism of the three of them often took on racist overtones, suggesting that black players didn't have the capacity or discipline to represent the nation at the highest levels. The next generation of Afro-Brazilian footballers, including Pelé, would often have to struggle to find their place and gain the recognition they deserved in comparison to white players. Barbosa was made to feel like he was a kind of curse. Not only was he taken off the team, but he was also barred from ever commenting on national team matches and from attending any national team practices for the rest of his life. In 1963, he apparently invited friends to a barbeque during which he burned the Maracanã goalposts in a "liturgy of purification." As he noted in an interview in 2000, in a country where the maximum jail sentence for any crime was thirty years, he had gotten "fifty years of punishment for a crime he had not committed."[36]

If there is one moment where the goalie has the best chance of earning redemption, and emerging as a hero, it is during a penalty kick shoot-out. Depending on your perspective, this is either the most riveting or the most absurd spectacle in soccer.

A penalty kick shoot-out is a relative rarity. In regular league play for professional teams, it is fine for a game to end with a draw, 0–0 or 1–1, since the rankings are based on a point system, with 0 for a loss, 1 for a draw, and 3 for a win. The same is true in the group stages that make up the beginning of international competition, where a selected set of teams—usually four—all play one another, and the top teams progress on to the next rounds. There are, however, some games that have to end in the elimination of one of the teams. In this case, if the game is still tied after ninety minutes, it goes into overtime. If it is still tied after two fifteen-minute periods of overtime, the game is decided in penalty kicks. The shoot-out works like this: teams alternate taking the same kind of penalty kicks that are given for fouls inside the box during regular play. One after another, the players step up and try to score.

In this dramatic sequence, all eyes are on the goalie, who has to stand up again and again and try to stop the other team from scoring. This is the moment when a goalie has the greatest chance of being hailed as a hero. Stopping even one goal, notably by successfully playing mind games—positioning herself oddly or unexpectedly, moving in a distracting way, or otherwise putting the opposing player off her game—can assure the goalie's team victory. The tables are turned, and for once it is those who are trying to score who bear all the responsibility.

That is partly because penalty kick shoot-outs are less about technical skills than a psychological game between the kicker and the goalie. Once, as I tried to explain baseball to a perplexed French visitor to my home in Durham, I finally hit upon this imperfect but still useful comparison: imagine the relationship between the pitcher and the batter as being a penalty kick shoot-out, repeated over and over again. What you are watching for is the drama of the relationship between the two of them, though the potential outcomes in baseball are much more varied than in soccer, where there is either a goal or not.

It shouldn't be that hard to score a penalty kick. The player shooting on goal has the advantage, at least in principle. The goal is huge, the goalie covering just a tiny part of it, and you can run up and kick the ball as hard and with as much precision as possible, with no distraction from defending players. You do, however, have to make a decision about where to kick and how hard. And you have to make that decision in a condition of tremendous stress, with everything depending on you. Most importantly, you have to make sure nothing about your approach or body language provides the goalie with a hint about where you are going to kick. If he picks up correctly on any such hints, the goalie is far more likely to be able to dive in the right direction and stop the goal. The situation is ripe for a kind of infinite regression of trying to read the other person while not letting them read you. Your mind can spin: does the goalie know what I am going to do? And if so, what should I do? Penalty kicks are, writes Wilson, a game of "bluff and double bluff."[37]

The penalty kick shoot-out has inspired its own share of literature. In his book *The Goalkeeper's Fear of the Penalty*—made into a film by director Wim Wenders—the Austrian novelist Peter Handke uses the protagonist's confrontation with this problem as part of a broader reflection on fate and choice. In the book, during a scene that takes place in the stadium, a character explains the dilemma of the goalie to a man standing next to him. The goalie knows where the kicker usually sends the ball. But he also knows the kicker may know that he knows, and so will decide to go the opposite way. "But what if the kicker follows the goalkeeper's thinking and plans to shoot in the usual corner after all? And so on, and so on." In a short story by the Argentinean writer Osvaldo Soriano, woven around what he calls "The Longest Penalty Ever," a penalty kick has to be retaken a day after a match is played, giving everyone too much time to think about which way the kicker might go. The goalie gets plenty of advice. One person tells him that the kicker "always" kicks to the right. "But he knows that I know," the goalie answers. "Then we're fucked," comes the reply. "Yeah, but I know that he knows," continues the goalie. "Then dive to the left and be ready," someone else suggests. "No. He knows that I know that he knows," the goalie responds—at this point so exhausted by the whole process of speculation that he goes off to bed. On the pitch, however, the outcome of the process of speculation can often determine the outcome of a game. When the goalie outsmarts the player taking the kick, it is as if the goalie has just scored a goal—and the crowd, for once, cheers for him as if he did.[38]

Every once in a while, in a penalty kick shoot-out, the goalie gets to actually score the winning goal. In at least one case, in fact, a goalie achieved perhaps the greatest feat in soccer: making both a critical save and the critical goal in one game. His name was Boubacar Barry, and he was the goalie for Ivory Coast in the final of the 2015 Africa Cup of Nations. As is surprisingly common in the Africa Cup of Nations, it went not just to penalty kicks but to a surreal and extended shoot-out that culminated in the two goalies taking shots against each other. Barry became a legend that day by first blocking the penalty kick from the Ghana goalie. Then he proceeded to step up, sweating, and kick the ball into the goal, winning the cup for his country.

Barry was, in a sense, a surprising hero. He plays for a good professional team in Belgium, but is not a very well-known goalie. He had been on the bench most of the tournament, and was in the final only because of an injury to the preferred, younger goalkeeper. He could have been forgiven, too, for being terrified. He had been in goal in the previous Africa Cup of Nations Final, in 2012, when Ivory Coast lost on penalty kicks to Zambia. Yet, despite all the pressure, he won the trophy by both blocking the goal and taking his final kick with tremendous poise—a small, humble figure somehow becoming a footballing giant.

That day in 2015, the legendary striker Didier Drogba, who for many years had been Barry's teammate on the Ivory Coast team, was watching at home. He had retired from international play and therefore had to watch the game on television rather than playing in it. He decided to film himself and his family as they watched the penalty kick shoot-out, producing what may be the best thing ever to be shared on the Internet.[39]

In the video, as he watches his teammates take their kicks from his living room, Drogba talks nonstop. He talks about those who have doubted Barry as a goalkeeper, clearly hoping they will be proven wrong. When Barry blocks the key penalty, Drogba cheers and then settles back in to watch as Barry takes his own kick. When Barry scores, Drogba and his wife explode into song and dance, unbelieving in the face of a miracle. It could be a film of any football fan watching a decisive penalty kick shoot-out involving his favorite team with a title on the line, except that it's not an ordinary fan; it's Didier Drogba. There is a certain sadness, or longing, about the moment. Drogba is experiencing vicariously a victory that had long eluded him when he was playing for Ivory Coast. The intensity of the video is partly the result of the fact that the viewer knows that Drogba wishes he were there with Barry. Or maybe it is that, in a sense, Drogba is there on the pitch as he kneels on the floor, almost praying in front of the television.

Barry was greeted as a hero back in Ivory Coast and paraded through the city. With classic modesty, when interviewed he explained, "I am not big in size or in talent. But I thought of my mother who loved me." In a sense, Barry at that moment was the ultimate goalie: a bit of an outsider, perhaps never appreciated and respected as he should be, but also—when it counted most—a savior.[40]

2

THE DEFENDER

"What is football?" an interviewer asked the defender Lilian Thuram in a 2006 interview. Thuram responded
simply: "It is the language of happiness." Years earlier, in 1999, he
described how he hoped, one day, to be able to play football the
way Miles Davis plays jazz. "We're not there yet," he added. "But
I haven't given up hope."[1]

While fans of many teams of course deeply appreciate a good,
solid defender, such players rarely become icons. In some ways,
defenders' work is simply less accounted for, perhaps less visible
than that of other positions. Goalies may be the loneliest players
on the pitch, but their successes and mistakes are vividly remembered. Great defenders, however, are rarely given the kind of adulation or mythological status that is bestowed on great offensive
players. There are few memoirs or biographies written about defenders. Yet defenders are pivotal to the structure of any team,
and the structure of the game itself. There are long-standing
debates about precisely what their role should be, debates that

raise larger questions about what is most important about soccer. Should the focus always be on what is effective and assures victory? Or should the beauty of the game be prized, perhaps even above victory?

Thuram is one of those rare defenders who became a global icon because of the role he played at a crucial moment in the history of French soccer, the 1998 men's World Cup. It began with a classic defender's mistake. As the second half of the semifinal between France and Croatia began, he was out of position: too far to the left and too far back. Instead of catching the Croatian striker Davor Šuker offside, he left him wide open in front of the goal. Šuker did not hesitate. He caught a beautiful volley and powered the ball into the goal.

Croatia's very presence in the semifinal match had something of the miraculous about it. The nation only became independent in 1991 after the breakup of Yugoslavia. This was the first time it had ever played in a World Cup tournament. The Croatian players surprised everyone, including themselves, by making it to the quarterfinal, where they met one of those teams you never want to have to play in a World Cup: Germany. Croatia's coach, Ćiro Blažević—who was from Bosnia—had prepared a detailed pre-match plan that he intended to present to the players. As he later recalled, "I was on my way to the dressing room with my theories, and there are a lot of mirrors in every dressing room. I looked at myself in the mirror and I was a kind of green colour. So I thought, 'Oh my God, am I going to die?'" The players, he noticed, "were the same green colour as me." He quickly realized there was no way they would be able to pay attention as he laid out his plan. "They were more and more green. . . . So I crumpled my theories and I threw them down," he said. "Fuck the theory." Instead, he just said: "You have to go outside today and die for the Croatian flag and all the people who have given their lives." Croatia beat Germany 3–0 in a riveting match. In the semifinal, after Šuker's goal against France, it seemed like they might be on their way to an even greater upset. If they won, they would not only defeat the host of the tournament, but also earn a place in the World Cup final.[2]

It was an uncharacteristic mistake for Thuram, who is considered one of the greatest defenders of his generation. He was born on the French Caribbean island of Guadeloupe on January 1st, 1972—a local newspaper printed his photograph because he was the first baby of the year. He was small and sickly, which Thuram later attributed to his mother Mariana's "difficult life." They were poor, and during the last months of her pregnancy she had to continue working, harvesting sugarcane in the fields during the day and then traveling several miles to the island capital to clean houses. Thuram grew up in the village of Anse-Bertrand, and he started playing football games, which he remembers "stretched into the night," in empty lots or the street in front of his house. When he was ten, his mother—like thousands of others from the French Caribbean—migrated to metropolitan France seeking a better life for her and her children.[3]

They settled in a housing project near the town of Fontainebleau, south of Paris, which was right next to a large forest. Thuram and his new friends "played the World Cup," scoring goals by sending the ball through a broken slat on the back of a bench in a stretch of grass between the apartment towers. Thuram later described growing up in this neighborhood as a wonderful experience. He celebrated the "multiplicity of cultures"—a Pakistani friend taught him the rules of cricket, Congolese families introduced him to African politics—and the "intensity and freedom" of the relationships with others he crafted there. In a 2006 interview, he was asked about his memories of growing up in Fontainebleau and responded, "Mixing: Moroccans, Algerians, Zaïrois, Spaniards. . . . They are good memories." His vision of his neighborhood runs strikingly counter to the usual media portrayal of such housing projects, which are often depicted as dismal and violent places. As a football star, he became a kind of spokesman for the communities, often of immigrant background, who live in these neighborhoods.[4]

Thuram had various dreams: as a child he wanted to be a priest, and he also has a long-running fascination with history. But he was an excellent soccer player, shining on a local youth team originally founded by Portuguese immigrants. He attended a local high school with a special focus on athletics, where one of his classmates there was Claude Makélélé, who would play with him on the French team and become a star midfielder. In 1989, Thuram was recruited by Arsène Wenger, who was then coaching Monaco, and began a professional career. He originally played midfield, but after a knee injury slowed him down, his coaches positioned him in defense. He was angry at first, but ultimately settled into the role. Thuram spent most of his career playing professionally in Italy—first for Parma and then for Juventus. Historian John Foot recalls that, in the midst of a period in Italian soccer rife with corruption scandals and fan violence, he found endless joy in watching Thuram as, "for the thousandth time in his career," he "trapped the ball, looked up, and passed it elegantly to a midfielder." Thuram, Foot writes, was always a reminder that there was something beautiful left in football.[5]

Defenders are not expected to be great at scoring goals, though the best among them can be dangerous in front of the opposing goal. Thuram, however, was notoriously bad at scoring. The only time he scored when he played for Monaco, he remembers, was when he accidentally sent the ball into his own goal when he made a bad pass backward toward his goalie. Goalie Fabien Barthez, who played with him for Monaco and later on the French national team, remembered that even when Thuram was right in front of an open goal, the defender would wait for someone else to come and pass it to him so he could shoot. But against Croatia in 1998, Thuram discovered some new capacity, perhaps buried within. He couldn't be responsible for France failing to get into the World Cup final on its own soil, after all. So as soon as the game restarted after Šuker's goal, Thuram streaked forward on the right wing, surprising the Croatian defenders. His teammate Youri Djorkaeff slid the ball forward to Thuram, who angled toward the goal and pummeled it in. It was a surreal moment; Thuram seemed transported in disbelief. It all happened so quickly that you can't even see the first part of the play on the footage from the game—the feed was busy showing replays of the Šuker goal.

Over the next twenty minutes, Thuram was everywhere on the field, stopping shots by the Croatian forwards but also making streaking runs up the field. As he told his mother after the game, he watched as his teammates—including star midfielder Zinedine Zidane and the young striker Thierry Henry—sent ball after ball "everywhere but in the goal." Twenty minutes before the end of the game, Thuram dribbled up the right side of the pitch. He gestured to Djorkaeff: I'll pass it to you, you pass it back to me. The one-two worked, and Thuram was able to send another ball streaking into the net. It was 2–1 for France. The score stood. Thuram had put France in the final of the World Cup for the first time in the nation's history and, in the process, redeemed his earlier lapse.[6]

His celebration of the second goal became an iconic image of the 1998 World Cup and of Thuram as a player. He slid to his knees and put his hand over his mouth, a finger posed on his lips, pondering, looking straight ahead. It was as if, in the moment, he was sitting there thinking philosophically: "What, exactly, is a goal?" Or, perhaps more precisely, "What is going on?" His teammate Marcel Desailly ran to him along with the rest of the team and asked him, "What is happening to you?" Thuram responded, "I don't know." For many of those who were watching in the stadium, in France, and around the globe, it felt like a miracle. His pose, wrote one observer, made it seem like "Lilian Thuram has risen out of this world. . . . Enlightened, inspired, Lilian Thuram is the messiah."[7]

Thuram predicted after the game that it would be another twenty-five years before he scored two goals in a game for France. Actually, he never scored again for the French national team: at the end of a career with a record-breaking 142 appearances, those two goals against Croatia were the only ones he had ever made. But because they were scored in such a surprising way, and on the greatest stage in world soccer, they instantly made him an icon. Crowds chanted "Thuram President!" as they thronged the streets of Paris. For some, the goals were also a strike against the far-right, anti-immigrant Front National movement led at the time by Jean-Marie Le Pen. Starting in 1996, he had declared that he thought there were too many "foreign" players on the team. This was an inaccuracy and a sleight-of-hand trick: anyone who plays on a national team has to be a citizen of that country, and the French players in the 1990s had almost all been born and raised in France. Le Pen was really just trying to single out the players who looked different—the black players of African or Caribbean ancestry, and those of North African descent like Zidane. Le Pen suggested they were not truly French and were even unpatriotic, accusing them of not singing the national anthem before games. This politicized the players, many of whom spoke out against Le Pen, and it made the team, and Thuram's triumph, a kind of symbol that suggested that France's diversity could actually be a strength. The night of the French victory over Croatia, among the crowds celebrating in the streets was a man named Moussa, an immigrant from Ivory Coast, who told a journalist that for him the game was "a way of saying to Le Pen that we blacks are not what he thinks. It shows that we are French, that we'll fight for France." Moussa continued, "France's battle is my battle. . . . This game was an act of vengeance against the Front National." Meanwhile, in the neighborhood where Thuram had grown up, the celebrations were intense. Hundreds of revelers marched there into the center of Fontainebleau. One man climbed up the façade of the Hôtel Napoléon, one of the town's monuments, and ripped down the French flag so that he and his friends could parade around with it in celebration.[8]

Starting in 1998, Thuram used his iconic status to become a political voice speaking out on behalf of racial minorities in

France. After his retirement from professional soccer in 2008, he created an anti-racism foundation, curated an exhibit about the history of racial representations, and wrote a book about global black history called *Mes étoiles noirs* (*My Black Stars*). Thuram is relatively unique not just for his intellectual and political activities but also because he became a widely recognizable star despite the fact that he was a defender.[9]

The role of the defender—and of defense—has always been a troubling and troubled one in soccer. Among many players and fans, there is also a sense that when a team's play becomes too defensive—that is, when the focus is on stopping the other team rather than on scoring goals—it can make soccer boring and even cynical. An overly defensive strategy feels like it is trying to stop everything that is beautiful and exhilarating about the game. Still, there is no way around the fact that defense is at the very core of soccer.

The structure of a team's defense is not always visible on television because the cameras usually focus on the ball, and all that is happening elsewhere on the pitch is harder to perceive. In a stadium, you can truly see the geometry of the game, the way the positioning of players far away from the ball might be stretching out the space on the pitch, creating openings. You can see the way that defenders are constantly working to reconfigure space by passing back to the goalie and therefore stretching out the game, or else moving out to the wings (the sides of the pitch) in order to move forward. When done well, such motion can make the game breathe and open up. And you can see how, conversely, when a team is focused on defending, packing players around the penalty box and goal in an attempt to stop the offensive work of a superior adversary, large stretches of the pitch begin to seem neglected, even lonely, with only the goalkeeper keeping watch.

Since its development in the nineteenth century, soccer has seen many waves of innovation in tactics. Styles of play that might now seem obvious, even natural—passing, organizing defensive players in specific positions on the pitch, pressuring players when they have the ball at their feet—actually had to be imagined and invented. In the mid- to late nineteenth century, English soccer mostly took the form of "kick-and-rush": most of the players on one team ran forward alongside their teammate who was dribbling the ball. "Head-down charging" was the prized approach according to soccer historian Jonathan Wilson, and "passing, cooperation and defending were perceived as somehow inferior." This was partly an inheritance from the versions of ball games that allowed players to carry and pass the ball with their hands. Soon, however, teams began to experiment with other ways of playing and arranging themselves on the field that allowed for a different kind of play.[10]

A formation is the arrangement of players on the field in a particular position. Formations are usually described with a numerical formula that explains where the ten players are to be located. The goalie is not included. The formation most common in the early days of soccer, to the extent that there was one, took the shape of something like a 1–2–7: one defender in front of the goal, two players in the midfield, and seven (if not more) in the attack. Since players tended to dribble forward, and in so doing had to physically confront opposing players, bigger and strong players had an advantage. Then, writes Wilson, in an 1872 game between England and Scotland, the smaller Scottish players "decided to try to pass the ball around England rather than engage in a more direct man-to-man contest in which they were likely to be out-muscled." It was, in a way, a strategic decision by players trying to find a way to win against the odds. Yet it was a turning point in the history of the game, and the passing style caught on in part thanks to the presence of increasing numbers of Scottish players on English teams.[11]

The idea of passing rather than dribbling was revolutionary. It changed the way the game was played, and the kinds of players who could play it. Defensive and midfield players began to take on a more important role. These players sought to control the game in the middle of the field, where more and more of the action took place as teams used passing and overlapping runs—a move in which a player without the ball runs ahead to receive a pass from behind and then moves forward across the pitch. Formations rapidly evolved to versions of a 2–3–5, with two defenders in front of the goal, three players in the midfield, and five up front in the attack. Some observers groused about the changes: one journalist in 1882 made fun of teams that kept players near the goal, claiming their only purpose would be to chat with the goalkeeper. But team managers increasingly focused on training their players to play in certain positions as part of a larger tactical framework. One manager at Sheffield United used twenty-two lumps of sugar on a table to show his players where they needed to be positioned.[12]

The idea at the core of the passing game was to make the ball do the hard work of moving across the pitch, rather than the players. Passing quickly between players was seen as a more efficient way to get the ball moving forward, rather than having one player dribble as far as possible. The focus turned to retaining possession of the ball and using passes between players to keep the ball away from the other team. As the defender Frank Buckley explained it in the early 1900s, the forward players "tip-tap the ball here and there, making headway by short, sharp transfers from one man to another." Soccer became a more cerebral and artistic game. A player for Newcastle United, Bob Hewison, described how the team's passing game required players with "individuality, brains, adaptability, speed." Only a "real artist," he went on, was able to play this way. "But there is no reason," Hewison added, "why there should not be a cultivation of the art, since it is the pure football."[13]

This new style of play was perfected across the Atlantic, in the Latin American country of Uruguay. British expatriates brought the sport there in the late nineteenth century, and it was rapidly adopted throughout the country. Uruguayan writers and coaches have argued that their unique school of football developed thanks to the conditions of freedom in which it emerged, notably in rural areas. As the manager Ondino Viera, who coached the Uruguayan national team at the 1966 World Cup, describes it, his country developed their style "alone on the fields of Uruguay," where a premium was placed on brilliant dribbling that made players "absolute masters, of the ball," intent on seizing it and "not letting it go for any reason." It was, in the words of the Uruguayan writer Eduardo Galeano, "a game of close passes directly to the foot, with lightning changes in rhythm and high-speed dribbling"—"chess with a ball."[14]

The Uruguayan team won the gold medal at the 1924 Olympics in Paris, stunning European teams and earning the admiration of the crowds who watched. "A revelation!" wrote the French novelist Henry de Montherlant. "Here we have real football." The French player Gabriel Hanot, who became the editor of the French sports newspaper *L'Équipe*, celebrated the Uruguayans' "marvelous virtuosity" and the way they created "a beautiful football, elegant but at the same time varied, rapid, powerful and effective." This style of play also expanded all the spaces on the pitch, including the midfield—a center of contest between players. Defensive players took on an increasingly visible and important role in the tactics of the team. Fast, sophisticated dribbling was important everywhere, as defenders could, in one move, set up an attack by passing to midfielders, who in turn could outmaneuver or outflank their opponents to move forward or pass to roving forwards. The role of the defender became more than stopping offensive plays; it became intricately tactical in its own way, and dependent on many of the same kinds of dribbling and positioning skills that attacking players used.[15]

During the same period, soccer was also developing rapidly in Brazil. One of the great early defenders there was a man named Domingos da Guia. He was born in 1911 in the factory town of Bangu. His grandfather had been a slave, and he and his brothers all worked in a textile factory, which, like many others in Brazil at the time, had a soccer team that workers played on during their leisure time. Da Guia's brother was considered the star of the team, but one day when the team's defender was injured, da Guia got his chance. His brother, writes Wilson, urged him to draw on his skills as a dancer, and he invented "a short dribble" that was an imitation of "the *miudinho*, that type of samba." Having played as a midfielder until then, da Guia brought a certain way of capturing the field in front of him, of understanding space and movement, to his role as a defender. Though it was a hard road, he carved out a professional career for himself, playing in Uruguay and Argentina before ultimately settling at the Brazilian club Flamengo. "He watched the patterns of a match develop, stepping in to intercept a pass or tackle an attacker at precisely timed moments," writes historian Roger Kittleson. Da Guia admitted that his skill with the ball was partly a form of self-preservation. He had always seen black players like himself "whacked on the pitch," and he knew he had to be a step ahead of the opposing team.[16]

The rivalries among Uruguay, Argentina, and Brazil would become some of the most intense and influential in the history of the game, driving long-standing debates about tactics, as well as the relationship between national cultures and playing styles. At its core, this debate was about whether soccer should emphasize what is beautiful or what is effective. There have always been those who have understood that, if the goal is to win a game—especially against a team that is technically superior—a good strategy is to focus on robust defense. If a team keeps a lot of players in front of the goal, uses physical challenges to break up offensive play, and focuses on not conceding any goals, it can eke out a 0–0 game. Sometimes, with luck, a player can make a break for the opposing goal and even win. What this means, of course, is that the game takes the shape of one team trying to get around a packed defense and the other absorbing attacks and seeking to shut them down. This strategy can be effective, and it frequently leads to ties and a few scattered wins, but for many fans it is incredibly tedious and frustrating to watch. As the French soccer journalist Jean Eskenazi put it: "How shall we play the game? As though we are making love or as though we are catching the bus?"[17]

If you want to cultivate an attacking style of play on a team, you need to configure the defense in a particular way. Although defenders of course need to be ready to stop attacks from the opposing team, they also play a critical role in creating the conditions for their own team's forward motion. This requires versatile defensive players who know not only how to stop the forwards from the other team. Just as important, or even more so, they need to know how to turn the game around, how to move forward and create space for midfielders and strikers toward the opponent's goal. The potential problem, of course, is that if defenders are not talented enough to hold on to the ball as their team moves forward into attack, they make their team vulnerable. If the forwards of the opposing team can gain possession from defenders with an open path to the goal, the results can be disastrous. Many a goal has been scored when an adventurous forward manages to steal the ball from the last defender and streak toward the goal, pulling away from the other players, with only the goalie to beat. The key to having an effective defense on a team that is geared toward attacking, then, is to have versatile defenders. The tactics of the team, however, also have to be calibrated carefully to successfully orient everything toward a strong attacking formation. "The whole history of tactics," writes Wilson, has been a "struggle to achieve the best possible balance of defense solidity with attacking fluidity."[18]

The renowned Argentinean manager Marcelo Bielsa, citing his mentor Óscar Tabárez, summarizes the "fundamentals" of soccer in this way: "1) defense; 2) attack; 3) how you move from defense to attack; 4) how you move from attack to defense." With these principles as the core, the issue becomes "trying to make those passages as smooth as possible." Doing so requires constantly thinking about how players are positioned and move on the field. The position of defensive players is critical in this regard, because it effectively determines how much room other players have to maneuver on the pitch.

There is a rule in soccer that constrains and shapes where players can be on the pitch at any given time: the offside rule. It is perhaps the most influential and important rule in the game. Often misunderstood, and frequently infuriating to players and fans alike, the offside rule is one of the most fundamental pieces of the grammar of soccer. On the most basic level, it prevents attacking players from getting too close to the opposing goal too easily and creates limitations on when and where they can move. Negotiating the offside rule is one of the most complex and absorbing features of the game both for strikers and defenders, an intricate dance that involves positioning and timing of the most nuanced kind. To appreciate and understand this dance is, on a basic level, to appreciate and understand soccer.[19]

A player is offside when she has moved too far toward the opposing goal, ahead of either the ball or the defensive players from the other team. In the current version of soccer, if you are an attacking player with the ball behind you, there must be at least two players between you and the goal—the goalie and the last defender. But it took a while to get to this version of the rule, with a few twists and turns along the way.

The term offside comes from the military, where in the nineteenth century an offside soldier was one who was no longer serving in his unit. Similarly, a soccer player who is offside is not allowed to touch the ball, and therefore no longer an active participant on the team. In a way, an offside player may as well be on the sidelines—though once she gets back into position she can immediately join play again. This can lead to one of the more frustrating sights in soccer: a player is in a perfect position, perhaps in front of goal, but cannot receive a pass or even get in the way of the opposing defenders. The only thing she can do, essentially, is stay out of the way.

How did the offside rule come to be? During the early nineteenth century, before soccer's rules were codified by the Football Association, most versions of games played at various English schools outlawed any forward passing of the ball, that is, kicking it ahead to another player. Therefore, the only way down the field was either dribbling the ball or passing sideways or backward. This is still how rugby is played: passes can only be made backward, which is why advances are often made in a diagonal line, with the ball being passed to the runner slightly behind as the formation moves up the field. In early soccer, if the ball was passed forward, anyone who touched it was considered offside and not allowed to participate in the game. As an early rule book from the University of Winchester put it, a player in such a position when the ball was kicked toward him was not allowed to "kick it himself nor try to prevent the opposite side from having a fair kick at it." Any ball kicked "in transgression of this rule *cannot* obtain a goal." According to the rules of Cheltenham College, an offside player must "immediately leave the ball alone" and could be kicked out of the game if he did not do so.[20]

The impact of these rules depended on other features of the game. It is not that hard to toss a ball backward as you run forward, because you can swing your arms backward. Doing this in a game where you can't carry the ball, and are using your feet to pass, is more challenging. You can turn around and pass of course, but if you are running ahead full tilt and try to pass a ball toward someone a bit behind you—unless you are skilled at flashy back-heel passes—there is a good chance you will end up on the ground. Trying to picture a soccer game without forward passing is quite difficult today, because much of what we love about the game—such as the rapid forward development of plays through dribbling and passing—would simply be impossible. Without forward passing, notes soccer historian David Goldblatt, a kicking game would seriously lack a "measure of complexity, three-dimensionality and depth."[21]

What was the solution? Simply allowing any kind of forward passing might lead to the opposite problem: players could just stand around in front of the opponent's goal and wait for a teammate to lob a high, long ball to them and then push it into the net. The middle of the field would become irrelevant and depopulated, and the resulting game a boring spectacle of volleying the ball. The compromise between these two options, slowly crafted over the course of the nineteenth and early twentieth centuries, was a set of offside rules that allowed players to pass forward, but only under certain conditions. These rules created a game in which you could move forward without the ball, and receive passes from players behind you, as long as there were still a certain number of players from the opposing team between you and the goal.

Probably the earliest version of the offside rule is in an 1847 rulebook from the elite Eton College. According to Eton's rules, a player could run forward to receive a pass, as long as there were more than three of the other team's players between him and the opponent's goal. It evocatively used the term "sneaking" to describe any play that violated these rules. "A player is considered *'sneaking'* when only three or less than three of the opposite side are before him and the ball behind him," the rules said. "In such a case, he may not kick the ball." Except for the fact that it didn't use the term "offside," this was close to what would become the established rule in the mid-nineteenth century. A similar measure seems to have been part of the 1848 Cambridge Rules, an early attempt to create a coherent rule book that could be used in games between universities. Here, too, there had to be "more than three" opposing players between the one who received a forward pass and the goal he was trying to reach. The rule stated clearly that the point was to avoid having a player "loiter between the ball and the adversaries' goal." What this meant concretely was that a player advancing up the field had to always be aware of the opposing players, and keep enough of them ahead of him to be able to receive a pass.[22]

It took some time before such rules came to be accepted across the board. The Sheffield Football Club, the first team created outside of a public school, did not have any rules against offside play in its 1855 rule book and allowed any kind of forward pass. Other schools continued to outlaw forward passing altogether. The rules agreed upon by the English Football Association after its founding in 1863 included an offside rule much like Eton's, with the slight change that it required "at least three" rather than "more than three" players between the attacking player and the opponent's goal. Once the position of goalkeeper developed in the 1870s, this meant that attacking players always had to keep two defenders, in addition to the goalie, between them and the opposing goal, unless they were in possession of the ball.[23]

The basics were in place, but there were plenty of refinements to come. In 1873, the rule was adjusted so that the determination of whether a player was offside was to be made not when they received the ball from a pass, but "at the moment of kicking." This meant that a player could now start to run past a defender once the ball was moving toward them. This added dynamism to the game, though the rule—in place to this day—also required intricate judgment on the part of the attacking player, who has to time his run perfectly, and the referee, who must judge whether a player has moved into an offside position before the ball is kicked. Because the kick might happen far away on the pitch from where the receiving player is located, this can feel like it requires superhuman powers of observation. The offside rule, quips philosopher Paul Hoyningen-Huene, is so complicated that "the referees need two independently moving eyes" in order to apply it. In time, the referee would get the help of linesmen, assistant referees who stand on the side of the field, in making such determinations. Yet the offside remains easily the most difficult to apply in soccer.[24]

By the 1880s, an attacking player was permitted to receive the ball, even if he was in an offside position, from what is known as a corner kick. A corner kick happens when a defending team, including the goalie, touches the ball last before it goes out of bounds behind the goal. In this case, the attacking team gets to kick the ball in from the corner of the field. Usually, teams try to volley the ball from the corner so that it will drop right in front of the goal, giving attacking players the chance to head or kick it in at close range. This is possible thanks to the exception to the offside rule, which makes it so that if a player heads or kicks a ball into the goal directly off a teammate's corner kick, it doesn't matter if the attackers are offside. Decades later, in 1921, the Football Association made a similar rule about the throw-in, allowing players to receive the ball in an offside position when it is thrown in from the sidelines. This rule, too, opened up new possibilities for attack. That is one reason why it can be useful to earn a throw-in—by kicking the ball off another player and off the pitch—when moving into attack. And though this is relatively rare, if a team has a player with a particularly strong throw, she can volley the ball from the sideline directly in front of the goal, in the same way as a corner kick, and players don't have to worry whether they are offside if they can head or kick it in off the throw. In both cases, the exception to the offside rule is only for the first throw or kick. Once the ball is in play again, players have to pay attention to their position. This can end up being very complicated for both players and referees, because it can be hard to figure out everyone's position in the tangle of players in front of a goal after a corner kick. As a fan, the application of the offside rule in these situations can be a bit bewildering, with goals scored but then disallowed by the referees. This is also a moment when referees often make mistakes, or at least calls that are hotly contested by those who feel they have been wronged in the seemingly never-ending struggle over the interpretation of offside.[25]

Originally, the offside rule applied to the entire pitch, which meant that defenders could move quite high up the field, even into the opponent's half, and effectively compress the other team and throw everyone into attack. In 1907, however, the offside rule was changed so it would only apply in the opponent's half. This created a new danger for an attacking team, opening up space for a counterattack. If a team throws all their players into the opponent's half trying to make a goal, a defending team can leave a few players close to the halfway line, but still in their own half. If one of their teammates can stop the attacking team and pass the ball back to them, he can then break with it toward the opposing goal with no defending players between them and the goalie. Because of this rule, it does not make sense for the last defenders to move past the halfway line, because they have to be in a position to stop any breaks from the opposing team. This makes the midfield a key area of contest between players.[26]

One of the most famous ways that teams attempt to capitalize on the offside rule is what is called the offside trap. This is when defensive players move up the field in order to catch opposing forwards behind them, where they can't receive the ball. One of the players who perfected this technique was a defender from Northern Ireland named Bill McCracken, who played for Newcastle United from 1904 to 1924. McCracken would stay close to the halfway line, keeping the attackers as far away as possible from the goal. A second defender from his team, in what was known as a sweeper position, stayed behind to catch any player who snuck past. McCracken was so good at catching players in an offside position that, as Wilson describes, contemporary cartoons depicted him "clapping his hands with glee at getting another offside call in his favor."[27]

It was an effective technique for basically stopping attacking teams in their tracks, and it caught on. Once it did, the number of goals being scored began to drop, and by the mid-1920s fans were getting restless after seeing too many 0–0 draws, and attendance was falling. The Football Association decided that it had to do something, and in 1925 made the final major change to the offside rule. It was a significant one, decreasing the number of players that had to be between an attacking player and the goal from three to two. This gave attackers a clear advantage: they only had to keep one final defender, and then the goalie, between them and the goal. McCracken's trademark trap could no longer be sprung. This rule change had an immediate impact, with a rapid increase in goals scored. The English Football League, founded in 1888 to organize games between professional teams in England and Wales, saw 6,373 goals scored from 1925 to 1926, after the rule change, compared to 4,700 the year before. Games were suddenly more surprising and unpredictable, to the delight of crowds.[28]

The period after this change in the offside rule produced tremendous and far-reaching innovation in how defense was organized. One of the main drivers of this was Herbert Chapman, who was born in Yorkshire and had a long career as a player and then as a manager. Chapman loved the beauty and spectacle of the game, and was worried that an emphasis on results was undermining what soccer was supposed to be. "The average standard of play would go up remarkably if the result were not the all-important end of matches," he insisted. "If we would have better football, we must find some way of minimizing the importance of winning and the value of points." Chapman worried—as have many fans, players, and coaches since—that as soccer became more institutionalized and tied to financial interests, there would be an obsessive focus on rankings and outcomes. In the process, the very things that made soccer beautiful and interesting—the dynamism and creativity of players, the possibility for experimentation with new styles of play that might be either brilliant or disastrous—would be taken over by a boring, industrial, and predictable way of playing the sport.[29]

As the manager of the Northampton Town team from 1902 to 1912, Chapman tried to find a way to make sure his team played with the "finesse and cunning" he valued while still winning matches. He realized that "a team can attack for too long," and began encouraging his players to drop back into their own half, which encouraged the other side's defensive players to move forward in support of their offense. This meant that, if an attacking play could be broken up and the defending players got possession of the ball, they could quickly mount a counterattack, moving into the space left open by the other team. Other managers were developing similar tactics, including a manager named Clem Stephenson who experimented with ways to render the offside rule less limiting by having players drop back into their own half "before springing forward." The key was to pull as many of the players from the opposing side toward your goal, but then have the skill and speed to burst past those players and whatever defenders were behind them, dribbling and passing the ball quickly toward the opposing goal.[30]

When he became manager of Arsenal in 1925, Chapman formalized what came to be known as the WM formation, so called because of the way Chapman arrayed his players on the field. In front of the goalie, he had three defenders, and then a bit farther up two more with defense roles. These became the M that made up the defensive formation. In front of them, in the W formation, were two additional players in the midfield, and then three attackers. The goal was to balance defense and attack, but also to provide strong control over both the center of the field and the wings. Though the formation featured four lines of players—it could be described as a 3–2–2–3—Chapman thought the W and M better captured the dynamism of the system.[31]

The defender in front of the goal, variously known as a center-back or center-half, played a critical role. He had to be very solid in protecting the goal so that other players could move more freely on the sides of the pitch. The key to the counterattack was in the wings, however, where players who could move quickly along the edge of the pitch stretched out before the opposing defense, and then had a better chance of dribbling or passing into the center so a goal could be scored. When first introduced, Chapman's tactic left opposing teams befuddled—as new tactics usually do—breaking up the usual patterns of play. It worked as well as it did, of course, because Chapman had a particularly talented group of players on his team. Arsenal's games became electrifying, involving rapid back-and-forth movement across the pitch as the team absorbed attacks and then created streaking counterattacks, often with players moving up the wings. The player Bernard Joy, who joined the team in 1935, wrote that the strategy consisted of "deliberately drawing on the opponents by retreating and funneling to our own goal, holding the attack at the limits of the penalty box, and then thrusting quickly away by means of long passes to our wingers." The soccer that resulted was, according to Wilson, "twentieth-century, terse, exciting, spectacular, economic, devastating." It was rapidly adopted by other teams and profoundly shaped the way the game has been played to this day.[32]

The tactic made its way to West Africa in the late 1940s, for instance, thanks to a Senegalese defender named Raoul Diagne. His father, Blaise Diagne, was an important political leader from the island of Gorée, Senegal, who served in the French Chamber of Deputies. Raoul Diagne began playing football in the elite schools he attended in Senegal, and at twenty moved to Paris to pursue his studies. There, he joined the Racing Club de Paris, a professional team, where he played as a central defender. He helped the team win a series of French championships during this period, and also played eighteen games with the French national team—the first black player to do so. A powerful defender, he specialized in sliding tackles, capable, as historian Bocar Ly writes, of "stretching out his leg and depriving an adversary who was already looking at the open space in front of him of the ball." After World War II, he returned to Senegal and joined the team at Gorée, off the coast near Dakar. He introduced the WM formation to the team there. The tactic helped Gorée to a series of important victories in the Senegalese championship, a competition between the best professional teams in the country that had been formed in the 1940s. In the wake of Senegalese independence from France, Diagne became the coach of the national team. He coached Senegal to their first victory against France in 1963, and in doing so became a national hero. Diagne had talented forwards and midfielders on his team, but his background as a defender and his sophisticated deployment of defensive tactics were key to his success as a manager.[33]

While crowds, players, and coaches have often enjoyed flowing styles of play focused on moving and counterattacking, these approaches only really work well when teams have the technical talent required for swift passing and velocity up the pitch. More defensive play can sometimes be ideal for teams with less technically gifted players. Karl Rappan, the coach of the Swiss national team in the late 1930s, put it bluntly as he looked back on his career: "The Swiss is not a natural footballer, but he is usually sober in his approach to things. He can be persuaded to think ahead and to calculate ahead." A team like Brazil could win, he noted, with "eleven individuals" with "sheer class and natural ability." But Switzerland could also win with "eleven average footballers," as long as they had a good plan. He developed a style of play called the *verrou*—translated literally as "bolt"—which focused on having a strong, solid defense. It worked: Switzerland defeated England 2–1 in a friendly match in 1938, a major upset, and made it to the World Cup that year. The tactic, however, was not actively adopted by many other teams at the time.[34]

It was in Italy that a more formalized and ultimately famous— and infamous—set of tactics focused around a highly defensive strategy developed in the second half of the twentieth century. The approach came to be known as *catenaccio*, which means "door bolt" in Italian, again using the metaphor of "shutting the door" on attacks. One of those who developed the approach was the Italian manager Gipo Viani. He had found inspiration from an unusual source: fishermen. One morning, taking an early walk past the harbor in his town in Italy, he watched a fisherman on a ship that had just come in from the sea haul in a net full of fish. Underneath it was another net, the "reserve net." Seeing this, Viani had a eureka moment, realizing that while there were always some fish that slipped the first net, they would always be caught by the second. His team, as Wilson puts it, similarly needed "a reserve defender operating behind the main defense to catch those forwards who slip through." This position became known as the *libero*. This player had the role of sweeping in front of the goal, usually remaining far back and providing an added layer of defense in front of the goalie, though the best players in this position were also versatile and able to effectively set up attacking plays.[35]

The power of this defensive style of play was on display during the 1970 men's World Cup in Mexico, when Italy made it to the finals thanks largely to its remarkably strong defensive formation. They were "so patiently defensive," wrote the Scottish journalist Hugh McIlvanney, that "they sometimes appeared willing to wait for opponents to grow old" before attacking the opposing goal. "Patience," for the Italy team, was "a weapon in itself." Though they ultimately lost to Brazil in 1970, Italy became men's World Cup champions in 1982 when they defeated a brilliant West German team 3–1 during a tournament that again showcased their powerful defense. For supporters of *catenaccio*, the deployment of a perfect, impenetrable defense represents the height of the sport. "A perfect game," wrote journalist Gianni Brera, a devotee of the style, "would finish 0–0."[36]

Other fans in Italy and elsewhere, however, have lamented more defensive styles of play, which are sometimes described as "anti-football." For soccer to remain interesting, they argue, there has to be dynamism, motion back and forth, and goals. More recent changes to the offside rule have made things a bit easier for forwards to attack. Traditionally, players were considered offside if they were exactly level with a defensive player. But in 1991 this was changed slightly, so that a player is only offside if he is actually in front of the defender. And since arms cannot be used in play, a player is only offside if his feet, legs, body, or head are ahead of the last defender. Though these seem like minor changes, they can have big effects, because calls for offside play often happen for very small infractions, such as a foot slightly in front of another player. Even a small advantage on the part of an advancing forward can open up space for a fast break in front of defenders. These changes, along with some other changes in the rules that more stiffly penalize various forms of tackling by defenders, have made it a bit riskier to try to use an offside trap against another team. This, in turn, has made attacking play more unpredictable and fluid.[37]

In the flow of a soccer game, the edge of play is often defined by the offside rule, and the way in which defenders use it in positioning themselves. It is there, in a sense, that possibilities are contained. Sometimes, if everything is timed right, a forward breaks at exactly the right speed, in just the right direction, as the ball is passed from behind. She has beaten the last defender, and ahead is a beautiful opening: just the goalie, and then the goal, beckoning. Then the geometry breaks open and everything is in motion, the forward rushing ahead, directly through the center of the pitch, or diagonally finding the right angle. The defenders, beaten, are rushing behind, but if they are just a moment too slow, and if the forward decisively hits the ball hard, or chips it over the goalie, the goal is made, the crowd erupts into cheers and groans, the decisive moment secured.

Sometimes, however, the defender has the last laugh. Perhaps the most infuriating and disappointing moment in soccer—a game with many such moments—comes when a beautiful run leads to a beautiful goal, and just as the spectators jump up, alight with joy, they begin to notice the referee on the sideline, holding up the dreaded flag that indicates the player was offside. The run may have been stunning, the ball kicked gorgeously, the net billowing and the goalie arcing to the ground, hands just a fraction too far away. It was perfect, ready to be replayed and remembered. But it doesn't count, because at the instant the play began, the forward made a mistake, or the defender played things just right, and the offside rule, the ancient law as interpreted by the referee, has decreed the goal illegitimate. And so, play starts again, the defenders creating their lines, limiting movement, ready to stop the advance, and the forwards looking for the moment that will send them into open space.

Through all of the tactical twists and turns in soccer, the role of the defender has remained pivotal in shaping how a team uses the space on the field. The greatest defenders have brilliantly deployed the tactics of their teams, serving both as the last line stopping attackers and as the root for offensive play. The star Argentinean forward Diego Maradona describes the ethos of the defender perfectly in his autobiography, *El Diego*. As a young boy, he first played as a defender, delighting in the freedom and power of the position. "I always was and I still am seduced by playing *libero*," Maradona writes. "You see everything from the back, the whole pitch is in front of you, and you get hold of the ball and you say . . . let's go that way . . . let's look from another perspective. You are the owner of the team."[38]

Today, as David Goldblatt writes, the rules outlawing tackling from behind and a more assiduous policing of physical fouls by referees have made it so that defenders "move more and kick less." They are organized to "defend space," and many teams use what are called "attacking fullbacks," who "are often the players who cover the most ground in the match, providing attacking options down the wing but also required to sprint back to return to their defensive duties."[39]

At their best, defenders impart a kind of serenity and confidence to the players around them and in front of them. This is what made Thuram such a powerful defender: when you saw him there, you felt that the team was strong, that whatever came at him he would be one step ahead. In the 2006 men's World Cup, during a semifinal against a Portuguese team showcasing the star attacker Cristiano Ronaldo, it at times felt like Thuram was literally everywhere at once, diving in front of the goal to block shots with his head, stopping attacks on the wings, roving around the back of the field as if he always knew what the opposing players were thinking. At other times, Thuram's role was to create calm in the midst of chaos and slow down the game when it needed to be slowed down. This was also one of the things that, decades earlier, da Guia brought to the Brazilian teams he played with.

As Kittleson writes, da Guia moved "in slow motion," while "all around him whirled in a frenzy"—a kind of island, "serene" on the pitch. It is that quality, in the end, that makes a defender a force on the team, opening up the possibilities farther up the field, so that the other players always know that, if the attack fails and the tide turns—as it always does—the defenders will be there.[40]

3

THE MIDFIELDER

Aleksandar Hemon was visiting Chicago in 1992 when war broke out back home in his native Sarajevo. Unable to go back, he stayed in the United States, watching "CNN extensively and voyeuristically as it covered the slow killing of my hometown" and feeling "thoroughly disconnected from the world around me." He had long played soccer in Sarajevo, but in Chicago at first he "couldn't find anybody to play soccer with." He writes, "Not playing soccer tormented me." He felt as if he were "at sea" and wasn't "fully alive." Then, riding his bicycle past a lakeside field one day, he saw a group "warming up and kicking the ball around." He asked if he could join.[1]

These weekly soccer games brought together players from "Mexico, Honduras, El Salvador, Peru, Chile, Colombia, Belize, Brazil, Jamaica, Nigeria, Somalia, Ethiopia, Senegal, Eritrea, Ghana, Cameroon, Morocco, Algeria, Jordan, France, Spain, Romania, Bulgaria, Bosnia, Ukraine, Russia, Vietnam, Korea" and even a "very good" Tibetan goalie. The games became Hemon's new home, the place where he fit within something bigger. In the midst of the joyful, chaotic games, he occasionally found "that moment of transcendence that might be familiar with those who practice sports with other people; the moment, arising from the chaos of the game, when all your teammates occupy the ideal position on the field; the moment when the universe seems to be arranged by a meaningful will that is not yours." It is a moment that almost always "perishes—as moments tend to—when you complete the pass." Yet, when making that pass to a teammate—"fully aware that it is going to be miskicked and wasted"—Hemon had that "pleasant, tingling sensation of being connected with something bigger and better than me."[2]

The Swedish novelist Fredrik Ekelund writes similarly about the "fantastic understanding" that he has felt often while playing in a "kickabout . . . the almost telepathic communication with the 'Other', the player who spots you, the player who—without you ever having met or exchanged a word—knows exactly where you want the ball, and at the same moment you, or rather I, know where he wants it played back to him." When you play, he writes, you can "forget yourself" and "feel bigger somehow," part of something unexpected, a web of connections and movement and possibility.[3]

The title of Hemon's memoiristic essay is "If God Existed, He'd Be a Solid Midfielder." With this phrase, Hemon captures something powerful about the position of midfielder. It is that player, he suggests, that best embodies the miracle of connection that Hemon found in his weekly games in Chicago. When all goes well, the midfielder is a fulcrum around which a team plays, the organizing force, the center to and from which all things pass. When you play as midfielder, writes Gwendolyn Oxenham, you have to be "everywhere, all the time. . . . All points connect through you." Midfielders can be a bit invisible to those who have recently come to the game, and yet in a sense they are the most riveting players to watch. "Where is the most work in a football game?" the Danish coach Sepp Piontek asked. "In the midfield. They are involved in attack and defense."[4]

What exactly is a midfielder? Since the development of the WM formation and the many other tactical formations that flowed from it, many players have occupied positions on the field that can be broadly thought of as "midfield." Today, commentators often talk about "attacking midfielders," who essentially serve as strikers, versus "holding midfielders" or "defensive midfielders," who stand as the front line of the central defense. In all of these different roles, however, it remains the capacity for flexibility, and for seeing and sensing the motion and pulse of the entire game, that makes for a strong midfielder.

The Brazilian Waldir Pereira, nicknamed Didi, helped shape the modern midfield position. In a photograph taken during the 1962 World Cup, Didi is pictured concentrating on a game of chess. It is a fitting metaphor, for at his best on the field he was always several steps ahead, finding ways to advance against the opponent without exposing the king—that is, the goal—behind him.[5]

Born and raised in Rio de Janeiro, Didi became one of the most prominent Afro-Brazilian players of his time. The great defender of an earlier generation, Domingos de Guia, noted that Didi's skills may have been honed to such high levels because he had to constantly overcome the racism of Brazilian society to earn himself a place at the highest levels of the sport. "If he had been white, he wouldn't have been so perfect and precise a stylist," de Guia claimed. Didi came of age in the wake of Brazil's traumatic loss in the 1950 World Cup, which had been blamed on Afro-Brazilian players, including the goalie Moacir Barbosa Nascimento. The Brazilian Football Confederation was determined to avenge this loss during the 1958 World Cup. The group claimed it was going to assure victory by using a "scientific" approach to training the team, hiring specialized trainers to oversee the diet and exercise of the players and bringing on a team psychologist to evaluate prospective players. Having blamed black players for the 1950 loss, the confederation also initially created a team made up entirely of white or very light-skinned players—with the exception of Didi, who was considered "absolutely irreplaceable" in the midfield.[6]

The attacking skills of the 1958 Brazilian team's strikers, including Pelé, are what have made it perhaps the most famous team in the history of soccer. But as Roger Kittleson writes in his history of Brazilian soccer, their goals were all based on the midfield work of Didi, who was the "conductor of the team." He controlled the ball brilliantly, but more importantly he controlled the larger flow of the game thanks to his masterful positioning. Didi's posture and passing, according to Kittleson, gave him "the air of an imperial magistrate." He was a "classic midfield general," prompting journalists to give him the nickname "Black Napoleon." As Eduardo Galeano writes, Didi was like a "poised statue of himself . . . standing at the center of the field," where he was "lord and master." He was adept at sending long balls forward, passing them high in the air across much of the pitch, perfectly placed so his teammates could score. For Galeano, Didi embodied one of the truths of soccer: that it was the ball that needed to run, not the player. He played "unhurriedly," and beautifully.[7]

Didi called on various powers to help him play. Before playing a championship match with his team Botafogo, for example, he promised his patron saint he would walk across Rio from end to end if his team won. They did win, and Didi went straight from the game in his uniform, fulfilling his promise, walking across the city that very night. His romance with a singer and actress from Bahia, Guiomar Baptista, was a frequent topic of commentary in the newspapers, and she handled his business affairs. He suffered so much from being apart from her that during the 1958 World Cup, when the Brazilian team was kept in a closed camp to prevent the distractions of contact with the outside world, he went on a hunger strike, insisting that he at least be allowed to talk to Baptista by phone. The coach refused, and Didi ultimately gave in and started eating again.[8]

Didi's technical skills were legendary. He had a "touch so subtle that he did not need to play quickly," Kittleson writes, "holding his position before maneuvering slightly to let adversaries rush futilely by him." He could be a rough player, giving strong tackles when needed to win the ball. "His preference, though, was to a play a beautiful, flowing game, running as much as he had to, but letting the ball run even more." He became famous for a signature move he developed called the *folha seca*, or "dry leaf." This was a way of taking free kicks that left goalkeepers confused and helpless. The ball, writes Galeano, "would leave the ground spinning and continue spinning on the fly, dancing about and changing direction like a dry leaf carried by the wind,

until she flew precisely where the goalkeeper least expected."
With a goal scored this way in a match against Peru in 1957, Didi
secured Brazil's qualification for the 1958 World Cup.[9]

When Brazil faced England early in that tournament, the
English team managers had understood, writes Jonathan Wilson, that "the way to stop Brazil was to stop Didi." They asked
one defender to "sit tight" on the Brazilian midfielder, and it
worked. England was able to scrape through with a goalless
draw. It helped the English that, at first, the Brazilian strikers
lacked spark. The team psychologist had judged which players
were suitable to be included for the tournament. Among those
he tried to disqualify was the striker Manuel Francisco dos Santos, nicknamed Garrincha. The psychologist deemed him too
much of a show-off. In a warm-up game against the Italian professional team Fiorentina before the tournament, Garrincha had
maneuvered around the goalkeeper with the ball but felt that
just kicking it into the empty net wouldn't quite be enough. So
he waited for the goalie to recover, then dribbled around him
again and, only then, finally scored. The psychologist also determined that the seventeen-year-old Pelé was "obviously infantile"
and lacked a "sense of responsibility." "You may be right," Pelé
politely told the psychologist. "But the thing is, you don't know
anything about football." Luckily for Brazil, and for soccer, the
coach ultimately overruled the psychologist, and both Garrincha and Pelé were on the field for a critical match against the
Soviet Union. The presence of the two dynamic strikers was a
vital boost, but their success in the tournament depended on the
tactical structure that Didi had already built for the team, from
its center.[10]

The plan was to shock the opponents with Brazilian skill from the first minutes of the game. "Remember," the manager told Didi before the match, "the first pass goes to Garrincha." Didi passed smoothly to Garrincha, who feinted as if he would move one direction, then went the other way around the Soviet defender, leaving him on the ground. He then slowed down so the defender could get up—and he could beat him again. And then he did it a third time, leaving the defender lying behind him once more. Garrincha then took a shot that hit the post. Soon after, Pelé shot and hit the crossbar of the goal, and a minute later Didi passed a beautiful through ball, which streaked far down the pitch past the defenders and reached a Brazilian player who rushed toward the goal and scored. The French sportswriter Gabriel Hanot called the beginning of the game "the greatest three minutes of soccer ever played." The understanding between Didi, Garrincha, and Pelé was almost uncanny, a brilliant display of motion and dynamism between midfield and strikers.[11]

Brazil's defeat of the Soviet Union was the beginning of a string of victories. They confronted a strong French team led by a brilliant player born and raised in Morocco, Just Fontaine, who scored thirteen goals during the World Cup, a record that still stands. But even France was no match for Brazil, who defeated them 5–2. Brazil marched into the final, facing the home team Sweden. Four minutes in, Sweden scored, and the Brazilian players were visibly shaken. As Brazilian player Mário Zagallo later recalled, the team anxiously thought they might be headed for a replay of the defeat of 1950. But Didi, writes Kittleson, "scooped the ball out of the net, put it under his arm, and walked as slowly as he could back to the center of the field." Along the way, he calmed the players by telling them the Swedes would be easy to beat: "I guarantee these gringos can't play at all." He then started the game back up by passing the ball perfectly over a Swedish defender so that it landed right at the feet of Garrincha. The Brazilian team was now ready to come back. They scored their first goal a few minutes later, and went on to win the game 5–2. As always, Didi's roving, serene play in the midfield opened up the space ahead and enabled the forwards to make goal after goal.[12]

A generation later, when Brazil shone once more at the 1970 men's World Cup, it was again a vital midfield player who led the team to victory: Gérson de Oliveira Nunes, known as Gérson. In his history of soccer tactics, Wilson notes that many soccer fans consider this tournament "the apogee" of the history of the sport, and the Brazilian team that won it as "the greatest side the world has known and probably ever will know." A Brazilian journalist went so far as to compare the significance of his national team's victory to the "conquest of the moon by the Americans" the previous year. Brazil's team had, in fact, gone through a NASA physical training program in preparation for the tournament. Both the moon landing and the World Cup were witnessed by unprecedented numbers of people because of the expansion of television, making them what Wilson calls "the first two great global events of the tele-cultural age." As with the moon landing, many observers considered the "majesty" of what happened on the pitch during the 1970 World Cup to be "somehow a victory for all humanity." "Our team was the best," Gérson explained simply. "Those who saw it, saw it. Those who didn't will never see it again."[13]

In 1958, the World Cup had been televised for the first time, so some viewers were able to see the brilliant play of Pelé and

Didi live. It aired in black and white, however, and without commentary. Occasionally, a clock was superimposed over the visuals of the field to indicate how much time was left in the game. Despite the very basic production of the spectacle, there was a vast audience. When France made it into the semifinal match that year, French people bought two hundred thousand television sets in the course of a few days—a substantial addition to the million sets already owned in the country. By 1970, television ownership was much more widespread globally, and broadcasts were coming in color. The World Cup was the ideal television spectacle. Brazil, effuses Wilson, "played in vibrant yellow with shorts of cobalt blue: they were perfect for the new age of color television. Under the iridescent heat of the Mexican sun, it seemed as though this was the future: bright and brilliant." What's more, for the first time, broadcasters used slow-motion technology to show replays of goals. All of this made the 1970 World Cup a kind of aesthetic revelation, as viewers began to learn to experience the game in new ways.[14]

If it was such a brilliant spectacle, of course, it was because the team was full of brilliant players. There was Pelé, the majestic Carlos Alberto in defense, and the forward Jairzinho—appropriately nicknamed Furacão, the hurricane—who scored in every game in the final round of the World Cup. Connecting all of this together was the midfielder Gérson, the player who set up many of Jairzinho's goals. As the team trained in Mexico, Wilson writes, Gérson "spent hours practicing clipping diagonal balls" to Jairzinho, "calibrating his left foot, making adjustments for the thinness of the Mexican air." The altitude shaped how the game was played during the tournament, slowing down the game, making it harder for the Italian players to pursue the Brazilian players and shut down their advances, and therefore creating space on the field that Brazil used to devastating effect.[15]

Brazil shone early during the 1970 tournament in a group stage match against England, the reigning men's World Cup champions. As Hugh McIlvanney wrote at the time, the game crystallized everything dramatic about the sport. The two most recent champions were facing off, bringing with them "their fierce pride in their separate philosophies of the game," and "the football world was watching for a sign." It was a "concentrated drama," with players going into the match "with the certain knowledge that the result will stay with them, however submerged, for the rest of their lives." Defeat would "deposit a small, ineradicable sentiment." Victory would leave "a few tiny bubbles of pleasure" that would "never quite disappear."[16]

After their team was eliminated from the tournament, Mexican fans adopted the Brazilian team as their own, and the night before the game there was a "raucous assault" on the Hilton Hotel, where the English players were staying. The Mexican police contented themselves with standing inside the doors of the hotel but did nothing to stop the all-night cacophony. The English team had helped to provoke this response, in part by having their own bus brought to Mexico from England, rather than relying on one provided by the tournament organizers. "Do you think we have not yet discovered the wheel or the internal combustion engine?" a Mexican observer wondered. While opposing fans kept the English from sleeping, the Brazilians were up worrying whether Gérson, who had pulled a thigh muscle in Brazil's first game against Czechoslovakia, would be able to play.

The midfielder was determined. "This is the match that stands between us and the World Cup," he declared, and even if he was going to "damage the leg badly" by playing, he was ready to do so to defeat England. The team doctor ultimately decided to keep Gérson off the field against England. Although it was a tough game for Brazil because of the excellent goalkeeping of Gordon Banks, the home favorites were ultimately able to pull out a 1–0 victory, and a rested Gérson was ready for the next games.[17]

Gérson, wrote McIlvanney, was pivotal for Brazil, and not just for his "brilliance as an individual." He shaped the entire team's motion through the "alertness with which he read situations, the subtlety of his running," and the "deadly variety" of his passes. He brought "a sophisticated tactical intelligence and a fierce, infectious will" to the field. "He, even more than Pelé, was the team's formative thinker on the field, compulsively driving, instructing and cajoling throughout the ninety minutes." Gérson was, in other words, a worthy heir to the great Didi and his role in the 1958 and 1962 World Cup victories.[18]

Brazil ended up facing Italy in the final. As he made his way to the game that day, McIlvanney wrote, "every joke seemed funnier, every face friendlier," everyone delighting at the "prospect of one of the last great communal rituals available to our society." There is a kind of electricity that only a World Cup can produce. Forty years later, I went to watch Spain play Holland in the final of the 2010 men's World Cup in South Africa and felt precisely the same way: each interaction and detail infused with delight and meaning, everyone sharing a similar, slightly stupefied grin that said, "I can't quite believe I am here, at the center of the world."[19]

The Mexican fans were fully behind Brazil in 1970—so it was essentially a home game for the visitors—and many observers were confidently predicting a Brazilian victory. One Rio columnist, Armando Nogueira, offered a "simple, technical reason why Brazil would definitely win." The Italians were using a sweeper— that is, a defender who stayed in front of the goal—and so they could not mark, or cover, all the Brazilian players individually. "The Brazil player they will not mark is Gérson," Nogueira predicted. "He will be deep in midfield at the start and they will leave him alone. He will have space, he will move through to shoot, probably score and certainly decide the match." Many such predictions, of course, are made before games and turn out to be totally wrong, and those who pronounce them hope afterward they will be forgotten. But Nogueira, it turns out, was right. The Italians left Gérson largely unmarked, leaving him open to build up Brazil's plans, to devastating effect.[20]

Pelé scored in the eighteenth minute, but before halftime Italy had scored, leaving the game 1–1. Throughout the half, Gérson was testing the Italian side, discovering weaknesses, but without fully exposing his own strategy of attack. Interviewed after the game, Bill Shankly, the legendary manager of Liverpool at the time, declared Gérson's patience during the first half of the game one of the most impressive things about the 1970 World Cup. Though Gérson had realized that he could create difficulties for Italy if he moved up, Shankly noted, he also "knew that if he did too much of it they would see what was happening and try to find a solution at the interval. So he waited until the second half. Then the Italians had no chance to discuss the problem. They were sunk." As McIlvanney puts it, Gérson came out into the second half of the game "like an arsonist who had been allowed to stoke up on matches and petrol" and was now "ready to set the game alight."[21]

In the sixty-sixth minute, Gérson scored a beautiful goal. He started it with a pass to the wing, and then moved forward into perfect position. He moved past a tackle by a defender and then sent forward a shot remarkable for its "clean force." McIlvanney writes, "It flew more than twenty yards in a killing diagonal and was still only waist height when it hit the far side-netting." Now it was clear that Gérson was "the central influence of the match, the hub of the wheel that was grinding Italy down." He soon set up another goal, lifting the ball toward Pelé, who was perfectly placed in front of the goal. Pelé headed the ball down in front of Jairzinho, who ran the ball into the net, putting Brazil up 3–1. Italy was now so confounded that a player delivered the ball at one point straight to Gérson, a move "about as profitable as throwing live grenades against a rubber wall." Before the game ended, Carlos Alberto had scored one more streaking goal.[22]

During the final minutes of the game, the Azteca stadium seemed about to explode. When the ball was sent into the stands, a fan grabbed it and didn't want to give it up. The German referee frantically signaled the sidelines—I need a ball!—and eventually one was produced. By then, however, someone had pried the ball away from the fan in the stands, and so for a moment there were two balls on the pitch. A fan ran onto the grass, as if to say, "We all know the game is over, and it is time to celebrate." When the whistle was finally blown, people thronged onto the pitch. Pelé was hoisted onto the backs of fans, a large Mexican hat was placed on his head, and he was galloped around the field almost as if he were riding a horse made up of human beings. At one point, Carlos Alberto, running around with the World Cup, dropped the gold top of the trophy, and a little boy picked it up and tried to run off with it until another Brazilian player pried it from his hands. It was a breathtaking, almost surreal, victory. The next day, Pelé woke up and thought maybe he had dreamed the whole thing. Even seeing his medal on his bedside table didn't fully reassure him. He called his wife to ask, "Are we really the champions?"[23]

McIlvanney penned perhaps the finest summary of what this moment meant:

> Those last minutes contained a distillation of their football, its beauty and élan and undiluted joy. Other teams thrill us and make us respect them. The Brazilians at their finest give us pleasure so natural and deep as to be a vivid physical experience. This was what we had hoped for, the ritual we had come to share. The qualities that make football the most graceful and electric and moving of team sports were being laid before us. Brazilians are proud of their own unique abilities but it is not hard to believe that they were anxious to say something about the game as well as about themselves. You cannot be the best in the world at a game without loving it and all of us who sat, flushed with excitement, in the stands of the Aztec sensed that what we were seeing was a kind of tribute.[24]

In retrospect, the moment seems even more vital because it ultimately represented a kind of "zenith never to be repeated" in the history of soccer, according to Wilson. After 1970, the game began to change, and the space the Brazilian team used so effectively during that tournament would evaporate as new developments pushed soccer toward a faster, more pressing game. In 1974, a "Brazilian midfield based on elaboration and passing" was overwhelmed in a game against a new force: the Dutch, whose development of "Total Football" transformed the game, the role of the midfielder, and the space of the pitch for good.[25]

It was, in a way, surprising that soccer was revolutionized by the Netherlands. In the 1950s, their national team was, according to Wilson, "barely even a joke." In his history of Total Football, David Winner connects developments in society, culture, and the tactics of soccer in Holland during the late 1960s and 1970s. Total Football, he argues, was the result of a convergence of developments in architecture and social experience, along with the presence of an innovative and brilliant group of players and coaches, first at one club, Ajax, and then on the Dutch national team. Among them, the most legendary was the midfielder Johan Cruyff. Lanky and long-haired, with an "anarchic attitude, and a love of provoking the establishment," he and those around him reshaped the very idea of what team, position, and play were on the pitch. Cruyff was an intellectual leader, full of "bizarre counter-intuitive ideas that were so brilliant that people followed his lead," as one admirer put it. Upon first seeing him play, one journalist called him "Pythagoras in boots." He was, writes Winner, "anti-system but, paradoxically, he had a system: one based on creative individualism." His influence was profound not only in Holland but in Barcelona, where he played in the 1970s and managed from 1988 to 1996. The style of today's Barcelona, considered by many the greatest and most riveting professional team in the world, is very much an extension and embodiment of Total Football.[26]

Total Football emerged at a time when European intellectual life was being shaped by a series of revolutionary new approaches to understanding human society. These movements included the structuralism promoted by the anthropologist Claude Lévi-Strauss, new approaches to language exemplified in the work of Roland Barthes, and the historical school known as Annales, which focused on *longue-durée* (long-term) processes and structures. All of these were united by a concern with understanding the ways in which a range of structures—discursive, ideological, material, cultural—shaped human thought and life, and the ways these structures both circumscribed and defined possibilities for change and, occasionally, opened up spaces for transformation. These broad intellectual currents also influenced design and architecture. In Holland, for instance, structuralist designers and architects sought out new ways of imagining buildings and cities. In 1963, Dutch designer Wim Crouwel created a "Total Design" studio, seeking forms of practice aimed at creating holistic and interrelated systems. The Dutch architect Aldo van Eyck argued similarly that "all systems should be familiarized, one with the other, in such a way that their combined impact and interaction can be appreciated as a single complex system."[27]

Total Football might be described as structuralism on the pitch. Like the new approaches to urban design and architecture, it was all about thinking of space in a different way. At its core was a "conceptual revolution," writes Winner, "based on the idea that the size of any football field was flexible and could be altered by a team playing on it." The principle was deceptively simple: when a team has possession of the ball, that team's goal is "to make the pitch as large as possible, spreading play to the wings and seeing every run and movement as a way to increase and exploit the available space." When the other team has possession of the ball, space has to be shut down, constrained, essentially "destroyed" to limit the motion of the other team. This is done by pressing "deep into the other side's half, hunting for the ball," and making strategic use of the offside rule by having defenders positioned as high as possible on the pitch toward the opposing goal, about ten yards back from the halfway line. Players, especially in the midfield, consistently rush forward toward the opposing goal, seeking to break up the play of advancing players from the other side. Midfielder Johan Neeskens played this role for Ajax, pursuing attacking players so ferociously that his "prey tended to try and retreat into their own half to try and get away from him." They couldn't, though, because he would keep following them even there. Other defenders soon followed his lead, and in time "Ajax hunted in packs," with "the defense so far forward that opposition would be caught offside if they tried to attack."[28]

The defining approach of Total Football was the development of players who could change positions in the midst of play, bewildering opponents and creating a constant shift in the spatial configuration of the pitch. Players had long moved laterally, from left to right, on the pitch as they advanced or defended. Sometimes they might switch places with players in their own position—for instance, a defender on the right swapping with a defender on the left. But Total Football developed a "revolutionary" approach where players changed longitudinally, moving from defense to midfield and even to offense rapidly in the course of play. As Cruyff's Ajax teammate Barry Hulshoff explained, "The player in attack can play in defense." While the defender "must first think defensively," he "must also think offensively." If a defender saw an opening, he could move into it, playing like a striker. In response, strikers might move back into a defensive role in case of a counterattack. Though the players did have positions to which they returned, and where they played best—Cruyff, for instance, was not a very good defender—this fluidity created a riveting and aggressive attacking style of all-consuming play. "Position-switching looked fluid and chaotic and gave opposing defenders a blizzard of movement and hostility to deal with," explains Winner. The approach was surprising to many other football teams when they first encountered it. As the British manager David Sexton explained, with their "pressing and rotation," the Dutch teams "created space where there wasn't any before," offering a potent alternative to what remained a relatively "rigid" tactical approach in England and elsewhere, which had been built around "straight lines and fixed positions." In part because more defensive styles of play, including Italian *catenaccio*, had become common and in-stitutionalized, many spectators were delighted to see the emer-gence of this more open form of soccer. It had elements of the creative and exciting style of the Brazilian teams of 1958 and 1970, but was played more quickly, and with more movement between positions and players, adding layers of uncertainty and experi-mentation that thrilled fans.[29]

Part of the strategy involved using the offside rule strategically to compress the size of the pitch. In the 1974 men's World Cup, for instance, Holland had to figure out how to play against Brazil. As Holland's star midfield player, Cruyff understood his team would never defeat skillful Brazilian or Argentinean players if they were playing "on a huge pitch." But the Dutch players could "reduce the space and put everybody in a thin band" by "squeezing the game" with an offside trap. The key was using the offside rule to create possibilities for offensive play by suddenly moving defensive players up the pitch. By catching a good portion of the opposing team behind the defenders, and therefore unable to receive the ball, the Dutch reduced the number of players they had to beat in order to make a goal. One of Cruyff's teammates on Barcelona recalled a practice session where he learned the strategy. All of the defenders would move forward so as to catch as many as four or five of the opposing players offside and unable to receive a pass. Then, these defenders charged the player with the ball. If they were able to gain possession, they had a numerical advantage and could rapidly move toward the opponent's goal. If it was difficult to create a chance, however, the defenders dropped back and could try the maneuver again.[30]

The Dutch defender Ruud Krol, a key fixture of both the professional club Ajax and the Dutch team during this period, explained that the players "always talked about space in a practical way. When we were defending, the gaps between us had to be very short. When we attacked, we spread out and used the wings." The tactic of changing positions made it possible to play an aggressive game partly because it diminished the amount of space a player had to run: rather than running up field to attack and then having to run back to return to one's defensive position, the defender could become a midfielder or forward for a time, because the forwards would have moved back into defense. In a way, no player had a position. As Krol put it, "The immediate position of play itself determined when and where the players moved within the game." But the preferred posture of the team was one of constant attack. "When we defended," explained Krol, "we looked to keep the opponent on the halfway line. Our standpoint was that we were not protecting our own goal, we were attacking the halfway line." In a sense, then, Total Football made all players into midfielders, demanding of them the versatility, vision, and dynamism required of this position.[31]

The Ajax players had an uncanny ability to adapt to the conditions of a given pitch, on any given day. In an intense showdown played against a Turkish team in Istanbul in 1968, the defender Piet Keizer decided to take advantage of the fact that, under a driving rain, the pitch had turned largely to mud. He lobbed a ball into a thick patch of it. The Turkish defenders had thought the ball would bounce, but because it just landed, stuck there in the mud, they ran past it. Cruyff, meanwhile, had understood that the ball wouldn't go anywhere, and he glided up to it and streaked forward to score a goal. A Kuwaiti emir who was watching the game approached Keizer afterward, so moved by his performance that he gave him the solid gold watch he was wearing. Similarly, in another rainy game in Greece, the Ajax players kept passing the ball into pools of water on the field, tricking the defenders who had not accounted for the fact that water would slow the ball down.[32]

Reporting on an Ajax game in 1972, one journalist wrote that the team had "proved that creative attack is the lifeblood of the game," and that a "blanket defense can be outwitted and outmaneuvered." In so brilliantly deploying a new style, he went on, the team "had made the outlines of the night a little sharper and the shadows a little brighter." In 1973, during a semifinal European Cup game against Real Madrid, Ajax midfielder Gerrie Mühren found he needed a little time before passing the ball to a teammate, so he stopped on the pitch and juggled the ball until the teammate arrived. It was, as Wilson describes, "a moment of arrogance, of joie de vivre" that "encapsulated" what Ajax stood for. As Mühren recalled, "The balance changed" in that moment in the game. "The Real Madrid players were looking. They nearly applauded. The stadium was standing up. It was the moment Ajax took over."[33]

At the center of this swirling storm was always Cruyff, moving, dribbling, making beautiful, curved passes forward. His playing was often breathtaking. The Dutch player Ruud Gullit vividly writes about playing against Cruyff at Ajax, watching him create a goal "as if out of nothing" by eluding one tackle after another and moving unexpectedly from the left side of the pitch to the far-right corner, then lobbing the ball a long distance over the goalie into the net. It was an "extraordinary goal" and even as an opposing player there was only one thing to do: "applaud."[34]

Cruyff, however, played an even more important role in the way that he constantly directed other players. As Winner describes, he was "like a conductor directing a symphony orchestra." The "most abiding image of him as a player is not of him scoring or running or tackling. It is of Cruyff pointing." When he began playing for Ajax at seventeen, he already was delivering "running commentaries on the use of space to the rest of the team, telling them where to run, where not to run. Players did what the tiny, skinny teenager told them to do because he was right." There was a sense that in his mind he always held a vision of possibility, of space opening up, of beauty unfolding. "It was as if," writes Winner, "Cruyff was helping his colleagues to realize an approximate rendering on the field to match the sublime vision in his mind of how the space ought to be ordered." A poem written in his honor—later turned into a song—placed Cruyff in a venerable genealogy of geniuses who saw the world differently, and so remade it: "And Vincent saw the corn / And Einstein the number / And Zeppelin the Zeppelin / And Johan saw the ball."[35]

Cruyff was a cultural phenomenon. He was adored by fans the world over, and many European intellectuals and artists were awed by him. The legendary Russian ballet dancer Rudolf Nureyev was "fascinated by Cruyff." As one of his Dutch colleagues, the choreographer and dancer Rudi van Dantzig recalls, Nureyev once declared that Cruyff "should have been a dancer." There was a "magnetism" about his "perfect control and balance and grace." Van Dantzig mused, "In a way, I think Cruyff was a better dancer than Nureyev. He was a better mover." Van Dantzig also compared the footballer's role to that of Maria Callas's in opera: "Cruyff was a Callas on the field," bringing something "very dramatic, like a Greek drama," to the pitch. Designer Dirk Sijmons, meanwhile, explained that there was something "spiritual" about Cruyff's playing, as if he were a "grandmaster of chess playing twenty games in his head simultaneously" but also endowed with a kind of "telekinesis." Sijmons continued, "He seemed to know where everybody would be in the next three seconds," and as he kicked the ball he was also "making sure his player would appear in that place at exactly the right time."[36]

The artist Jeroen Henneman saw a parallel between Cruyff's play and what painters of his generation were seeking to do in their explorations of abstraction. Henneman also saw "something spiritual going on" at Ajax because of the beauty produced on the pitch. "It is in the grass, but also in the air above it, where balls can curl and curve and drop and move like the planets in heaven." There were moments of perfection and an occasional miracle, such as the beautiful, arcing, curved passes that Cruyff made in order to allow strikers to get behind a line of defenders. "A pass like that is not hit very hard, but it must be very precise," Henneman said. "It's a beautiful thing, a beautiful curved ball, and it is effective. It is also quiet, modest." Henneman, writes Winner, was "beguiled by the extraordinary shapes unfolding on the pitch, patterns of movement and passing that had never been seen in football before." The playing was "very artistic," in part because it was focused on process, on beauty, more than on the goal. It made the center of the field, the space of the midfielder, the center of a swirl of movement and change that was like a dance. "Goalscoring was the possibility, but the real aim was the beauty of football itself," wrote Henneman. It might not have been so beautiful to fans if it didn't also lead to stunning victories. But Henneman and other commentators were also suggesting that, ultimately, what drew them to soccer was similar to what might draw them to great art: a desire to be surprised and moved by patterns and motion, to see in a moment of grace on the pitch a hint of something greater, something magisterial, about the human condition.[37]

The influence of Total Football was vast. It moved with Cruyff, who brought its approach to Barcelona—a team that in many ways still embodies the style of play he helped envision and develop—and it persisted in various iterations of Ajax and the Dutch national team. Since Total Football and the approaches it inspired emphasized pressing and faster movement, the fitness and speed of players became an increasing focus of training routines. In time, this generated an increasingly scientific approach toward the development of players to make sure that they would be physically ready for the demands of this kind of soccer. One study concluded that the amount of distance traveled during games by players doubled between the mid-1970s and the mid-1990s. Soccer since the 1970s, then, has become a faster and more fluctuating game than that played by the Brazilians in the middle of the century. Players are moving up and down the pitch at increasing speed, and the game is changing direction more frequently too.[38]

Midfielders, however, remain as central to the flow of the game as they did in the time of Gérson and the 1970 Brazilian victory. The greatest midfield players are still able to create a sense of calm and pace at the center of the storm. The man considered one of the greatest players in the history of the sport, Zinedine Zidane, was a midfielder who led France to their only World Cup victory in 1998, playing alongside Lilian Thuram, and had a storied professional career in France, Italy, and Spain.[39]

By 2005, Zidane had become legendary enough that he became the subject of a remarkable experimental film: Zidane: A 21st Century Portrait. The filmmakers placed seventeen cameras in different parts of the Santiago Bernabéu stadium in Madrid and filmed Zidane during an entire game. The film focuses on him whether he is on the ball or not, and it captures one of the most curious things about being a player, which is that you almost never touch the ball. The film offers a rich portrait, too, of what it means to be a midfielder, for much of what we watch is Zidane's work positioning himself, ready to create an opening for him to arc forward. During much of the game, he is walking slowly. At one point, the camera focuses on him sliding his cleats across the turf, and the microphones capture this tender sound.[40]

Most of the film is accompanied by a variety of sounds generated in the stadium, carefully mixed together—the chants and cheers and moans and drums of the crowd, but also sounds emanating from Zidane and other players, including words, breathing, grunts and groans when someone is fouled, and the swift brushing of running, along with the thud of kicking the ball. This is layered over with a soundtrack by the band Mogwai that comes and goes in organic relationship with what is happening on the pitch. The film gives us a feeling that we are inside the game, and perhaps even inside Zidane's mind as he plays. In fact, the filmmakers offer a few lines taken from interviews with Zidane, which scroll over the screen at certain key moments. In one of them, Zidane describes what it sounds like on the pitch: "When you step onto the field, you can hear and feel the presence of the crowd. There is sound. The sound of noise." But, Zidane goes on, "when you are immersed in the game, you don't really hear the crowd. You can almost decide for yourself what you want to hear. You are never alone."

In 2002, Zidane scored what many consider to be his greatest goal, helping Real Madrid defeat Bayer Leverkusen in the final of the Champions League. The Spanish writer Javier Marías, a devoted Real Madrid fan, celebrated the goal in the Madrid newspaper *El País*. "Among memorable goals," he began, "there are great ones, there are wonderful ones, and there are supernatural ones." Zidane's fell into the last category. "Supernatural goals have an air of gratuity, of the unthinkable, of gift," Marías writes. "They seem like gifts fallen from the sky."[41]

It was supernatural in part, writes Marías, because it was "unexpected by everyone, including Zidane." The game had been tied since early in the first half, and Real had been mostly chasing the ball. The Spanish commentators were distracted, talking about other things, as Zidane's teammate, the Brazilian player Roberto Carlos, ran toward a pass sent to the far-right corner of the pitch. Carlos seemed intent on simply not losing the ball to the defenders, when he popped it up backward—a high volley, seeming uncontrolled, streaking up into the air, that looked to Marías like a "clearance-balloon." He writes:

> It never occurred to anyone that it might end in a goal. Not to the goalie or Leverkusen's defense, who didn't have time to be alarmed. And not to Roberto Carlos, or even Zidane. He didn't look for the ball, as I said, nor did he go to the spot where he anticipated it was going to fall. No, he circled the edge of the penalty zone, and while the clearance-balloon went up and up, very high, the idea of a goal still didn't enter his mind. When did it come? When did it finally become intentional? Exactly when the ball stopped rising and hovered in the air. It was then that Zidane, who knows gravity and speed, understood that there was no other route in the air than the vertical toward the ground. And he saw that it would fall exactly where he was. Only then did it occur to

him, only then did he decide it (if the last verb can be applied to what was never meditated—not by the German players or the Madridistas). Only then did Zidane understand the chance, the improvised, the unexpected nature of the ball: it was supernatural, a gift fallen from the sky. He did the rest. At times he also seems to have fallen from the sky. That's how he recognized it, and the gift became flesh, and then verb.[42]

As the ball descended, Zidane was at the edge of the penalty box. He swiveled with his left leg out and, with perfect timing, sent the ball looping past the defenders and just below the crossbar, the goalie still far away as the ball streaked into the top of the net.

This was not Zidane's only miraculous goal, however, not by far. In 1995, Zidane was playing with Girondins de Bordeaux against the Spanish team Real Betis, when he scored from the midfield. Zidane recounted the goal, which he considers one of the three or four best in his career, in an interview and suggested there was something mystical about the whole sequence. The goalie had lobbed the ball up to the midfield, where it glanced off another player's head and landed right in front of Zidane. At halftime, other players had pointed out the opposing goalie was often positioned far up outside of goal. Zidane raised his eyes for a second and saw that this was indeed the case. He thought, "There's only one thing to do." Of course, there wasn't only one thing to do: most players in the situation would have just tried to control the ball and start building from the midfield. As Zidane admitted, it happened so fast that he wasn't sure if "I'd scored the goal or if I got help." He continued, "You do ask yourself, how is this possible? So I say to myself: maybe I got help, from somewhere—from who?" As he said this, he looked up, enigmatically, a small, mysterious smile on his lips. From the middle of the field, having taken just two steps, he sent the ball on a beautiful arc all the way across the field and into the back of the net.[43]

For a midfielder, this kind of supernatural goal scored from the halfway line both captures the essence of the position and surpasses it. His focus is almost always about working up through the midfield, painstakingly passing and dribbling forward to open up space ahead, or battling for the ball to stop an advance. He tries to control the midfield so that, ultimately, he or other forwards can score from in or around the penalty box. Midfielders like Zidane clearly harbor a dream, though, that they could skip all that once in a while and score from where they are, in the midfield, making a clean, unstoppable shot through the sky. This is the version of the Hail Mary shots sometimes made at critical moments in football or basketball. In soccer, these goals appear as moments of delightful madness, sudden and impulsive decisions on the part of players who, for an instant, let go and think: Why not?

For goalkeepers, of course, the idea of being scored on in this way is terrifying, and it is one of the reasons some hesitate to move up the field, outside their box. Such goals scored from the midfield are rare, of course, but when they do happen they leave the goalie looking particularly silly. One of the most shocking such goals was scored by the Spanish striker Mohammed Alí Amar, also known as Nayim, during a match between Real Zaragoza and Arsenal. Nayim unexpectedly scored a game-winning goal from just in front of the halfway line in the final seconds of extra time. Arsenal goalkeeper David Seaman dove backward and touched the ball, but ended up sitting in his net. He was, as Wilson writes, "ridiculed for the rest of his career" for letting the ball in from such a distance.[44]

In international games, such goals have been very rare. In the 1970 men's World Cup, during Brazil's first game against Czechoslovakia, Pelé tried to lob the ball toward the goal from the halfway line. It arced beautifully through the air, but it didn't go in. Pelé was applauded, though, just for trying to make such a crazy and ebullient goal. Afterward, asked whether his shot had been "an attempt to realise a lifelong ambition," he smiled and nodded happily. Forty-five years later, another player tried the same thing in a World Cup tournament—this time in the final match—and succeeded. Her name was Carli Lloyd.[45]

As she recounts in her autobiography, Lloyd always had a thing for making goals from the midfield. At the end of practice, she would line up a few balls on the midfield line. "I look towards the empty goal, about fifty yards away," she remembers. "I take a few steps back, sprint up to the first ball, plant my left foot beside it, and swing my right leg into it as if it were a sledge-hammer, pounding it as far as I can." She would do this again and again, trying to reach the faraway goal, and sometimes making it.[46]

Lloyd grew up in Delran, New Jersey, and was recruited to play on the US under-twenty-one team when she was a student at Rutgers University. Then, at the age of twenty-three, she joined the US Women's National Team, which competes in the World Cup. April Heinrichs, the coach of the national team, had been impressed with the way Lloyd struck the ball, "dead center," making it fly "in a way that is very difficult for a goal-keeper to handle." Lloyd had earned a reputation in college for being a tough and physical player, a "one-man wrecking crew" in the words of one coach whose team faced her. With a powerful ability to help shape the space and movement on the pitch, she is always a few steps ahead, positioning herself and placing her passes perfectly. The outcome of a game can often depend, Lloyd writes, on "the smallest of events—a tackle in midfield, a high pressure run that forces a sloppy pass, a sprint to keep the ball in bounds"— which means pushing herself, "finding gears I don't know I have." Lloyd's tactical sense is accompanied by a strongly physical form of play. "I always make a point to have a crunching tackle early in the game," she declares. "It's a part of my game plan." The goal is not to be "dirty," but just to "let my opponents know what they are going to be up against when they are pressing the attack in midfield." Doing this can "set the tone for an entire game."[47]

By the time of the 2011 World Cup, Lloyd had become central to the US team. She was their most precious midfield player. In the team's showdown with Brazil, she played a pivotal role, in the final seconds, by setting up one of the greatest goals in the history of the sport. With the US behind 2–1, in the last minute of extra time, she received a pass in the middle of the field. She took three quick touches, and then passed it with perfect timing to Megan Rapinoe, who was running up the left wing. "*Quick, Pinoe, let it fly*," Lloyd thought as she sent the ball forward, she recalls. Pinoe did, sending a long beautifully curved pass that arced perfectly in front of the goal. Abby Wambach was right there, and headed it into the net.[48]

Though it was Wambach's goal, it was the brilliant play of Lloyd and Rapinoe in the midfield that made it possible. They provided the vision, timing, and execution that allowed the team to score the latest goal in the history of the Women's World Cup. It was pure beauty. As journalist Alicia Rodriguez wrote at the time, "Rapinoe's Cross" was one of those that "players practice their whole lives and never hit quite right. . . . I am tempted to change my name to 'Rapinoe's Cross,' so that years from now, when non-soccer fans ask me how I got such a strange name, I can tell them to watch the clip. And they will watch, and they will be astounded." She concluded, "I will be dreaming of that cross in my sleep for weeks."[49]

The US team won on penalties against Brazil and went on to defeat France, earning a place in the final against Japan. The team's run electrified audiences back home. More people in the United States watched the final than any other soccer game before it in history. It was a riveting match against a tactically brilliant Japanese team—"masters of the one-touch pass," as Lloyd puts it—led by attacking midfielder Homare Sawa. Just as the US team had against Brazil, Japan drew even with the US after a goal scored by Sawa in the waning seconds of the game. This time, however, the US lost on penalty kicks, in part because Lloyd missed her shot.[50]

At the 2013 Olympics, Lloyd shone once again. US coach Pia Sundhage had benched her at the beginning of the tournament, but soon realized she was vital to the team. In the final against Japan, played in Wembley Stadium in London, she received a pass from Rapinoe in midfield, and saw a "stretch of space." With a few touches she managed to keep finding room, pulling the defense with her, and then, as she writes, "let it rip, across my body, across the grain." She sent the ball flying just inside the left post, putting the US up 2–0. Although Japan came back with a goal, a brilliant save by Hope Solo delivered the win for the US team. Sundhage admitted graciously that she had been wrong to doubt Lloyd. "I am really happy that she is more clever than I am," Sundhage said, smiling, in an interview.[51]

The next challenge for the team was the 2015 Women's World Cup, to be held in Canada. Under the stewardship of a new coach, Jill Ellis, Lloyd affirmed her role as the team's central midfielder and was pivotal during the competition. Battling through a few shaky games early on, the team made it to the semifinal. There, they faced a strong Germany, which had just defeated France. I was in the stadium in Montreal that day. It was packed with US fans who had traveled to Canada for the match. We were all talking to each other, on the subway, on the way to the stadium, outside, waiting in line for food: "Where are you from?" I met three women from California traveling together, a referee from Iowa, people who told me tales of going to the 1995 Women's World Cup in Sweden. A mother and her ten-year-old daughter marched through the tunnel from the subway, the mom smiling and saying, "I really can't believe we're here. We made it." That was, in a way, the feeling that infused everyone. In the stadium, the sound was different than that of most soccer matches. It was the sound of voices of many different ages, of children and elders, but most of all of both men and women, boys and girls. Many young women had come with their teams, wearing their own club jerseys, looking on with a mix of admiration and ambition. Young girls lined the stands, leaning down and high-fiving everyone as they walked past, cheering, jubilant, completely at home. That day, the US Supreme Court had issued its decision on gay marriage, an issue important to many of the players on the women's team, and many fans. Some had come ready to celebrate the Supreme Court's decision on marriage equality as they rooted for the team. One fan was draped in an American flag with the white stars on the blue background but the bars in the color of a rainbow. People kept wanting to take a picture of her, or with her, and she happily obliged. Later, in the stands, one woman held up a sign: "Rapinoe Marry Me—In All 50 States!"

The US played confidently from the first. There was a paced serenity about the team as it kept creating its own space, its own openings, showing that mastery that turns the pitch into a place of possibility. A kind of seriousness, but also a quiet pleasure in the small victories that began to pile up, one after another. When the US earned a penalty kick against Germany, it was Lloyd who stepped up to take it. In goal was Nadine Angerer, one of the greatest goalies in the game. Yet there was a sureness, and an intensity, in Lloyd's posture and eyes that was amazing to watch. Her eyes focused on the goal, she stood behind the ball for what seemed like forever. "I have already visualized the PK the night before," she recalls. She knew where she was going to place it. "I am leaning forward, slightly bent at the waist, eyes fixed on the ball, nothing else." She sent it billowing into the net. There followed a humorous moment of brief panic in the stands. The giant screens announced "GOAL" followed by the word "BUT," and people breathed in all at once as if someone was about to take it all back. The French-speakers in the stands had to reassure them. Montreal is a bilingual city, and *but* is how you say goal in French.[52]

With their win over Germany, the US was once again in the final of the Women's World Cup, and once again facing Japan, four years later. Many of the same players were on the pitch on both sides, and the respect between the teams was palpable. But the beginning minutes of the game were among the most remarkable in any World Cup final, a festival of goals that harkened back to some of Brazil's games in the 1958 tournament. Except in this case, three goals came from Lloyd, and she accomplished each in a different way. The first one came after just three minutes, when Lloyd sprinted into the box on a diagonal run, coming in from the midfield, catching a beautiful pass from Rapinoe and powering it into the net. Two minutes later, when the US was given a free kick, Lloyd flew into the penalty box again and knocked the ball into the goal. "Who can even believe this is happening?" she recalls thinking. "It is almost an out-of-body experience," the "greatest start to a game the US has ever had." It got even better: in the fourteenth minute, the midfielder Lauren Holiday scored, making it 3–0.[53]

The Japanese players huddled and then restarted the game, moving the ball quickly, connecting ten passes. But Lloyd was pressing and managed to intercept one of the passes at the middle of the pitch. She looked up to see who to pass to, and noticed something, far down the pitch. The Japanese goalkeeper was way off the goal line, very far up. Lloyd decided to try for the goal. She had, after all, practiced just such midfield scoring for a long time. "It's worth a shot," she told herself. She pushed the ball far enough to "take a full swing at it." As she sent it up, she knew it had "just the right trajectory, high enough to carry but low enough" that there was no time for the goalie to skitter back and catch it. Lloyd, furthermore, was "shooting from the shadows" and the goalie was "looking straight into the sun." The goalie reached and touched the ball, but couldn't stop it and it swept into the net. "We have entered the realm of the surreal," Lloyd recalls thinking. She was "running and laughing," and Solo ran across the field to hug her and asked: "Are you even human?" And there was, in that moment, something of the beyond at work, a bit of God, perhaps, in the work of this solid midfielder.[54]

4

THE FORWARD

The pass came in to the Irish forward Stephanie Roche fast, about knee high, and she had her back to the goal. But she bounced it off her right leg, then kicked it up into the air with her left. She was just outside the penalty box, and as it arced above her, she twisted and volleyed it straight into the net. It was an exhilarating move, acrobatic, unflinching, direct, and graceful all at once.

When the moment comes, a forward cannot hesitate. She has to believe that she can score, even from an unexpected place. That is why forwards are also often called strikers: the goal needs to come like a bolt of lightning. Their feats on the pitch make them the most celebrated of soccer players. Their contributions can easily be counted, evaluated, and compared. What they accomplish is, of course, only possible because of all the other members of the team, and yet the magic of the final touch, of the motion that puts the ball into the net, represents the climax of the game. This also means that they carry a great deal of pressure, for in a way everything comes down to whether they can do precisely the right thing at precisely the right moment in precisely the right way. When a glorious team effort has built up play and placed the ball at the forward's feet in front of the goal, everything perfectly set up, and then she fails, it can feel like a waste. And yet if she carries that burden too heavily, she is more likely to fail than succeed. A forward has to be a bit reckless, willing to take the risk of failing spectacularly—sending a ball looping over the goal and into the crowd, or a few feet outside the goalposts—so that sometimes she can succeed spectacularly. She has to accept that everything leads to her, to perhaps even love that fact. Strikers can seem arrogant and narcissistic at times, but there is a way in which that is precisely what the game demands of them. It is fascinating to watch how different forwards carry themselves in this role, and how they make it their own.

"I knew it was a good goal," Roche told a journalist after the game. She posted a video of it on her Facebook page and sent it to some friends. From there it spread as people shared what came to be known as a "wonder goal," and soon a million—and then a few million more—people had watched. Thanks to the attention on social media, a few months later FIFA selected Roche's goal as one of ten nominated for the Puskás Award. The award, for the best goal of the year, is named after a Hungarian player of the 1950s and 1960s, Ferenc Puskás, who scored over five hundred goals in his career. The winners of the award are chosen from ten nominees by a public vote, and Roche won second place, behind a goal scored by the Colombian player James Rodriguez during the 2014 men's World Cup. Strikingly, Roche beat out one of the most celebrated goals from that tournament, a diving header scored by the Dutch player Robin Van Persie.[1]

Roche's recognition was all the more surprising given the fact that, when she scored her goal, there was only a tiny crowd watching. She was playing for Peamount United, an Irish women's team based in the village of Newcastle in South Dublin. It is one of the leading women's clubs in Ireland, and many of its players—including Roche—have competed internationally for the country. Like many women's teams throughout the world, however, it has only a small local following. Roche's goal was seen by so many thanks only to social media. Although the situation has improved somewhat in recent years, media coverage of women's soccer has long been paltry. The continuing marginalization of the women's game is not an accident. It is a legacy of institutional choices made as long as a century ago, when the men in charge of English soccer decided there was something dangerous about watching women score goals.

There has been very little work on the history of women's soccer, but we do have enough traces to know it is as old as the game itself. By the 1880s, enough women were playing the sport that it was possible to organize international competitions. In 1872, a match was organized between men's teams representing England and Scotland. Less than a decade later, the same rivalry was played out by women's teams, with matches in Edinburgh, Glasgow, Manchester, and Liverpool. Although a women's game in Glasgow was broken up when a group of men invaded the pitch, the games mostly drew large and sympathetic crowds. A few years later, in 1889, a Canadian women's team traveled to

Liverpool to play against English teams. In March 1895, Lady Florence Dixie—the daughter of a marquess and a "keen advocate of women's rights"—created the British Ladies' Football Club in London, with the goal of supporting tours by women's teams throughout Britain. She invited women to come play "a manly game" and therefore show "it could be womanly as well." Their first event was a matchup between teams representing the north and south of London. Another game in Newcastle soon after drew eight thousand spectators, a large crowd for the period.[2]

Women have consistently faced criticism and opposition from those who believe it is inappropriate for them to play soccer. In nineteenth-century Britain, critics argued it was immodest for men to watch women running about on a field. To dampen this criticism, women played in elaborate attire that must have made it quite hard to run and kick the ball. An 1895 report from Manchester described players in "full black knickerbockers fastened below the knees, black stockings, red berretta caps, brown leather boots and leg-pads," and "a short skirt above the knickerbockers." Some men involved in soccer organizations went further, claiming that playing soccer was bad for women's health. The real source of their anxiety was something else, however. They worried that the existence of women's teams posed a threat to the masculine image of male players and of soccer itself. In 1902, the English Football Association outlawed men's teams from playing against "lady teams," presumably fearing the embarrassment that might result from men losing to women.[3]

During World War I, women's soccer nevertheless boomed in England, when women who had been recruited in large numbers to work in war-related industries embraced the tradition of the factory-based soccer team. It had been common since the nineteenth century for British factories to field soccer teams of their male workers, who competed against teams from other factories. During the war, however, these men's teams were depleted by the departure of many men for the trenches. One day in October 1917, during the lunch break at the Dick, Kerr company in Preston, Lancashire, a woman named Grace Sibbert and her friends started making fun of the male players on the factory team, which had lost a series of games. "Call yourself a football team?" Sibbert taunted. "You're useless; we could do better than you lot!" The male players, embarrassed, challenged the women to a match. Sibbert and her friends agreed. They enjoyed the game so much that they created the Dick, Kerr Ladies football club. On Christmas Day 1917, they organized their first game, a charity event to raise money for a local hospital for wounded soldiers. They faced off against a women's team from a nearby foundry, drawing a crowd of ten thousand. It was, as Gail Newsham writes in her book about the team, the "start of what was to be the most phenomenal success story in the history of women's sport."[4]

The Dick, Kerr Ladies team organized other charity games over the course of 1917 and 1918, drawing crowds of between two and ten thousand. It was clear, one newspaper noted, that there was "distinctly a public for ladies' football." When the war ended, the team and others like it decided to keep playing. In 1919, a fourteen-year-old named Lily Parr came to work at the Dick, Kerr factory and was soon recruited to the team. She was a consummate forward, relentless and physical in attack. She eventually became the star of the team and, according to Newsham, can be considered "probably the greatest woman footballer of all time."

In a career that stretched from 1919 to 1951, she scored at least nine hundred goals.[5]

Parr was an imposing figure on the pitch, writes Newsham, "almost six feet tall, with jet-black hair, her power and skill were admitted and feared wherever she played." Parr was "big, fast and powerful." A 1921 newspaper article described the young player as the greatest "football prodigy" in the country, not just because of her "speed and excellent ball control" but for her strength, which enabled her to "brush off challenges from defenders who tackle her." According to a 1923 match program, she could "take corner kicks better than most men and [score] many goals from extraordinary angles with a left foot cross drive, which nearly breaks the net." Her long-time teammate Joan Whalley recalled how strong her kick was. She could "lift a dead ball, the old heavy leather ball, from the left wing over to me on the right and nearly knock me out with the force of the shot." One male professional goalkeeper found out just how strong her strike was. He told her that while she might look impressive against other women, she couldn't score a goal against a man. Parr decided to test the hypothesis. She told him to stand in goal, then took a shot that was so fast and strong that "as he put his hands up to catch the ball, his arm was broken by the force of her kick." Parr "smiled to herself as she heard him say to his teammates, 'Bloody hell, get me to the hospital as quick as you can, she's broken me bloody arm.'"[6]

By 1920, Dick, Kerr was the most successful women's team in England and began connecting with women's teams in other countries. They invited a team representing France to play them at Preston. The British women greeted the visitors by singing La

Marseillaise as their train came into town, and the two teams then played in front of a crowd of twenty-five thousand before going on a tour that ended with a game in Chelsea's Stamford Bridge stadium. The goalkeeper for the French team later returned to join Dick, Kerr, making it an international squad. Soon after, the team journeyed to Paris, where they played in front of a crowd of twenty-two thousand so animated that the game ended in a pitch invasion by French fans angry at a refereeing decision. After another game played in Roubaix, which had a large population of British soldiers and workers, the Dick, Kerr players' were carried off the field by delighted fans after a victory. The tour helped to propel the growing popularity of women's soccer in France.[7]

On the team's return to England, they were more popular than ever. They played a charity match in Leicester at night. Searchlights were used to illuminate the pitch. On Boxing Day 1920, they played at Goodison Park in Liverpool, the home stadium of the Everton men's team. A massive crowd of fifty-three thousand packed into the stadium to see Dick, Kerr take on the hometown women's team. Another ten to fourteen thousand spectators were outside, unable to get in. By 1921, they were playing two games a week, traveling all over Britain. Because they were not paid as players, they continued to work in the factory. Sometimes the women left for matches in the afternoon, played, and then returned home the same night in order to be back on the job early the next morning. They were part of a huge, thriving network of an estimated 150 women's teams in Britain by 1921. Dick, Kerr was considered the best of them. In a game against an all-star team of players from throughout the country played in Leicester, a crowd of twenty-five thousand watched as Parr scored a hat trick in the first half and then two more goals in the second, ensuring a 9–1 win for her side.[8]

While male spectators were thronging the games, some powerful men in the world of professional soccer were getting nervous. About nine hundred thousand spectators had gone to see the Dick, Kerr Ladies club over the course of 1921. Meanwhile, many men's teams were struggling to draw crowds anywhere near as large. The women represented the threat of competition, and the leadership in the English Football Association fretted that soccer was starting to be seen as a women's game. On December 5, 1921, the Football Association unanimously passed a resolution that declared: "Football is quite unsuitable for females and ought not to be encouraged." Clubs belonging to the association should, they went on, "refuse to use their grounds for such matches."[9]

Overnight, Dick, Kerr and other women's clubs found themselves banned from most of the stadiums in the country. The Football Association went even further in trying to marginalize the women's game; referees credentialed by the association were instructed not to referee women's matches. The association's stated reason for the ban was to protect women's health and fertility, which they claimed could be harmed by playing soccer. A few doctors came out in defense of women's soccer, questioning this reasoning. As one physician noted, "Football is no more likely to cause injuries to women than a heavy day's washing." Many supporters were dismayed. "Why have the FA got their knife into girl's football?" people asked on the streets of Liverpool. "Are their feet heavier on the turf than the men's feet?" But the decision was made, and the broad power of the Football

Association meant that the expansion of women's soccer was stopped in its tracks.[10]

Women's soccer in Britain went, if not quite underground, then to other grounds. "We play for the love of the game and we are determined to carry on," Dick, Kerr captain Alice Kell wrote. Women's teams came together to create an independent Ladies' Football Association. The English Football Association ban, however, made it very difficult to find venues and referees for their games. The project of a women's league foundered. The Dick, Kerr Ladies found another way to keep playing, however, organizing a new tour abroad, this time to North America. "They certainly rule English football," Kell noted of the Football Association, "but not the world, thank goodness."[11]

The English Football Association continue to go to great lengths to quash women's soccer. Angry that Dick, Kerr was organizing an independent tour, the association members attempted to derail it by convincing their Canadian colleagues to refuse to organize matches with the team. In the United States, however, Dick, Kerr was welcomed. There were few women's teams there at the time, but a number of men's teams agreed to play the British women. There were games in New Jersey, Rhode Island, and in New York City, where Dick, Kerr played Centro-Hispano, a team made up of Latino immigrants. A brass band played the American and British anthems as the two teams marched onto the field. There were seven thousand spectators and a lot of goals: the game ended 7–5 for Centro-Hispano. From there, the tour took Dick, Kerr to other cities including Washington, DC; New Bedford, Massachusetts; and Baltimore, Maryland. The team drew larger crowds than usual for men's games in the United States and also attracted more women to the stands.[12]

Kell noticed that the men's teams in the United States played a different, more physical style of soccer. "There isn't the same combination," she wrote. "It's all individual play out there. They don't pass the ball around like we do, so the players all try to get through on their own." Tackling was rough: "When a forward is coming along with the ball the full-back doesn't bother much about the ball if he can get the man." The British women also encountered that curious offshoot of soccer, American football. Visiting a college campus, they walked past a football practice. The odd-looking, oval-shaped ball came flying toward them, and Parr kicked it back—sending it over the posts at the end of the field. The coach joked that this was clearly a fluke, and Parr, characteristically, took up the challenge: she kicked it again, farther and higher. On their visits to some US campuses, the British women also met with athletics staff who were considering setting up women's soccer teams on campus. It would ultimately take fifty years—and the passage of Title IX—but in time colleges became the focal point of the explosion of women's soccer in the United States.[13]

On their return home to Lancashire, the Dick, Kerr players were greeted by local officials, one of whom said he was sorry about the ban on women's football, adding that he hoped the leaders of the Football Association would soon see the error of their ways. They didn't: the ban in England lasted until the late 1960s. Given England's central place in the administration of the sport at the time, the association's decision had global implications. Following England's lead, similar bans were put in place in other countries in Europe and Latin America over the next decades. The German Football Association formally banned women's soccer from 1955 to 1970. Even when the ban was lifted, for several years the association required women to play sixty-minute games, in flat shoes rather than cleats, and with smaller balls than the men. In Brazil, women's soccer boomed in the early twentieth century as it had in England, with as many as forty teams just in Rio de Janeiro. The Brazilian Football Federation banned women's soccer in 1941, however, a policy only lifted in 1979. While the country has produced probably one of the greatest forwards alive today, Marta Vieira da Silva, along with many other talented players, persistent lack of support and funding on the part of the federation has held back the team over the past decades. In 2017, frustrated players on the Brazilian women's national team wrote a detailed letter outlining a history of unequal treatment at the hands of the federation, with some retiring from the team in protest.[14]

Such prohibitions, of course, could never stop women from playing the game they loved. As Dick, Kerr player Alice Norris recalled, though it was a "terrible shock" when the English ban was handed down in 1921, "we ignored them when they said that football wasn't a suitable game for ladies to play." In Britain and throughout the world, women found other grounds for practice and playing, and in time they organized independent networks of teams. Parr became a nurse and continued to live in Preston, where she played until 1951. Since her death in 1978, she has gradually been recognized as a pioneer and founder of modern soccer. Still, unfortunately, we only have descriptions of a few of her goals, and only a few images of her playing remain. We are left to imagine her streaming up the pitch, cutting around defenders, sending an arcing cross into the net, as she scored her hundreds of goals, embodying the determination and recklessness of a great forward.[15]

In soccer, forwards are the consummate authors of goals. And each goal is its own story, perhaps even its own poem. In a way, the work of the forward can seem evanescent. Some like it that way. As Jonathan Wilson describes, there is a story told in both Argentina and Uruguay of a player "skipping through the opposition to score a goal of outrageous quality and then erasing his footsteps in the dust as he returned to his own half so that no one else could ever copy his trick." Although every goal is celebrated in the moment, most of them are forgotten. The forward knows, however, that there is always the possibility of scoring a goal that will become legendary, that if he writes one that enters the canon of soccer, he will also at the same moment be greeted into the pantheon of those who have written the greatest passages of the game.[16]

No one knows this better than Diego Maradona, whom many consider the most important and influential player the game has ever seen. He scored two of the sport's most remembered goals in the course of one game during the 1986 men's World Cup. Both were such memorable works of art that they were given titles. The first, the "Hand of God," might just be the most infamous goal ever scored, while the other, known as the "Goal of the Century," is often considered the greatest goal in soccer history. There will always be a debate about whether Maradona is *the* greatest soccer player the game has ever seen—and of course future players will have something to say about that. There is little doubt, though, that he is the most interesting, culturally significant player in the history of the sport, a kind of endless tornado whose life on and off the pitch is a mix of delirium, brilliance, excess, absurdity, and redemption.

During his years as a player, Maradona was pugnacious and controversial. He struggled with drug use for much of his life, and was often at odds with coaches and FIFA. He was also a perpetual trickster. "Maradona had a habit of sticking out his tongue when he was on the attack," writes Eduardo Galeano. "All his goals were scored with his tongue out." His life was "one long improvisation on the field," making him a kind of "talisman of Argentina soccer." He was, in the words of Mexican journalist Juan Villoro, "the greatest and most impulsive artist ever to grace the game." It is a struggle to even begin to represent Maradona, though the Serbian director Emir Kusturica offers a mighty effort in his 2008 documentary about the player, *Maradona by Kusturica*. The frenetic, swirling film takes us into the Church of Maradona (whose acolytes complete their marriage ceremonies by reenacting the Hand of God), offers us footage of Maradona leading anti-US demonstrations in the 1990s alongside Venezuelan president Hugo Chávez and Bolivian president Evo Morales, and shows the player singing alongside his daughters a bittersweet, mournful, but ultimately exultant song of regret and apology for his years of cocaine addiction. If Maradona had not ended up a soccer player, Kusturica notes, he would have become a revolutionary. And in his way, he was.[17]

"Playing football gave me a unique peace," Maradona writes of his childhood in the Buenos Aires suburb of Villa Fiorito. His family was poor, and he and his seven siblings sometimes had to dodge the leaks from their roof when it rained. His father, Don

Diego, worked in a mill "pounding cattle bones from four in the morning to three in the afternoon." As a young child, Maradona received a soccer ball from a cousin. It was, he writes, "the best present I've ever received in my life. . . . I was three years old and I slept with it hugged to my chest all night." As he grew, he played with neighbors at a place called Siete Canchitas—seven little pitches—on the "enormous patches of waste ground" and "really hard earth." Maradona recalls, "When we started running, we stirred up so much dust that we felt as if we were playing at Wembley in the fog."[18]

The forward attributes his early success to the simple fact that his father made sure he always had at least one good meal every day. "That's what made me different from the others: I had good legs and I ate." Yet he was clearly always hungry to escape a life of poverty. Soccer was for Maradona, as for many other players in history, a way out and a way up. He embodied the fearlessness that a forward needs to succeed. He was willing to try to score in any way imaginable, willing to invent new ways of moving in pursuit of the goal, and he didn't hesitate when there was an opening. By the time he was twelve, Maradona was already stunning defenders and crowds with his goals. Galeano describes one: "Several players tried to block his path: he put it over the first one's tail, between the legs of the second, and he fooled the third with a backheel. Then, without a pause, he paralyzed the defenders, left the keeper sprawled on the ground, and walked the ball into the net." Interviewed on film as a boy, Maradona declared to a journalist that his dream was to play in the World Cup for Argentina. It now seems prophetic, but of course, as he admits in his autobiography, "it was the same dream every child had." And, as his years dogged by depression and addiction suggest, in his heart there was always fear, too, that he would fail.[19]

Starting at age fourteen, Maradona made his way up through the divisions of Argentinean soccer, from the ninth to the first. As he went to his debut with the first-division team Argentinos Juniors in October 1976, he hoped to get some prize money so he could buy "a second pair of trousers." Putting him on the field, the coach told him, "Go on Diego, play like you know how . . . and if you can, nutmeg someone"—meaning that he should kick the ball between a player's legs and then run past them, a particularly humiliating way of outplaying a defender. Maradona did: with his back to the defender covering him, he received the ball and then turned and kicked it between his legs. "It went clean through and I immediately heard the *Ooooolé* . . . of the crowd, like a welcome," Maradona recalls. He also quickly learned that the defenders at that level didn't mess around. "I had to jump in time; you had to dribble round a player, jump over his kick and continue with the ball. If you don't learn that, after the third kick you can't go on." Part of the glory of Maradona on the pitch was watching him leap and twist, lightly, sometimes like lightning, as he tried to survive the onslaught of defenders who understood that the only way to stop him was to take him down. Maradona never forgot that debut. "That day," he writes, "I touched the sky with my hands." One newspaper article about the teenager's meteoric rise declared, "At the age most kids hear stories, he hears ovations."[20]

Maradona was so beloved in Argentina because he embodied a celebrated way of playing soccer, one that placed a premium on the spectacular, the beautiful, and the playful. The pure energy condensed in his body, the endless forward propulsion, the tension, always destabilized defenders who were never sure what he would do next. That is the mark of the great forward. It enables him to recalibrate an entire game, placing the opposing players on the edge of panic, always conscious that even the smallest of errors can be an opening for their roving opponent. At the time, Maradona writes, "there was a big fight between those of us who played and those of us who . . . ran. And I was something like the standard-bearer for those who loved having fun with the ball." He constantly complained that referees did not protect him against fouls by defenders, and so allowed cynical, physical play to destroy the beauty of a creative attack. After he was seriously injured by a defender while he was playing for Barcelona, a headline describing the incident complained that Maradona was "forbidden to be an artist." Like many other forwards, Maradona could easily be accused of being a pouting megalomaniac, not to mention paranoid and narcissistic. He regularly, childishly declared he was sick and tired of the way he was being treated and was leaving. As the Argentinean journalist Daniel Arcucci pointed out in 2008—when Maradona came out of retirement for a short spell as the manager of the national team—the player had "first announced he'd had enough in football in 1977." Yet everyone knew not to take him seriously. Soccer was his life, and his lifeline, and even when he disappeared for a time, he always came back.[21]

Maradona lived and played at the crossroads of a long-standing debate in Argentinean soccer about precisely how the game should be played in a way that best embodied the national character. The country had tight links with Britain in the nineteenth century, and was the first in Latin America to adopt soccer, with a game recorded in 1867. Employees of the large British banks and companies in Argentina played the game, and Argentinean elites sent their children to English-language schools where soccer was part of the curriculum. It was in these schools and in athletic clubs set up by British and Anglo-Argentine residents that the game took root. The first league was formed in 1891, and the Argentine Football Association founded in 1893. But the anglophone elite soon found its dominance of soccer challenged. Between 1895 and 1914, the population of Argentina doubled with the arrival of European immigrants from Italy, Spain, Portugal, and Germany. Soccer was a way, notes historian Joshua Nadel, to make these immigrants "part of the nation," but it was also a way for them to "show their superiority over the elite 'Anglos' who were seen as controlling the national economy." Soccer, explains Galeano, was a form of communication not just among various European migrants but also between these migrants and those arriving in Buenos Aires and other cities from the Argentinean countryside. "Thanks to the language of the game, which soon became universal," he writes, "workers driven out of the countryside could communicate perfectly with workers driven out of Europe." As the migrants from Europe and rural Argentina transformed Buenos Aires, soccer became a crucial cultural idiom. By 1914, there were about five hundred clubs in the city of Buenos Aires alone.[22]

Wresting soccer from the English—and transforming it by developing new styles of playing rooted in Argentinean culture— gave the game a potent and enduring social meaning. Players in the country, writes Wilson, developed their own style of play, in which "power and discipline were rejected in favor of skill and sensuousness." As Nadel notes, Argentinean writers during the period crafted an image of a particular kind of player, a *pibe*, a poor kid who "taught himself to play the game on the empty fields of the Buenos Aires suburbs." There, the "holes, roots, rocks created an obstacle course for the *pibe*, who by playing on this uneven ground learned how to retain possession of the ball." The skills developed there made for a kind of "star player defined by his ability to keep the ball at his feet and to use a series of feints to go through opposing defenses." Galeano argues there was also a link between soccer and another popular form of performance developed at the time: the tango. "Dancers drew filigrees on a single floor tile," he writes, "and soccer players created their own language in that tiny space where they chose to retain and possess the ball rather than kick it, as if their feet were hands braiding leather. . . . The ball was strummed as if it were a guitar, a source of music." Although some criticized this style of soccer as being too individualistic, by the 1920s it had come to be seen as just as quintessentially Argentinean as the tango.[23]

In time, this style of play became known in Argentina as *la nuestra*—our style. It was driven by the joy of attacking, and therefore focused on spectacular play by strikers. The games were festivals of goals: between 1936 and 1938 there was not a single 0–0 game played in the highest-level Argentinean league. In the novel *On Heroes and Tombs*, the writer Ernesto Sabato offers an anecdote from the 1920s that crystallizes what many in Argentina thought soccer should be. During a game, a striker named Manuel Seoane set up a play with his teammate Alberto Lalín. "Cross it to me, man," Seaone said, "and I'll go and score."

The plan worked perfectly, Seoane got the ball, shot, and scored. As he ran back to celebrate, he said, "See, Lalín, see?!" His team-mate responded, "Yes, but I'm not having fun." Scoring goals in a predictable way wasn't really worth it. Instead, the key was developing a style that was beautiful and exuberant, that made fans gasp and cheer because of its inventiveness and creativity. This is what would give soccer meaning as an expression of a broader, bold Argentinean culture, a way of being in the world, something Maradona exemplified more than any other player.[24]

"We went out on the pitch and played our way: take the ball, give it [to] me . . . this, that and the goal came by itself," explained Juan Carlos Muñoz, a forward who played on the Argentinean team River Plate in the 1940s. Fans called the team the "Knights of Anguish" because it often "took a long time for the goal to come." In front of the goal, the forwards did their best to score, but "in the midfield we had fun. There was no rush." This was perhaps an embrace of one of the fundamental truths about being a forward. A forward's work is, in its purest sense, the point of the game: to score goals. Yet a forward's dominant experience is one of building and building toward a goal, but never reaching that goal. For every score that is made, there are so many more misses and failures. There are yawning volleys over the bar and strikes where just a fractionally different angle would have made all the difference. The rarity of goals is part of soccer's fundamental truth. The Argentinean style was meant to accept that and turn it into a form of pleasure. The game is about the process, the pleasure of building up something through intricate movements and passes, each of them beautiful and pleasurable in their own way. Instead of always being focused on the goal, why not accept that soccer should really be about enjoying the play?[25]

In the late 1970s, César Luis Menotti, the manager of the Argentinean national team, sought to anchor his leadership of the team in this understanding. He was an unlikely figure to represent his country on the international stage. Argentina was in the hands of a brutal, right-wing military dictatorship, and Menotti was, as Wilson describes, "left-wing, intellectual, a philosopher, and an artist"—an "ineffably romantic figure," a "pencil-thin chain-smoker with collar-length hair, graying sideburns, and the stare of an eagle." According to Wilson, Menotti saw soccer as "a means of self-expression, a way for a player or a coach to live out their ethical beliefs." For him, the team was "above all an idea." Like those who celebrated Total Football during the same period, he was worried that coaches were too oriented toward victory, and therefore destroyed the "festival" that should be at the heart of soccer. Focusing only on the outcome of each matchup led to a style that avoided risks and diminished the beauty of the game. After all, Menotti noted, most teams in any given competition ultimately lost, so winning should not, and could not, be the only objective. "In a thirty-team championship," he said, "there are twenty-nine who must ask themselves: what did I leave at this club, what did I bring to my players, what possibility of growth did I give to my footballers?" Menotti's goal was therefore to make sure that efficacy was never "divorced from beauty." As a coach of the professional team Huracán in the early 1970s, he managed to make the team embody their name. "To watch them play was a delight," one journalist noted. It brought fans back to an earlier day of Argentinean soccer, full of "one touch-moves, nutmegs . . .

one-twos, overlaps." After Huracán defeated one team in Rosa-rio 5–0, the opposing fans applauded them in gratitude for the beauty of their play.[26]

Argentina hosted the 1978 men's World Cup, and its government sought to use the tournament to legitimize its dictatorial rule and present an image to the world that hid its human rights violations. Nevertheless, the Mothers of the Plaza de Mayo, who protested silently with photographs of their children who had been disappeared by the military, were able to use the event to gain international attention for their cause. Given his politics, Menotti was in an ambiguous position. He knew that he and his team were being used to stoke nationalism and silence opposition. But, he argued, by playing a kind of soccer that was "free and creative," the team could offer the people of the country "a reminder of the free, creative Argentina that existed before the junta." Before the final game, he told his players, "We are the people. We come from the victimized classes, and we represent the only thing that is legitimate in this country—football. We are not playing for the expensive seats full of military officers. We represent freedom, not the dictatorship." Menotti's team defeated the Dutch in an intense final in Buenos Aires.[27]

The eighteen-year-old Maradona was not on the team in 1978. But in the coming years, the young striker would become the standard-bearer for Argentinean soccer. He embodied the quick-moving, theatrical style long celebrated in the country. By the time of the 1986 men's World Cup, he was the most celebrated player in the world, and he captained the Argentinean team. Hugh McIlvanney captured the wonder, and surprise, of Maradona in his dispatches from Mexico that year. Compared to other "truly great goal-scoring attackers in the history of football," such as Pelé or Johan Cruyff, Maradona might "at first glance" look like "a Jeep among racing cars." Although short and stocky, he was masterful at the "sinuous infiltration of the crowded penalty areas of the modern game." He was, writes McIlvanney, a "Formula One machine all right, a phenomenon capable of reducing the best and swiftest defenders to impotent pursuit, of leaving them as miserable stragglers baffled by astonishing surges of acceleration and the most remarkable power steering in sport."[28]

Maradona was in fact very fond of fast cars. At the time of the 1986 World Cup, he was playing professional soccer for Napoli, leading the team to unprecedented success in the Italian league. He was beloved in Naples for the defeats he inflicted against much-hated rival teams from the north of Italy. These teams looked down on Napoli. One banner at a game read, "Welcome to Italy: now wash your feet." When Maradona helped lead the Napoli team to victory, writes Villoro, it "defied all logic." The team was seen as "an African horde" from "the lofty climes of the Milan dressing room." But they were winning nevertheless. Maradona had also become a global icon. A poll taken at the time determined he was the "best-known person in the world." Not surprisingly, automobile companies were eager to have Maradona seen in their latest models. "I asked for cars that weren't available and soon afterwards I would get them delivered," he recalled. Once, representatives from Mercedes brought him a new high-end model—the first to come into Italy—as a gift. He tried it out, but it was an automatic, so he wasn't interested. He did keep several other sports cars, including a Lamborghini, a Rolls-Royce, and a black Ferrari F40—"the only one in the world at the time." They came in handy as Maradona negotiated a busy season of professional play and World Cup qualifying matches for Argentina in 1985. After a game in Turin against Juventus, he sped away in one of his sports cars—"I can't remember which one," he writes—and drove 250 miles to the airport so he could take the plane to Argentina to play a qualification match in Buenos Aires the next day. Maradona played the game, scored a goal, and got back on the plane for Rome, playing a match for Napoli before again crossing the Atlantic to play in Argentina.[29]

Maradona recalls how much trouble a young Peruvian defender named Yordy Reyna had given him during a World Cup qualifier. Reyna had been given the order to never leave Maradona's side. He "followed me everywhere, to the loo practically, it was madness!" At one point Maradona needed medical attention and Reyna "followed me to the edge of the pitch." Years later, Reyna and his teammates sent Maradona a signed ball when he was receiving medical treatment in Cuba. "Aged forty and in Havana," Maradona jokes, "and I still couldn't shake him off!" Maradona almost always could beat one defender—even one as dogged as Reyna—but he admitted that early in his career he had trouble with what was called "zonal marking." This approach has defensive players cover a particular zone on the pitch rather than follow a specific player. While this requires good coordination between defenders, it often frustrates forwards, who find all the space in front of the goal they are attacking carefully covered by the opposing team. In 1980, the England coach Ron Greenwood had success containing Maradona with such an approach in a game at Wembley. "If you tried to mark Maradona one-for-one," he told his players, he "would murder you—isolate you and leave

you stranded." What Maradona wasn't used to was "people coming at him from all sides." So, every England player near him
should "attack his possession, creating the effect of coming at
him from all angles . . . and chasing him from the back." Because
they were able to contain Maradona, England was also able to
move into the attack and won 3–1 against Argentina.[30]

By 1986, though, Maradona was a more mature player and
seemed unstoppable as he led his team through the early stages
of the men's World Cup. His teammate Jorge Valdano described
Maradona as "the soul of our team," and "our great offensive key."
When Argentina earned a place in the quarterfinal against England, it felt almost as portentous as a final. In 1982, Britain and
Argentina had gone to war over the control of the Islas Malvinas,
also known as the Falkland Islands. The Argentinean government had seized the territory, which was held by Britain, and
British prime minister Margaret Thatcher dispatched troops to
take it back. The war was on the minds of the Argentinean players as they went into the match. "Of course, before the match,
we said that football had nothing to do with the Malvinas War,"
and that "football and politics shouldn't be confused," Maradona
recalls. But, as had been clear during the men's World Cup held
in Argentina in 1978, politics was always involved in the tournament. In the game against England, the political stakes were very
clear. Maradona and the other players went in seeking a kind of
revenge on the pitch. The players knew that many Argentinean
"kids had died there, shot down like little birds," he recalls. "In a
way, we blamed the English players for what had happened, for
all the suffering of the Argentine people." It felt very personal:
"We were defending our flag, the dead kids, the survivors."[31]

Maradona scored two goals that day, authoring two sacred texts in the history of soccer. The first goal came in the fifty-first minute. Maradona was moving forward when he played a one-two with Valdano, who had to kick the ball quickly to Maradona, under pressure from the English defenders. The "dud ball" floated toward Maradona at a height he couldn't reach with his head. In a moment of inspired madness, he jumped up with his fist up behind his head, and punched the ball into the goal with his hand. An English defender immediately appealed for a handball, but Maradona acted the part of a goal scorer brilliantly. As he recalls, he made "a beeline towards the stand where my dad was with my father-in-law to celebrate with them." He admits, "I was a bit stupid, because I was celebrating with my left fist outstretched and watching what the linesmen were up to out of the corner of my eye." The referee might have seen that and suspected something was going on. In fact, Valdano looked over at Maradona and said "*shhh!* with a finger over his lips." Then the referee signaled that the goal would stand. "I got a lot of pleasure" from the goal, Maradona admits gleefully in his autobiography. "Now I am able to say what I couldn't then. At the time I called it the 'hand of God.' Bollocks was it the hand of God, it was the hand of Diego! And it felt a little bit like pickpocketing the English."[32]

Maradona had scored a few goals with his hand before. He had gotten away with it once, as a young player, though on another occasion the referee had caught him. "He advised me not to do it again," Maradona remembers. "I thanked him, but I also told him I couldn't promise anything." He thought of that referee after he scored in the World Cup: "I don't know if he cheered our victory over England or not." Maradona had long criticized referees for not protecting him on the pitch against fouls by defenders. It was probably with an ironic smile that he told a BBC reporter who asked him about the goal, "It was one hundred percent legitimate because the referee allowed it and I'm not one to question the honesty of the referee." Of course, there were then, and are now, and will always be, many who see the goal as perhaps the pinnacle of cynicism and dishonesty in the sport. At the time, though, McIlvanney—a Scot rather than an Englishman—pointed out that if the tables had been turned, few English fans would have refused the gift. "Of course," he writes, Maradona "could have set a noble example to the youth of the world. . . . He would have been an international hero. But would his teammates have seen him in that light?" It made good sense for Maradona to accept "condemnation from the rest of us," McIlvanney concludes, rather than suffer the "resentment and disapproval" of his teammates.[33]

Maradona's Hand of God goal is so famous, and still talked about, precisely because it tore at the fabric of soccer's spectacle. It represented a clear breach in the always falsifiable but nevertheless often deeply held belief that there is fairness and logic and reason to be found in soccer. The moment exposed then, and continues to expose now, some deep truth about the game, and about ourselves. The way we interpret and react to it perhaps says more about us, in the end, than it does about Maradona. For those devoted to the idea that soccer should, ultimately, aspire toward fairness and fair play, the Hand of God goal represents perhaps the worst violation of the norms of the game, something to be condemned and avoided. And yet it remains celebrated by many fans, not just Argentina, because it captures what they love about

soccer—the moments of madness and unpredictability, the possibility of a rebellion against form and rules, and the fact that it
can create a space for a figure like Maradona to do something
completely crazy and get away with it.

The place of the Hand of God in the history of soccer would
also, undoubtedly, be very different if it was the only goal scored
that day. Instead, perhaps in a bid for redemption—though he
would no doubt never admit that himself—Maradona did something truly extraordinary four minutes later. He took it upon himself to score a goal entirely alone.

"Here's how it went," he recalls. "I started off from the middle of the pitch, on the right; I stepped on the ball, turned, and
sneaked between [Peter] Beardsley and [Peter] Reid. At that
point I had the goal in my sights, although I still had a few me-
ters to go." He then passed another defender, and there was just
one more between him and the goal. He was looking over at
Valdano, wanting to pass to him, but the last English defender
was sticking too close. "So I faced him, then threw a dummy
one way and then another, towards the right." Maradona got past
him, then did the same with the English goalie, smoothly rolling the ball into the net. It was, Maradona later wrote, the "goal
you dream of as a kid." Back on the dusty ground in Villa Fiorito
where Maradona had played as a kid, "we used to say that we'd
made the opponent dizzy, that we'd made them go crazy," and
that was what Maradona had done to the English. "I wanted to
put the whole sequence of that goal, in stills, blown up really big,
above the headboard of my bed," and—alongside a picture of his
first daughter, an infant at the time—add an inscription that said
"*My life's best*. Nothing more."[34]

The sound and images from that goal remain perhaps the most legendary in the history of soccer. The commentator Víctor Hugo Morales called the goal on Argentinean television, and the way he described it, the gathering acceleration and pitch of his narration, is itself a kind of work of art. After Maradona scored, Morales improvised a spontaneous poem to the glory of soccer: "I want to cry! Holy God! Long live soccer! Golazooooooooooo! Diegooooooool! . . . What planet did Maradona come from, to be able to get past so many English players? . . . Thank God! For soccer, for Maradona, for these tears." Recently, the musical group Gotan Project invited Morales to reconstitute his call of the play in a tango-inspired celebration of Maradona called "La Gloria." The song brings together layers of Argentinean history—tango and soccer coalescing into one form, with the verbal brilliance of Morales incorporated and therefore acknowledged as a form of music itself.[35]

As Argentina moved through the 1986 World Cup, Maradona remembers, "Each game brought more joy." They defeated Belgium and won a place in the final against West Germany, which had defeated France in the semifinal in a riveting match. By then, everyone in Mexico and throughout Latin America, and many places beyond, was rooting for Argentina, and specifically for Maradona. "Never before in more than half a century of World Cups has the talent of a single footballer loomed so pervasively over everybody's thinking about the final," McIlvanney writes. It was not just that Maradona was seen as the best player on the planet, but also that there was a "potent sense of declaration inherent" in his actions on the field during the World Cup. Ahead of the final, according to McIlvanney, his "vast" public had a clear "conviction" that he had "chosen the Aztec stadium as the setting for the definitive statement of his genius." The Germans were good, yes. But the only way to defend against Maradona, as McIlvanney puts it, probably involved "putting a white cross over his heart and tethering him to a stake in front of a firing squad. Even then there would be the fear that he might suddenly dip his shoulder and cause the riflemen to start shooting one another." Two billion would watch the final around the world, and "surely all but a tiny Teutonic minority are going to will him to succeed." Argentina triumphed in the final, and Maradona's childhood dream of holding the trophy for his country was finally realized. It was an apotheosis of sorts too, securing him a permanent and in many ways untouchable place in the pantheon of the sport.[36]

Years before, in October 1981, Maradona traveled to West Africa on a tour with the Boca Juniors. He was just at the beginning of his career, but already famous. "The world knew me," he recalls in his memoir. When the team arrived in Abidjan, Ivory Coast, a massive crowd was waiting to see him. "I'd never seen anything like it before and I don't think I ever lived through it again in my whole career." Crowds stepped over the "machete-wielding police" surrounding Maradona and hugged him, crying out "Die-gó, Die-gó!" Twenty-five thousand people came to watch the team play in the Abidjan stadium. He recalls how, at lunch, a little boy came up to him and called him *pelusa*—a childhood nickname. He was amazed that a child in Ivory Coast would know this small, sweet detail about him.[37]

At the time, there was another little boy living in Abidjan, a three-year-old named Didier Drogba. Perhaps the electricity around the visit of Maradona left its mark on him, for in time

Drogba would grow up to be a great forward, one of the greatest of his generation. Drogba was a very different kind of forward than Maradona: a strong presence at the front of his team, always roving around the penalty area, powerful in the air. He was, in his way, the consummate modern striker—there, again and again, when he was most needed to finish a play, to do exactly what was needed for his team. Drogba's style was perhaps more suited to the world of football in the 1990s and 2000s, in which speed and physicality overshadowed the playful, twisting, technical play of a Maradona. But like Maradona, Drogba ultimately became a symbol to his country too.

Like that of many other well-known contemporary soccer players of African background, Drogba's story is one of immigration, and of finding a home on the pitch in a life lived between nations. When Drogba was five, his parents sent him to live in France with his uncle Michel Goba, a professional soccer player. Looking back, Drogba describes this experience of being "uprooted" at a young age as a defining one, though he "never forgot those roots" in Ivory Coast. Following his uncle's itinerant career, he grew up in different small towns in France, first in Brest, then Angoulême, then Tourcoing on the outskirts of Lille. Drogba stood out; he recalls that some friends "would even rub my skin to see if I really was that colour!" In Dunkirk, Goba—by then Drogba's legal guardian—got him on a youth football team. On Sundays, they went down to the beach where his uncle showed the young boy "all sorts of tricks," such as "how to use my body against a defender, and how to time a jump effectively." Drogba recalls, "When I saw him jumping up for a ball, I used to think that he stayed in the air forever, as if he was flying."[38]

Eventually Drogba was reunited with his family when his mother and father emigrated to France as well. There were eight of them in a one-room apartment. His father discouraged him from playing football and urged him to focus on his studies. However, when his father came to watch him play, he realized it was on the pitch that his son, so shy and taciturn at home, was truly himself. "Who are you really, Didier?" his father asked him. "Who *are* you? Because the guy I saw out there, he was happy, talking, directing people, gesticulating, enjoying himself." Drogba writes, "It was true. . . . The football pitch was the only place I could be myself, the only place where I felt truly free." Drogba began to develop a knack for being in the right place at the right time in order to score, every forward's goal.[39]

Drogba writes with gratitude about various managers who taught him who he was as a player. An early manager in France told him, "You don't need to play the full ninety minutes. For you, five, ten minutes are enough. . . . You can play ten minutes and make a difference." Drogba's manager on the French professional team Guingamp, Guy Lacombe, "taught me a lot about placement, movement, pace," the forward recalled. Later on, when he was playing for Chelsea, coach Guus Hiddink reminded him that he could "stop running around all over the place. . . . 'You're a striker, you don't have to do that. Just stay up there and finish the actions.'" Drogba's most important connection was with the manager José Mourinho. Working together for Chelsea, the two claimed the greatest trophy in European professional soccer, winning the Champions League in 2012. Throughout his career, both in professional and international football, Drogba continued to have that transformative presence on the pitch; he often came on as a sub in a game and changed everything. "I have been lucky enough to score a few goals that mattered," he writes, with a modesty unusual for a forward.[40]

In a sense, Drogba was a kind of specialist, valued as a player who could be depended on to finish a play with a goal. What mattered most was what he did at the key moments, the way in which he could receive a ball, turn quickly and decisively, and power it into the goal. It was his ability to do so at moments when everything was on the line that made him so valuable. Sometimes, it seemed as if he were saving up his strength and concentration for just such a moment. In this sense, Drogba embodied the forward as a figure who, in an instant, can change everything. His effectiveness at finishing plays with a goal, of course, reconfigured the game in many ways. Opposing teams had to deal with the constant threat Drogba posed as he roved toward the goal. A star forward like Drogba also shores up the defense for all the other players on his team. Such a player has to constantly and carefully be watched, controlled, and contained by opposing defenders and midfielders, which ties up players who might otherwise move into offense.[41]

Drogba's ascent began in earnest when he was recruited, at the age of twenty-five, to Olympique de Marseille. The city of Marseille is famous for the intensity and devotion of its soccer fans. He was given a jersey with his favorite number—11—and greeted on his first game with a giant banner that said "Drogba, score for us." Playing in front of the sixty thousand fans in the Stade Vélodrome, "it almost felt unreal for me to be wearing that pale blue shirt," Drogba writes, "about to run into this incredible stadium." Before an important game, he went to the hilltop basilica in the town, leaving his Olympique de Marseille jersey there in the hopes that this would "give us a bit of divine fortune." The shirt was accepted as a gift and hung up to the right of the entrance to the basilica, alongside an Olympique de Marseille pennant—"but sufficiently high up to deter anyone from making off with it!" Drogba became famous in Marseille for the way he celebrated his goals. "Whenever I scored," he writes, "I broke into a bit of coupé-décalé, a popular dance in Ivory Coast and in the Ivorian community in France, based on Ivorian pop music."[42]

In the lower divisions in France, Drogba had suffered from the physicality—at times brutality—of play. At Marseille, he gained that peculiar kind of flattery that marks a good striker; he heard defenders "making some comments along the lines of the only way to stop me was to kick me. . . . That comment, for me, was the greatest compliment they could have given me!" It was, however, as a player at Chelsea, working with Mourinho, that Drogba reached the pinnacle of his career, when he played a central role in securing the team's victory in the Champions League competition. It was a particularly sweet win, for Chelsea had made it to the final of the competition before, in 2008, but suffered a bruising defeat at the hands of English rivals Manchester United. Drogba had played in that defeat and remembered it well. In the locker room after the 2012 victory, draped in the Ivory Coast flag, he delivered a long speech directed at the Champions League trophy. "Why? Why have you avoided us for such a long time?" he asked it accusingly. He told the long story of the many "almosts," the defeats Chelsea had experienced in the Champions League before, concluding with "everything we'd had to do in this match in order, finally, to be able to claim this trophy as our own." He later wrote, "Some of those who witnessed my speech told me afterwards that it almost felt like a religious experience." A brilliant striker on the pitch, Drogba also proved he was a striking orator off it.[43]

It was, however, as a player on the Ivory Coast national team that Drogba made his most important speeches. Though a dual national, with both French and Ivory Coast passports, Drogba was never selected to play on any of the junior national teams in France. His uncle, however, had once played for Ivory Coast. "I really wanted to continue the family tradition and pull on the jersey for 'The Elephants,'" Drogba writes. "Even when I was young, I used to get goosebumps whenever I heard our national anthem." He recalls his first match with the national team, an Africa Cup of Nations qualifier, in September 2002: "What is seared in my memory forever is the excitement of walking out into the cauldron of heat that was our national stadium, the Stade Félix Houphouët-Boigny." The "atmosphere" was different than "anything I had ever experienced." Fans had packed the stadium since ten in the morning, with artists and musicians performing, and "everyone had been joining in."[44]

Ten days later, a civil war began in Ivory Coast. Over the next years, there were periods of cease-fire followed by bursts of fighting, and French and UN peacekeeping troops were deployed to the country. Drogba became captain of the Ivory Coast team in 2005 and led them to qualification for the 2006 men's World Cup. As the team was celebrating, Drogba approached the cameraman filming the scene for Radiodiffusion Télévision Ivoirienne and asked him for the microphone. "We had always said that if we managed to qualify, it would be for the people, a way to ask them to bring peace back to Ivory Coast," Drogba recalls. As the star forward, he was the most visible player on the team, and he understood himself as its spokesman. "Spontaneously, with no forethought or prepared speech," he gathered his teammates around him in front of the camera and said, "My fellow Ivorians, from the north and from the south, from the centre and from the west, we have proved to you today that the Ivory Coast can cohabit and can play together for the same objective: to qualify for the World Cup." Then, asking his teammates to get down on their knees and pray, he continued: "We ask you now: the only country in Africa that has all these riches *cannot* sink into a war. Please, lay down your arms. Organise elections. And everything will turn out for the best!"[45]

When the team arrived home in Abidjan, there were huge crowds waiting at the airport and "crazy" celebrations. His parents were waiting for him, and they were deeply proud, "not so much because of our qualification—that was almost secondary—but for the message I had sent out for peace." Drogba's words had been played and replayed on television and aired on the radio for days. As the team made their way through the city to the president's house, there were throngs of celebrants in the streets, on rooftops, joyously waving flags and honking horns. It seemed that, "at least for the time being, bitterness between people was being suspended. There was still a long way to go until real peace was achieved, but it was a start."[46]

Although the team had a disappointing performance at the 2006 men's World Cup, Drogba was chosen as the African Player of the Year in 2007. In March of that year, a cease-fire was brokered between rebel forces in the north of Ivory Coast and the government. Drogba had an idea: What if he traveled to the rebel stronghold in the north, in Bouaké, to present his trophy? And what if Ivory Coast played their next game—an Africa Cup of Nations qualifier—not in Abidjan but in the north as well? Drogba brought the idea to the head of the Ivorian Football Federation and then to the president of Ivory Coast, and both agreed. On March 28, 2007, Drogba traveled "into the rebel heartland of Bouaké" in an "open-topped car," escorted by soldiers. He met with the leader of the rebel group Forces Nouvelles, Guillaume Soro, who was soon incorporated into the government as prime minister as part of the resolution of the conflict. Drogba felt full of "pride in our country and hope for the future." He remembers, "One elderly lady ran alongside the car for the entire journey." He was "just a footballer, one from humble origins," but felt that he was contributing to "rebuilding a unified country."[47]

The Africa Cup of Nations qualifier, against Madagascar, was set for June 3 in Bouaké. Some teammates were worried about the journey into rebel territory, but Drogba reassured them. "I went there, I saw them, they love football, they love the team, and they have always supported us, even when we were losing. So we have to go." The team blazed against Madagascar, winning 5–0, with Drogba scoring the final goal. "The game itself became a symbol of an attempt to heal divisions. I saw soldiers from the army watching alongside soldiers from the rebel forces." Footage of the game, broadcast throughout the country, offered a different image of what was happening in the north and encouraged people who had fled the region to return. "People were heard to say, 'If Drogba has been to Bouaké, it means it's safe to return.'" Drogba had left Ivory Coast as a child, found a place for himself as a young man on the pitches of provincial France, and ultimately climbed to the heights of the international game. He has continued to journey, playing in China and Canada. Yet his most important moment on the pitch—the place where he had always felt most at home—was probably when he played in Bouaké in 2007, and in so doing was able to help bring displaced people home.[48]

Drogba's career developed during a time when the cost of players, especially forwards, increased vertiginously. In the contemporary game, forwards are the most expensive members of professional teams for, as David Goldblatt puts it, "overwhelmingly they are the goal scorers and goals remain rare and difficult to come by." There are times when the focus on the forward can hamstring a team. That was the case for years on the Portuguese national team, led by star forward Cristiano Ronaldo, who in both his pure brilliance on the field and what his critics see as his megalomania, perhaps best exemplifies what the position means today. The Portuguese team, however, has had disappointing showings in international competition, in part because they often seemed too focused on Ronaldo, working less as a coherent team than a forward with ten other players around him.[49]

This can happen to other national teams when a star forward becomes too central to their tactics. During the 2015 Women's World Cup, for instance, the US women's team entered with a strategy built around the star forward Abby Wambach. There was a logic to this. She was the FIFA player of the year in 2012, and is the all-time greatest goal scorer in American soccer history, having scored a total of 184 goals in international competition, far greater than any male US player. Yet by 2015, she was not as potent a striker as she had been during the 2011 Women's World Cup, and the team at times seemed to be foundering because of too great a focus on her at the expense of other players. Manager Jill Ellis made the difficult decision to pull Wambach off the field, starting other forwards instead, and the team's play improved markedly. The change in tactics was critical and enabled the team to win the competition.

Something similar happened in the final of the 2016 Men's European Cup, though inadvertently. The game pitted Portugal against a favored French team, which was soaring from a victory over Germany in the semifinal. There was a surreal feel to the game because the staff at the Stade de France, which had been targeted by terrorists in November 2015, decided to leave the bright lights illuminating the field on overnight to make it easier for security to police the stadium. They hadn't counted on how nature would react. The lights served as a massive beacon, and brown moths from all over the region had been drawn to the stadium. There were so many that you could see them fluttering all over the pitch, sometimes landing on players.

All eyes were on Ronaldo, with Portuguese fans hoping this would be the moment of his final ascension to the heights of the game. Early on, however, he came down, seriously injured, and motioned to the sidelines that he needed to be taken off. He had tears in his eyes, and as the camera focused in on him you could see a moth poised on his shoulder, almost as if it was whispering to him, maybe consoling him. Maybe the moth understood something we didn't. At the moment it happened, it seemed like a complete disaster for the Portuguese team, portending a certain victory by the French. Instead, it was a blessing. With Ronaldo gone, everything changed about the game, and the French team, geared up to contain him, seemed unsure of what to do. And another Portuguese forward, Ederzito António Macedo Lopes, known as Eder, realized it was his moment.

Eder was born in the former Portuguese colony of Guinea-Bissau and moved to Portugal as a child. He was nowhere near as famous as Ronaldo, having played professionally in France and, at age twenty-eight, nearing the end of his career as a striker. But with Ronaldo injured, he took control of the Portuguese attack. In the second overtime of a 0–0 game, roving the edge of the penalty box, still far from goal, he decisively turned and kicked a beautiful volley into the French net. Portugal won the game 1–0, and the tournament, bringing home the country's first major trophy from an international competition. Everyone had assumed Ronaldo would be the hero of such a victory, but instead it was a much less well-known player, born in Africa, who became a national hero. It was a moment rich with history and meaning. Portugal's greatest footballer, the forward Eusébio da Silva Ferreira, known as Eusébio, was also of African background, born in Mozambique. He is considered one of the greatest soccer players in history, and led the Portuguese national team from 1961 to 1973. But even he had never won a trophy for the country. He died in 2014, and on the way back from their 2016 victory in Paris, the Portuguese team took a photograph of their trophy with a photograph of Eusébio propped up on it. The lineage from Eusébio to Eder, foregrounding the place of Africa in Portuguese—and European—soccer, was made powerfully clear in this moment.[50]

At their best, forwards embody the beauty of soccer as a language. Out of their motion, their decisions, the tiny choices they make about where they are and how they kick the ball, come the goals that create the rushes of emotion that tie fans to the sport. A forward can divide the story of the game into a before and an after, changing the narrative in an instant. In a game where goals are comparatively rare, often frustratingly so, there is always something a bit uncanny and unexpected about a goal. Nick Hornby writes that there is "the thrill of seeing someone do something that can only be done three or four times in a whole game if you are lucky, and not at all if you are not." And some goals—particularly those that secured a historic victory—become seared in the memories and consciousness of fans, who can call up the intricacies of the moment easily, describing it as if it is replaying before their eyes.[51]

The depth of feeling generated at these moments is one of the reasons that forwards inspire startling levels of devotion and awe from their fans, becoming icons in a way that few other modern figures do. A forward, ultimately, is the person who reminds us how to turn a possibility—of a goal, of a victory, of happiness— into a reality.

5

THE MANAGER

In early 1958, Mohamed Boumezrag, a retired professional soccer player, began traveling around France to recruit players for a new team. He met in secret with top professional players throughout the country. One after another, the players agreed to quit their current teams, including the national team, and join his. They were to disappear, all at the same time, and travel to Tunisia. There, they would announce that they were forming a soccer team to represent the nation of Algeria. Boumezrag had convinced the players, all of whom had been born in that French colony, that they could use their soccer talent as a weapon in the war for their country's independence.

Boumezrag was born in Algiers in 1921. His family was very politically active: his grandfather was an imam from the town of El Asnam, in the interior of the country, and had spent decades in prison because of his resistance to French colonization. During the time Boumezrag was growing up, a vibrant set of political movements in Algeria had criticized the colonial order and demanded more political rights for Algerians. He was interested in politics, but he also had a passion for soccer, playing with teams in Algiers and elsewhere. As a teenager, like many other players from North Africa, he moved to France and began playing for some of the country's best professional teams. He was recruited by the Girondins de Bordeaux, and during World War II played for L'Union Sportive de Mans, where he also served as the team's manager, before retiring from soccer in 1946. When, in the early 1950s, a new and more militant anticolonial movement developed in Algeria, led by an organization called the Front de Libération Nationale (FLN), Boumezrag joined the underground.[1]

In 1956, Boumezrag began to dream about creating a team for Algeria. There were many players from Algeria at the top levels of French soccer, a number of whom were supporters of the FLN. Among those he successfully recruited, the biggest stars were Mustapha Zitouni, who played for Monaco, and Rachid Mekhloufi, who had helped his team, Saint-Étienne, become champions of France the preceding year. Mekhloufi and Zitouni had been recruited to play on the French national team in the 1958 World Cup: as colonial subjects, they could represent the French empire on the international stage, as many players, including Raoul Diagne, had since the 1920s.[2]

Boumezrag's pitch to Mekhloufi, Zitouni, and other players was simple. For four years, Algerian insurgents had been fighting for independence. The war had become increasingly brutal, and countries around the world were interested in its outcome. In a time of rising movements for independence throughout the globe, the FLN was seeking recognition from foreign governments. But most nations still viewed the group as an internal rebel movement that France had the right to repress. What could legitimize the FLN's claim to represent a nation? Boumezrag thought he knew: a soccer team. Therefore, he was asking his recruits to do more than just play. He was asking them, by playing, to declare that Algeria was their nation, and that they were willing to represent it on the international stage.

It was a difficult choice for the players, most of whom were married to French women and many of whom had children. They were well-paid professionals, beloved in the towns where they lived and played. Mekhloufi, unsurprisingly, made a plea regarding the timing of Boumezrag's plan, asking him, "Couldn't we leave *after* the World Cup?" But Boumezrag convinced Mekhloufi that it was precisely by depriving France of his services as a player that he could make the strongest statement.[3]

Boumezrag had an eye for the theatrical, and understood well how attached French fans were to their soccer teams. He wanted to do something dramatic to increase awareness of the Algerian conflict in France. He asked all the players he met with to simply disappear, without announcing their intentions in advance. This was necessary in part so that they wouldn't get stopped and arrested by the French authorities, who were actively working to suppress pro-independence activists in France. It also, however, would hurt teams in a particularly vivid way. On match day, some of their star players would simply not show up. People would wonder, where had they gone? And then would come the answer: They had joined the fight for independence. They were now playing for their own country.

It worked. All but two of the recruited players made it out of France and to Tunis, and their action was front-page news. In a collective statement, the new team declared that because France was "fighting a merciless war" against the people of Algeria, they refused to support "French sport" in any capacity any longer. Together, they now officially represented the FLN, and the Algerian nation in the making, in the world of soccer. They immediately began organizing games with other countries. FIFA, which was dominated at the time by European members, declared that any country that agreed to play with or against the Algerian team would face sanctions. Morocco and Tunisia, recently independent nations that were not yet part of FIFA, agreed to play the FLN team. So did a few other countries in the Middle East—and eventually in Southeast Asia and the Soviet bloc—that were part of FIFA, which ultimately did not follow up on its threatened sanctions.[4]

Arranging games, of course, was one thing. Winning them was another. Boumezrag was not just a political organizer, however, he was also an experienced coach with a group of deeply talented players. Although few had played together before, they immediately clicked, playing what the historian Michel Nait-Challal describes as "intelligent, twirling" soccer, driven by a "flamboyant and inspired attack." In some countries, the team's first games were sparsely attended, but once word spread about how amazing they were, crowds tens of thousands strong thronged to see them play. Wherever the players went, they sang the Algerian national anthem—written by an FLN prisoner—and hoisted the flag of the independence movement. They traveled to Southeast Asia, where they were hosted by the North Vietnamese and met Ho Chi Minh and General Võ Nguyên Giáp, the commander who had defeated the French armies at Dien Bien Phu and secured independence in 1954. The FLN team defeated all the

Vietnamese teams they played, including the national team, and Giáp good-naturedly offered a kind of transitive theory of revolutionary victory: "We defeated France, and you defeated us, so you will defeat France!"[5]

He was prophetic. In 1962, Algeria won its independence from France. The victory had come on the battlefield, but also through diplomacy, and the FLN soccer team had played a key role in transforming the image of the movement. As they toured around the world, they became highly visible representatives for the cause of independence. They drew massive crowds because they played beautiful soccer, but in the process they shared the story and symbols of the Algerian struggle. With the war over, Mekhloufi—who had kept in touch with his French teammates during the 1958 World Cup—returned to play for Saint-Étienne. Other players remained in Algeria. Boumezrag did as well, continuing as the manager of the national team, which joined the Confederation of African Football and became part of FIFA in 1964. He had been able to do something that no other manager can claim: he'd not only created a soccer team, but he had helped create a nation in the process.[6]

Boumezrag had created a team out of nothing, gathering his players together and providing them with a common goal that inspired them. Though his political contribution was unique, his accomplishment exemplifies the multifaceted role played by the manager in soccer. Unlike the roles of the players, which are relatively well defined, a manager's job is less clear, and there are many different ways of both doing it and talking about it. The manager is a recruiter, a trainer, a tactician, a theorist, a psychologist, an artist, and even a spiritual leader.

In formal terms, the manager is the rough equivalent to a head coach in basketball and American football and the manager in baseball. Yet soccer's uninterrupted flow and continuous clock leaves the manager with relatively little power in the course of a game. Unlike coaches in American football, soccer managers don't organize or call plays as the game progresses. Unlike coaches in basketball, they cannot call a time-out to settle things down or reorganize. They can't do anything to stop the clock, in fact, which rushes relentlessly forward. They can yell, of course, notably at the referee, who polices the sideline near them and sometimes polices the managers, warning them to stay in their area. During the game, the only significant decision a manager can make is which players to substitute on, and what instructions to send on with them. This is a relatively limited power, since the manager can usually only substitute three players over the course of the entire game. He mostly has to sit—or stand—and watch, just like the rest of us, never knowing what is coming next.

The manager's real work happens before and after games, in the in-between time that defines what happens on the pitch. In contemporary soccer, managers are seen as essential, and are the focus of intense observation, criticism, and speculation. Yet their power can be, and often is, overestimated, for they have devoted themselves to trying to control what is ultimately uncontrollable: the game of soccer.

In his analysis of soccer, the philosopher Jean-Paul Sartre offers a useful way of thinking about the manager's role. He argues that, on a soccer team, the distinction between rights and duties, often seen as separate in political philosophy, essentially become meaningless. Each player has a function on the team, and his duty is to fulfill that function to the best of his ability, because in doing so he enables other players to also fulfill their functions. At the same time, each player has the right to expect that every other player will fulfill his duty for the team. That is because any "particular movement, pass, or feint" taken by a player only gains its meaning in relation to "the use made of it elsewhere in the undertakings of other members of the team." The sum of these actions only becomes meaningful through its relation to a common goal, which is pursued through the totality of all the actions on the part of the team. The act of playing, then, is a form of *"creative freedom in the common individual"*: a player is free, and creative, in the sense that he decides how to carry out a specific action, but his individual choices only matter to the extent that they are part of the common team effort. In the flow of a game, which involves "the perpetual reorganisation of the field by the players," what matters is the constant "reshaping of the group by the group." Each specific action aims at a kind of transcendence, a hope that it will gain meaning through a series of other actions that will ultimately lead to a goal, and a victory.[7]

The manager's role is best described as a kind of mediation. The manager has to represent the group to the group, making clear the common goal and how to achieve it, and explaining to each individual on the team what the group needs. Managers often inherit a group of players when they are brought onto a team, but they also are sometimes able to help constitute the group by recruiting certain players. In doing so, however, the manager has to figure out how a new player will fit into the team and play a particular function in a way that will elevate the team as a whole. Doing so successfully means absorbing and analyzing a swirling series of factors: not just the technical abilities of given players, which can be known only through their past performance, but also their future actions, and precisely how they might impact the alchemy of a team. In all of this, psychology plays a central role, for the ability of a team to succeed depends on the players' sense of being a group, of sharing a common goal, at any given moment. One of the more fascinating things to witness in soccer is the moment when a team begins to disintegrate psychologically, when individuals lose their sense of a common goal, when their bodies seem to slump, the players no longer look at each other, and a kind of resignation sets in. At moments like that, a manager can do little but watch, and try to figure out what happened and how to fix it for the next match.[8]

Each day, managers struggle to assert their authority, attempt to figure out what tactics to use and how to explain them to players, and hope they won't get fired if the team loses the next game. Like other aspects of the culture of soccer, the role of the manager emerged slowly. Initially, there was no manager or coach at all. Whoever created a team, such as the heads of a factory or the committee of a local club, picked players and organized training sessions. It was, in the words of historian David Goldblatt, a "working environment that was more like an artisanal craft workshop than a factory floor." It was Herbert Chapman, the Arsenal coach and developer of the influential WM system that transformed the tactics of the game starting in the 1930s, who was what historian Jonathan Wilson calls "the first modern manager." Chapman was "the first man to have complete control over the running of the club, from signings to selection of tactics to arranging for gramophone records to be played over the public-address system to keep the crowd entertained before the game and at half-time." It was a role that brought together what we associate with the general manager in American football, baseball, or basketball with the work of a coach who directly trains players and decides tactics. Early in his career as a manager for Northampton Town, Chapman noticed his players arguing about a card game during some of their downtime outside practice. He decided that there were probably more useful ways for the players to spend their time, so he instituted regular "team talks" that included extended discussions of tactics. This seems natural today, but was innovative at the time. With Arsenal years later, Chapman expanded this and had his players "gather round a magnetic tactics board to discuss the coming game and sort out any issues hanging over from the previous game." He involved the players in the discussions, having them debate their ideal positioning on the field every week. Chapman was, as one journalist at the time noted, "the first manager who set out methodically to organize the winning of matches." His dream, one that has been shared by managers since, was that data, analysis, and planning could increase the probability that a team would win in any given match and over the course of a season. His success with Arsenal suggested he was right.[9]

Chapman consistently scouted out opponents before games, so that he could tailor his team's tactics specifically to take advantage of weaknesses on the other side. He did this too obsessively, in the end. On January 1, 1934, he "caught a chill" during a game. Rather than staying home to rest, he decided he had to go scout out Arsenal's next opponents and then some potential players during the following days. The famous manager caught pneumonia and died a few days later, at the age of fifty-five.[10]

Chapman's model of leadership, however, lived on in English soccer and beyond. Managers took on pivotal roles in defining the tactics of teams and recruiting, evaluating, and training players. Beyond the clubs themselves, however, managers were relatively unknown. Only in the 1970s, with increasing media coverage of soccer and the expansion of televised matches, did some managers become widely recognizable figures. One of the icons of the era was Bill Shankly, who managed Liverpool from 1959 to 1974. He was a working-class Scot who had not received formal training, but obsessively oversaw everything from travel to innovative training methods. As Goldblatt writes, "He established a model of team-building rooted in his early years in a small mining community in the west of Scotland." His vision was one of "simple football. . . . Pass the ball to someone else in red and then take up another position in which you can receive it." It was a vision that "prioritized team over individual performance." He brought a "profound sense of solidarity" to the club, notably by keeping the players' wages relatively equitable to avoid a sense of hierarchy among team members. At one point, he likened soccer to socialism, "everyone working for each other, everyone having a share of the rewards."[11]

Shankly was extremely successful. He brought Liverpool out of England's second division and turned it into a club, as Goldblatt writes, "with a truly global profile, a byword for its own distinct tradition of playing and supporting football." Journalist James Corbett explains that Shankly led Liverpool "like a revolutionary leader, casting his personnel not just as footballers but soldiers to his cause, and became a folk hero to the fans." He was also, Corbett notes, "football's Muhammad Ali, a charismatic maverick whose utterances had an unexpected, undeniable poetry." Shankly crystallized his philosophy in a quote that has become one of the most famous in soccer: "Some people believe football is a matter of life and death. I'm very disappointed with that attitude. I can assure you it is much, much more important than that."[12]

During the same period, other managers pioneered "scientific" approaches to running a team. One of the most influential was Russian manager Valeriy Lobanovskyi, who was in charge of one of the USSR's greatest teams, Dynamo Kyiv, for nearly two decades starting in 1973. He also coached the USSR national team. Lobanovskyi studied engineering and computing at the Kyiv Polytechnic Institute, and this shaped the way he saw the game. As Wilson explains, he saw soccer as "a system of twenty-two elements—two subsystems of eleven elements—moving within a defined area (the field) and subject to a series of restrictions (the laws of the game). If the two subsystems were equal, the outcome would be a draw. If one was strong, it would win."[13]

The Russian manager focused on the fact that "the efficiency of the subsystem is greater than the elements that compose it." Soccer was "less about individuals than about coalitions and the connections among them." Lobanovskyi's close collaborator Anatoli Zelentsov, a scientist and professor at the local university, captured the idea through a powerful natural metaphor. "Have you seen a hive of bees fly? A hive is in the air, and there is a leader. The leader turns right and the hive turn right. It turns left and all the hive turn left. It is the same in football. There is a leader who takes a decision to move, say, here. Every team has players who link coalitions; every team has players who destroy them. The first are called on to create on the field, the latter to destroy the team actions of the opponent." The role of the manager was to make sure that such coalitions and connections were constantly being made by the players. This meant making sure the players were capable both of reading the game well enough to know what to do in a given situation and of using their technical abilities to carry it out.[14]

Working together, the two Russian coaches trained their players to focus on what they called "coalition actions," such as offside traps and overlapping runs on attack. "The most important thing in football," Lobanovskyi once said, "is what a player is doing on a pitch when he's not in possession of the ball, not when he has it." That was because it was the actions taken by the coalition of all the players that determined what was possible for the player with the ball. As in Total Football, Lobanovskyi cherished a certain "universality" in his players, the ability for all of them to both defend and attack. This would enable them to work as effective "elements" in the system they created for the team.[15]

Part of his success depended on an extremely sophisticated method for gathering data about games in order to analyze what had happened and improve the tactics of his team. Lobanovskyi created a complex mathematical rubric tracking the various actions carried out by his players—passes, tackles, shots on goal, runs with the ball, interceptions, defeats of opponents—and posted the results on a bulletin board after every game. This gave him a kind of power, probably at times overbearing, over his players. If he criticized a player, he backed up his criticism with empirical data that the player could see and could not dispute. He considered himself the master of this data, and the only one who could really understand and analyze it. If a player tried to respond to a criticism, saying, "But I think . . . " Lobanovskyi would shout back, "Don't think! I do the thinking for you! Play!"[16]

There is a struggle in the heart of most managers between different visions of their relationship to players. Some truly see themselves as the pivotal figures in a team's play, those who determine the tactics and train players to carry them out. These kinds of managers see their role as very clear-cut: they are supposed to deploy players in such a way as to win games, using whatever tools they have at their disposal. The manager Alan Durban, angry at journalists who criticized the way his team Stoke City was playing, famously told them to look elsewhere if they were looking for something pretty. "If you want entertainment, go and watch clowns," he said. Other managers emphasize their desire to create something entertaining and beautiful for their fans, focusing more on the creativity and independence of players, and on creating an environment in which players can ultimately thrive because they feel free to experiment and express themselves on the pitch. That was the case of the Russian coach Eduard Malofeev. He sought to infuse his players with joy and love of the game. Asked once in an interview what he did each morning, Malofeev replied "that first he thanked God he was alive, then he got out of bed and jumped up and down to celebrate the fact." His goal was to create what he called a "sincere football," and he wanted to make sure his players were able to express their individual styles of play. Most managers try to navigate between these various approaches. They understand that they have to guide the fitness and training of players, and develop a good set of tactics for games. Yet they also seek to create a space where players can thrive as individuals and express themselves joyously *and* effectively on the pitch. In this sense, they have to struggle with the broader debate over tactics within football, between playing to win and playing fluidly and beautifully. For managers, of course, this is far from a theoretical debate, since their jobs are often on the line.[17]

Managers sometimes describe what they do by comparing it to the work of various kinds of artists. Arrigo Sacchi, manager of one of Italy's top teams, Milan, as well as the Italian national team of the 1990s, declared that the goal of soccer should be to strive to create a great work of art, to offer "ninety minutes of joy to people." He explained, "I wanted this joy to come not from winning, but from being entertained, from witnessing something special." "Football is born in the brain, not the body. Michelangelo said he painted with his mind, not with his hands." If the pitch was Sacchi's canvas, players were his colors, and he expected them to be intelligent so that they could follow his broader plan. Not content with merely comparing himself to Michelangelo, in another context Sacchi also described himself as a conductor: "I didn't want solo artists. I wanted an orchestra. The greatest compliment I received was when people said my football was like music." In another interview, he reached for a different artistic metaphor: making a film. "A good manager is both screenwriter and director," he said. "The team has to reflect him."[18]

As all three metaphors used by Sacchi suggest, he saw himself as the only one who could really see the big picture and therefore create a beautiful work of art out of the constituent parts of his team. "Many believe that football is about the players expressing themselves," he explained. "But that's not the case," at least "not in and of itself. The player needs to express himself within the parameters laid out by the manager. And that's why the manager has to fill his head with as many scenarios, tools, movements, with as much information as possible. Then the player makes decisions based on that." The players he sought out were those who could understand their role in the bigger plan while having the skills and talent to work out what they were meant to do within it at any given moment. "I didn't want robots or individualists," he said. "I wanted people with the intelligence to understand me, and the spirit to put that intelligence in the service of the team."[19]

A manager wields great power, determining the prospects of a player, opening up possibilities or closing them down. There can be a ruthlessness, even cruelty, to this process. Sacchi, for instance, could be withering in his assessment of players. He recalls his work late in his career at Real Madrid, evaluating young players being trained in the team's soccer academy. In these academies, which most professional teams now have, young players who show promise are given intensive training by staff, with the hopes that some of them may end up being stars on the team when they are older. "We had some who were very good footballers. They had technique, they had athleticism, they had drive, they were hungry," Sacchi said. And yet they were not quite good enough for him. "They lacked what I call knowing-how-to-play-football. They lacked decision-making. They lacked positioning. They didn't have the subtle sensitivity of football: how a player should move within the collective." Sacchi doubted that some of them could learn these skills. While "strength, passion, technique, athleticism" were all important, according to Sacchi, they are only a "means to an end, not an end in itself." They only have meaning in relation to the goal of "putting talent in service of the team, and by doing this, making both you and the team greater." There was a difference between being a "great footballer" and "a great player." Sacchi's vision was perhaps best exemplified in a style of training session he held with Milan. As one scout from an opposing team described it, "They played a game with a full eleven on a full-sized pitch against nobody and without the ball!" As Sacchi recounted, "We would line up in our formation, I would tell players where the imaginary ball was and the players had to move accordingly, passing the imaginary ball and moving like clockwork around the pitch, based upon the player's reactions."[20]

The Argentinean manager Marcelo Bielsa—who since 1990 has led Argentinean and Chilean national teams as well as professional teams throughout Latin America and Europe—gets his players to a similar level by using what he called *repenitización*. The term comes from music, where it is used to describe sight-reading, or "the practice of playing a piece without having rehearsed it first." Applied to soccer, the term conveys both improvisation and urgency. *Repenitización* is a key to Bielsa's philosophy as manager. As Wilson describes, "It demands players repeatedly do things for the first time, a paradox that perhaps suggests the glorious futility of what he is trying to achieve." Bielsa put it differently: "The possible is already done. We are doing the impossible." There can be something overbearing and abstract, of course, about the vision of the manager. "If players weren't human," Bielsa declared at one point, "I would never lose." Here

Bielsa, like Sacchi, portrays himself as a kind of all-seeing mastermind of the game, seeking out players to fulfill an ideal perhaps only ever truly achieved in his own head.[21]

Managers sometimes have difficulty conveying their ideas to players, especially if they develop too many fancy new terms to describe the act of playing. Cláudio Coutinho, a former military officer who managed the Brazilian national team in the late 1970s, made much of the fact that he was going to transform the way his players approached the game by insisting that they embody "polyvalence." Although all this meant in practice was that he wanted his players to be flexible and versatile, moving between different positions as needed, describing this through a new term was part of his attempt to position himself, notes Roger Kittleson, as someone offering an "ultra-modern technical approach." When they first heard the term, however, many of the players responded with confusion, saying "Poly . . . what?" One player recalled a session where Coutinho was trying to explain a play using his newly developed technical jargon. He told one of his players how to combine with another player, the great Brazilian midfielder Roberto Rivellino, like this: "Rivellino is going to retreat to the penalty box arc, right next to the zone of reason, then you immediately look for the right flank, giving preference to open spaces. Then you overtake him at speed, trying an overlapping towards the future point, and that way you receive the ball in front of the goal." When Coutinho asked the player if he understood, the player replied, "I only got 'Rivellino.'"[22]

Other managers explain their aims more simply. Pep Guardiola, who came up through the ranks in the Barcelona academy as a player and later became legendary as the team's coach, articulated his philosophy in this way: "In the world of football there is only one secret: I've got the ball or I haven't." It was fine for other teams not to want the ball, Guardiola quipped, but "Barcelona have opted for having the ball. . . . And when we haven't got the ball we have to get it back because we need it." In part because he had been trained at and played for Barcelona, Guardiola was one of those who excelled at embodying and communicating a particular style of play to his team, helping Barcelona to become the reigning club in Europe under his leadership from 2008 to 2012.[23]

The stress involved with playing at the highest levels of soccer is intense. Sometimes, the most important thing a manager can do is just try to keep players calm and ready to focus on the game. Pia Sundhage, the Swede who managed the US Women's National Team from 2008 to 2012, once explained at a press conference that sometimes, when her players were getting too stressed before a match, she would pull out her guitar and play a song for them: Simon and Garfunkel's "Feelin' Groovy," with its classic opening lyrics: "Slow down, you move too fast." Sundhage's song offered a reminder that, in the end, what might be most critical for an elite team's success was serenity and confidence as they approach the game, knowing they can't ultimately control the outcome, but can still seek both victory and a kind of transcendence by enjoying their time on the pitch. Later, when Sundhage announced she was leaving her position in the United States to coach Sweden's national women's team, she sang Bob Dylan's "If Not for You" as she bid farewell to her players.[24]

Today, managers of national teams as well as professional clubs operate in an extremely high-stakes and high-pressure context, endlessly scrutinized, viciously criticized, and only occasionally lavished with praised for their achievements. In professional soccer, the financial stakes have skyrocketed in recent decades, largely as a result of increasing revenues from broadcasting rights. For instance, in the case of the English Premier League, probably the most watched league on the planet, such revenue makes up about half of teams' total income. Another quarter comes from stadium gate receipts and concessions, and the rest largely from corporate sponsorships and selling licensed products such as team jerseys.[25]

The English professional soccer teams are not franchises like sports teams in the United States, including Major League Soccer. They are rooted in a location from which they cannot be moved. The more apt comparison to US sports might be to college sports, since those teams are tied to institutions. English clubs did not start as businesses, but as associations located in a particular place. This "old theatre of English football," writes Goldblatt, was only gradually turned into a "globally attractive television spectacle." This involved a process he describes as "a modern institutional enclosure." This is a reference to the seventeenth-century process through which English elites took over lands that had previously been held as commons—used freely by a community for grazing and logging, for example—and put them in private hands. So, too, clubs began as a kind of common property of a locality, and their growth—notably through the construction of stadiums—was often sustained by public money. In the past decades, however, in England and elsewhere in Europe, a process of "stealth and legal maneuver" has moved most of these teams into "private hands in the forms of holding companies." The money that comes into clubs depends on a brand that only has meaning because of its history in a specific location and the accumulation of support by generations of fans from that place. Yet, today the most famous of English teams are also truly global brands. This means that they attract significant financial investment not so much because of the potential profits but because of the "status and glamour" associated with such symbolically powerful institutions. Clubs in England can receive "massive capital injections," as they increasingly do from foreign investors from the Middle East, Russia, and the United States.[26]

English soccer, like that of other European nations, is organized around a system known as "promotion and relegation." There are four divisions, and teams can move between them. The top three teams in any division at the end of the season are "promoted" into a better division, while the lowest-ranked teams in each division are "relegated" downward. The gains that come with promotion, particularly to the top division, the Premier League, are huge, because a team gets much more money from broadcasting rights when it is in the top division. This money, in turn, can be used to recruit better players and therefore be more competitive. Teams in the Premier League compete for the biggest prize: the European Champions League. The top four teams of the Premier League get to compete in this continental championship, which gives teams even more global visibility, and therefore access to larger streams of money.

Of all the participants in a professional team, it is the manager who is usually seen as most deserving of praise, or blame, when it comes to the fate of a team in this system. The place where the manager has the most control is in player recruitment.

Team academies play a crucial role here. Lionel Messi, for instance, was trained from a young age in the Barcelona academy before becoming a star player on the team. Yet most players on the wealthiest teams are recruited from elsewhere through something known as the transfer market.

The way the transfer market works is, on the face of it, relatively simple. When a player is under contract with a given professional club, he can only move elsewhere if his current club gives him permission and releases him from his contracts. "Transfer fees" evolved as a way of facilitating these moves. A team might not want to let a player go, but for a bit of money they might change their minds. Early on, transfer fees were quite modest: the first recorded one, from 1902 in England, was one thousand pounds. By the 1960s, the sums had increased dramatically, to the hundreds of thousands of pounds. Diego Maradona set a new record in 1984 with his transfer to Napoli from Barcelona, which cost five million pounds, about seven million dollars at the time. But this was just the beginning. In 1995, the Belgian footballer Jean-Marc Bosman won a case he brought to the European Union Court alleging that the rules—in place at the time in a number of countries—that limited the number of foreign players who could be recruited were a violation of the laws of the EU. After that, player movement within Europe became even easier, and as a result the transfer fees expanded exponentially. In 2001, Zinedine Zidane was recruited by Real Madrid from Juventus for forty-five million pounds. By 2009, when Real Madrid recruited Cristiano Ronaldo from Manchester United, they paid a record eighty-nine million pounds. The numbers continue to go up and up, vertiginously. In the summer of 2017, the French team Paris Saint-Germain, bankrolled by Qatari investors, paid a jaw-dropping transfer fee to acquire the Brazilian star Neymar da Silva Santos Júnior from Barcelona—253 million euros, about 300 million dollars. Each summer, soccer fans intensely track the news of potential moves, hoping their team will gain a star player, or fearing they will lose one. While transfers take place between continents, with promising Latin American and African soccer players being brought into Europe, the biggest amounts are exchanged between the wealthy soccer clubs of Europe, particularly the Italian, Spanish, French, German, and English leagues.[27]

The vertiginous expansion in transfer fees has reshaped the global economy of soccer on many levels. Today's global soccer economy is in many ways structured around the transfer market, with lower-division teams and less prominent leagues in places like Belgium and Switzerland acting as feeders to more prominent, richer teams in other European countries. Such teams train players in their academies and also recruit promising players, often from Africa and South America, offering them relatively low-paying contracts. Most of these players do not succeed at the professional level, but all it takes is one among dozens to get a significant offer from a wealthier club for the feeder club to make a windfall through a transfer fee. The smaller team can then use this fee to recruit better players and improve its standing and perhaps move into a higher division, which might bring higher revenues from television rights and increased visibility as a global brand.[28]

It is a high-stakes game. In their withering economic analysis of the many mistakes made by clubs and managers in the transfer market, journalist Simon Kuper and economist Stefan Szymanski single out Arsenal coach Arsène Wenger as a manager who has been markedly clever in navigating this system. Nicknamed "the professor" because of his degree in economics and the fact that he is "addicted to statistics" about players, Wenger has been the manager at Arsenal since 1996, a remarkably long tenure in today's soccer world. He was viewed with skepticism by at least one player when he was first hired. Tony Adams, who was then the captain of the team, recalls thinking, "What does this Frenchman know about soccer? He wears glasses and looks more like a schoolteacher." Having previously coached in Japan, Wenger criticized the English diet. "I think in England you eat too much sugar and not enough vegetables," he declared. There was, notes David Kilpatrick, always "a touch of xenophobia" in criticisms of Wenger. Not only was he a nerdy-looking Frenchman, but he also voraciously recruited foreigners, to the point that he could frequently field an Arsenal team without a single English player.[29]

What Wenger understands, Kuper and Szymanski argue, is the fundamental truth that in modern soccer "you need data to get ahead." Wenger is particularly interested in information that can help him decide which players to acquire for his team. He knows that past performance tends to be overvalued, meaning that clubs "pay fortunes for players who have just passed their peak." While he keeps his defenders on the team longer, Wenger transfers midfielders and forwards from the team at a younger age, often making a tidy profit in the process. Again drawing on empirical study, Wenger also emphasizes factors that shape the success or failures of players, including diet and psychology. Perhaps his greatest recruit was Thierry Henry, a talented French striker of Caribbean descent. Henry came from Juventus in Italy, where he had "languished," and Wenger converted him into what Kilpatrick describes as "the English Premier League's most lethal and poetic striker." Over his eight years at Arsenal, from 1999 to 2007, Henry scored 174 goals, many of them breathtakingly beautiful.[30]

Wenger has led his team to seven victories in the Football Association Cup, a competition open to all professional teams in England, the most of any manager in history. During Wenger's first year in charge of the team, 1997 to 1998, Arsenal both won the Football Association Cup and was the number-one ranked team in the Premier League. He repeated this feat in 2002. In 2003–2004, Arsenal played the entire season without ever losing a game in the English Premier League, earning the title "the invincibles." It was not just an unprecedented feat; it was done in style. Arsenal under Wenger, effuses Kilpatrick, plays with "aesthetic brilliance," seeking victories but also carrying out "the even more noble pursuit of inducing a sense of ecstasy." In 2009, Wenger explained that he was proud of having cultivated a "philosophy, a style of play and a culture of how you want to play the game." Though recent years have been frustrating for Arsenal and Wenger, with many vocal fans calling for his ouster, the team owners have kept him on, seemingly believing in his project. Kilpatrick, both a devoted fan of the team and a philosopher, expresses his admiration by claiming if the German philosopher Friedrich Nietzsche were alive today, he would certainly root for Arsenal. For Nietzsche, soccer could only be "justified as an aesthetic phenomenon," and therefore must be played "artistically—in a creative, imaginative, and positive manner—with a sense of the game's potential for beauty."[31]

Modern managers like Wenger manage not only players but, as Goldblatt writes, also an increasingly large staff that includes specialized coaches, psychologists, "scouting and computing departments," and even "acupuncturists, faith healers and translators." Directors of football and the executives of teams, meanwhile, have taken over some of the financial roles once held by managers. Perhaps the biggest shift, notes Goldblatt, is that "the balance of power between coaches and players has shifted." The increased pay and mobility of players have decreased the authority of managers. This makes their job complicated. "Operating inside a network rather than a hierarchy," a team manager must, writes Goldblatt, be "a manager of complexity, consensus and coordination." The question of how a manager relates to a new star recruit, for instance, can play a decisive role in how a team does in a given season. As a result, fans follow and are fascinated by managers, finding their "dilemmas and problems" in some ways more interesting than those of the players. With the rise of social media, as well as an expansion of sports commentary on radio and television, the decisions of managers are constantly analyzed, critiqued, and dissected. Fans who fancy themselves better qualified than managers to make such decisions have an outlet in fantasy leagues, where they get to create their own teams by recruiting players, starting with a given budget. These dream teams compete against each other in virtual leagues based on how the players do during the season. The actual performance of players in their games determines how well these virtual teams do, because players earn points for goals scored, and defenders and goalies earn points for preventing the other team from scoring any goals. The manager, however, is gone—replaced by you.[32]

What makes for a good manager? Kuper and Szymanski criticize the way clubs choose them. Men's teams almost never consider hiring a woman as a manager, and as a result overlook a significant pool of potential talent. Instead, again and again, they choose a white man "with a conservative haircut, aged between thirty-five and sixty, and a former professional player." They argue that the tendency to hire former players overlooks the fact that "playing and coaching are different skill sets." As they note, the manager who can probably be considered the most successful in soccer's history, José Mourinho, who has coached Real Madrid, Chelsea, and Manchester United, barely played professional soccer. Once asked about this, Mourinho replied sardonically, "I don't see the connection. My dentist is the best in the world, yet he hardly ever has a toothache." Failed players, Mourinho went on to suggest, might be better coaches in part because they have had "more time to study." Sacchi, who had never been a professional soccer player, explained it this way: "A jockey doesn't have to have been born a horse."[33]

For managers to have a real impact on a team, they need to be in their position over the long term, the way legendary manager Alex Ferguson was at Manchester United from 1986 to 2013, or the way Wenger has been at Arsenal. This kind of longevity, however, is growing rare. In the hypercompetitive and fluctuating world of contemporary soccer, managers have become as itinerant as players, hired and fired at a startling rate. On average, managers only last a year and a half in the Premier League, and the majority of first-timers are fired between six months and a year after starting. Even as their authority and influence has decreased, managers have seen their wages go up dramatically. Wenger and Zidane, who now coaches Real Madrid, each make about eight million pounds per year, while Guardiola now makes a record salary of fifteen million pounds per year coaching Manchester City.[34]

As certain professional teams have become global brands, their managers have become media stars alongside players. In the 1990s, the field of play in soccer was altered for the first time since the 1920s, to add a "technical area" for the coach to stand in. This was originally meant to contain them, keeping them from getting too close to the pitch. Yet, as Goldblatt notes, the managers now have a "stage all of their own," a little box by the side of the pitch where they can stand close to, but still a few steps away from, the game. This "grassy podium" becomes an "invisible cage," where the manager's "tics and neuroses are given center stage." This makes the manager's curious role all the more visible. He is on the pitch, in a way, but he is not part of the team that he leads. In fact, his "zone" is policed by an assistant referee who often is in conflict with managers who "persistently escape the narrow compound" in moments of celebration or rage, providing entertainment for fans in the stands and viewers at home. Every once in a while, a manager gets sanctioned and sent away from the pitch, having to watch the game from some seat or box up in the stands, even more distant and powerless than usual. Some managers—including, often, Wenger—eschew the box and remain seated on the bench, whispering with their assistants, accepting their basic inability to do all that much to influence the course of the game.[35]

Watching managers' expressions of delight or despair, the ups and downs of their emotions, can be one of the most entertaining parts of the modern soccer spectacle. Mourinho takes notes on a little notepad, and you want to know, what is he writing? Manager fashion is also a good topic of discussion. At which boutique in Barcelona, you wonder, does Guardiola shop to get those hip suits? Silvia Neid, the manager for the German women's national team from 2005 to 2016, had an intense serenity that seemed to channel energy to her team, and her artsy German T-shirts added an element of intrigue to her presence on the sidelines. Watching the furrows in Wenger's brow, along with his inimitable, tight-lipped expression of exasperation, is a spectacle in itself, and the joy in seeing him smile, as he does every once in a while, is contagious. Watching Zidane as a coach may not be quite as spectacular as watching him as a player, but once you get used to seeing him in a suit rather than a jersey, the same intense gaze and, occasionally, beautiful smile that punctuated his presence on the pitch shapes his presence on the sidelines.

Managers are asked to understand, and try to control, all the factors that go into preparing a team to go onto the pitch and win. When they are good at what they do, their efforts can pay off. And yet they are also reminded continually that, in the end, soccer cannot be controlled. Once the whistle blows and the game begins, the manager mostly watches—surprised, disappointed—along with the rest of us. During the game, the manager might see with satisfaction that something is actually working according to plan, but she can just as easily witness her team fall apart, unable to respond as a game slips from her hands. The manager lives at the heart of the mystery of the game.

Reflecting on his career on his sixty-seventh birthday, Wenger imagined trying to explain his way into heaven. "If God exists and one day I go up there and he will ask: 'Do you want to come in? What have you done in your life?'" Wenger admitted wryly that "the only answer I will have is: 'I tried to win football games.' He will say: 'Is that all you have done?' And the only answer I will have is: 'It's not as easy as it looks.'"[36]

6

THE REFEREE

In February 2007, an eleven-year-old girl named Asmahan Mansour was about to go onto the pitch during a tournament in Quebec, Canada, when the male referee working the game told her she couldn't play. The problem was her attire, specifically something that he claimed might endanger her and other players: her head scarf. Mansour lived in Ottawa and had long played there while wearing the head scarf, or hijab. No referee had identified this as a problem before. But the Quebecois referee clearly had a different opinion.[1]

In justifying the decision, he invoked the Laws of the Game, the official rules governing soccer around the world. There are a total of seventeen laws, starting with the field of play and its markings and dimensions, and ending with the corner kick. Each of the laws, however, includes many different parts—the current document totals 210 pages. It is the job of the referee to apply and enforce all these laws during the course of a soccer match, a task that requires a lot of interpretation on the referee's part. This is true of officiating in all sports, of course, yet the referee in soccer carries an extreme level of responsibility. Except in cases where a new technology called the Video Assistant Referee (VAR) system is being used, soccer referees generally don't have access to video replay, and so they have to make decisions entirely based on what they see in the moment. The referee on the field works with assistant referees, usually three of them, and can consult with them on decisions. Two of these assistants run up and down the sidelines of the pitch during the game and are especially crucial in determining whether a play is offside. The referees can consult together on decisions, but the expectation is that they will do so quickly in order to avoid interrupting the flow of the game.

The Laws of the Game offer guidelines, but they require interpretation. There are considerable gray areas surrounding what is considered a foul and how it should be punished. Because of the low-scoring nature of the game, referee's judgments frequently have a dramatic, even decisive, effect on the outcome. It is strikingly easy to think of games in which an error by a referee—for instance, a penalty kick given when it shouldn't have been, or not given when it should have been—has been the difference between a team's winning and losing. As a result, the calls made by referees are constantly contested by players on the pitch and managers on the sidelines. Calls are dissected and critiqued by commentators and fans. Some are remembered ruefully for years, even decades. To be a referee is to carry the burden of knowing that any of the many decisions made in the course of a match may end in controversy.

Still, the Quebecois referee likely could not have predicted the eventual consequences of his determination that Mansour's hijab was a violation of law number four. This rule states: "A player must not use equipment or wear anything that is dangerous to himself or another player (including any kind of jewelry). All items of jewelry are potentially dangerous. The term 'dangerous' can sometimes be ambiguous and controversial, therefore in order to be uniform and consistent, any kind of jewelry has to be forbidden." Just as the rule's wording foreshadowed, what began as a judgment call by a referee in a girls' tournament in Quebec became a major controversy in international soccer. The referee's verdict ultimately involved FIFA in a contentious and long-lasting debate about Islam, gender, and sports.

The referee's decision was controversial from the moment it was made. The tournament involved three hundred girls' teams from throughout Canada, including four from Ottawa. When Mansour's coach walked over to the bench and told her that the referee had decided she had to either take off her hijab or stay on the sidelines, her teammates were outraged. In what one report on the incident called a "swift show of solidarity," they declared that if she couldn't play, none of them would. The three other teams from Ottawa joined in the strike. Several dozen young girls had immediately taken a stand in support of Mansour. She initially felt guilty, expressing regret that the incident meant her team didn't get to play in the tournament. Ultimately, however, she spoke out against the referee's decision. "I think it's pathetic, really," she noted in one interview, because the head scarf was "tucked in my shirt." It was difficult to imagine a scenario in which this would lead to her getting strangled. As she put it in another interview, she just wanted "to play soccer."[2]

What had motivated the referee to make the decision? In Quebec at the time, as in France, there were ongoing debates surrounding the question of whether women should be allowed to wear head scarves or burkas (which cover the entire face and body) in public settings. These debates may have influenced the referee who, as newspapers reported, was also Muslim. Politicians were quickly drawn into the debate over the referee's decision. One, Jean Charest, rapidly weighed in to support the ban on Mansour playing in a hijab. Charest was then criticized by other politicians who defended Mansour's right to play wearing a head scarf. Mansour quickly became well known in Canada, her story covered in the nation's major newspapers. One Ottawa man criticized Mansour and told her she should "rise above petty things like wearing a hijab" and just get on with sport, but other readers came to her defense.

As the referee's decision quickly became a lightning rod for a broader debate in Quebec and beyond about the hijab, a widening web of soccer officials found themselves having to weigh in. A few weeks later, the matter was brought before the International Football Association Board (IFAB), the FIFA-affiliated board that issues the official rules of soccer, so its members could provide guidance to referees on whether a hijab constituted a danger to players.

IFAB was originally formed in the 1880s in order to facilitate international matches between England, Scotland, Wales, and Northern Ireland. At the time, there were still some differences between the rules of the game issued by the football federations of these countries. The federations decided to create the board in 1886, each country appointing one of its four members, to create a consistent set of rules that would govern international games. In 1904, when FIFA was formed to coordinate international soccer competitions, that organization accepted the authority of IFAB to continue to determine the Laws of the Game. In 1913, FIFA gained a foothold on the board, taking two new seats alongside the four occupied by the UK federations. These four federations, however, remained aloof from FIFA and didn't participate in the first World Cups in the 1930s. In 1947, however, they joined FIFA, on the condition that Scotland, Wales, Northern Ireland, and England could compete individually in international tournaments. They also kept their four seats on IFAB. Finally, in 1958, FIFA gained an additional two seats on the board, now made up of eight members. This configuration remains in place to this day. While the FIFA seats rotate among different member nations, the United Kingdom's four countries each have permanent seats on the board. Because changes to the Laws of the Game require six of IFAB's eight members to vote in favor, the UK federations remain the dominant force on IFAB. This is one reason why soccer, among global sports, has one of the most conservative approaches toward changing the rules.[3]

The formal link between IFAB and FIFA has been key to the latter organization's global dominance over the sport. When national soccer federations wanted to join FIFA in order to participate in international competitions, the organization demanded that they adhere to the rules as set by IFAB. This has also given FIFA power over the training and selection of referees for international competitions. FIFA's self-appointed power as the guardian of the rules, and therefore, in a sense, the game, is the basis for its extraordinary reach and prominence today. During the 1970s,

FIFA evolved from a small, Geneva-based, European-dominated organization whose main point of existing was to organize the men's World Cup and other tournaments into something much larger and more powerful.

The mastermind of this transformation was João Havelange, who was president of the organization from 1974 to 1998. The first non-European head of FIFA, Havelange presided over a vast expansion of FIFA's range. Part of his strategy was cultivating links with the large bloc of new members from recently independent African nations. For these countries, joining FIFA was about as important as joining the United Nations as a way of demonstrating their existence on the world stage. Havelange won his election to the FIFA presidency in part by getting the African nations to vote for him, and in return promised that his organization would provide support for the development of local federations and their infrastructure. The African bloc demonstrated its power in the 1980s by successfully getting apartheid South Africa kicked out of FIFA unless it agreed to send racially integrated teams to the men's World Cup. FIFA had at once become truly international and, in a new sense, truly political.[4]

During the same decades, FIFA got access to huge new streams of money by charging more and more for television rights to competitions. This change in FIFA was part of a global change in sports culture, one in which teams gained a major new source of revenue in the form of broadcasting rights. The increasing privatization of television stations in Europe in the 1980s and 1990s substantially increased the profits to be gained from selling these rights. In Italy, Silvio Berlusconi managed to bring together the power of TV, football, and politics in a way that transformed his country's institutions and culture. He used his ownership of one of his country's most successful soccer teams, Milan, as well as the country's largest media company, to launch a political career. The name of his political party, Forza Italia, evoked a familiar chant sung by fans of the Italian national soccer team. In some ways, FIFA has done the same on a global scale, becoming the odd Frankenstein's monster of an institution that it is today. It is partly an international organization, with more members than the UN, as its spokesmen often proudly state, thanks to the membership of places like Palestine, New Caledonia, and Wales. It is also a corporation, governing large amounts of cash. And, beyond that, it has become a kind of supranational authority, one with the power to actually push around national governments, and indeed force them to concede forms of legal and geographical sovereignty in return for the right to host a World Cup.

Given FIFA's reach and power, and the intense controversies surrounding the wearing of the hijab in different societies throughout the world, it was inevitable that Mansour's case would take on a political dimension. The implications went far beyond a simple question about whether someone can play in a hijab. And yet, in its first consideration of the question, IFAB seemed startlingly ill-equipped to address the problem in an articulate way. In March 2007, after what was described in the press as a "heated" discussion, a representative of IFAB emerged to declare vaguely, "If you play football there's a set of laws and rules, and law four outlines the basic equipment. It is absolutely right to be sensitive to people's thoughts and philosophies, but equally there has to be a set of laws that are adhered to." When pressed to explain what the board had actually decided about whether a player can wear a hijab, the representative had no clear answer. The board had decided not to decide. Referees were left with the burden of determining, on a case-by-case basis, whether the hijab was to be considered "dangerous." The officials, a reporter noted sardonically, "made clear they were not going to change the existing rules—or explain them."[5]

There was something about this moment that crystallized the daunting role the soccer referee takes on. IFAB makes the rules, but these rules only take on meaning through the decisions made, again and again, by referees on the pitch. Training to become a referee is intense, particularly for those who aspire to work in high-level professional matches or international tournaments. It is extremely difficult work. Referees are asked to be mind readers, philosophers, judges, expert negotiators. And counselors, telling people to calm down. And humorists, using a joke here and there to lighten the mood. As if that isn't enough, they also have to be prepared to be scapegoats, on the receiving end of virulent verbal and sometimes physical abuse by players and fans.

What would the game be without the referee? If you are an optimistic anarchist, you might argue it would be better, that the players would somehow work things out, as indeed they do every day in pickup games throughout the world. If you are more pessimistic about human nature, though, you might easily conclude that it would simply be a melee. The fact is that the referee may actually be the most essential person on the field during any soccer match. If the game is to have rules, someone has to enforce them. In fact, in any given game, many calls by the referees are relatively straightforward, though that doesn't usually keep players from protesting them. By making these calls decisively, referees enable the game to flow. Without the hundreds of quick decisions they make during any match, the whole exercise would be a farce, one in which everything is up for grabs. Referees represent the idea of soccer as a structure, and of the pitch as a place with defined processes and limits. Without the referees, there could be no game.

What makes soccer fascinating to watch, after all, is that the players have to find a way to move the ball around the pitch without violating the many rules that limit what they can do. Players have to be endlessly creative precisely because of the constraints placed on them by the referee. The referees have to constantly police the boundaries of not only what is acceptable, but also what is possible. In doing so, they make the game the unpredictable drama that it is.

Referees do many basic but fundamental things during the course of a game. They blow the whistle to start and end the game. They oversee the substitution of players from the bench, deciding when to stop play to do so. In most games, a referee holds up a small panel showing the number of the player who is coming off and the one who is entering the pitch. Even such seemingly simple decisions can have important consequences. Given the relatively constant flow of the game, a team can gain an advantage if play is stopped to make a substitution. If a team is winning late in a game, they'll often make a substitution just to gobble up a little time, with a player sauntering slowly to the sideline, and the referee having to urge her along. These moments are just one of many where the referee has to balance carrying out his duties with the need to ensure the flow of the game is not interrupted.

Referees are given a near-absolute power to punish players for their infractions on the pitch. They do so in various ways. If a foul is committed by one player against another, the referee can stop the game and give the team that was unfairly treated a free kick. If a foul is particularly egregious, because it has placed another player in serious physical danger or has had a dramatic impact on the course of the game, it can be additionally sanctioned with a card. There are two kinds of cards: A yellow card is a warning of sorts, and the player is allowed to keep playing. A red card means that the player has to leave the game, and her team has to play the remainder with one fewer player. If a player gets a second yellow card during a game, that is the equivalent of a red card, and she also has to leave the game. Though the rules about this vary depending on the international competition or league, these sanctions usually disqualify the player from a certain number of subsequent games as well. These aspects of the punishment can sometimes be appealed and altered. During the game, however, the referee's decisions are absolute and cannot be appealed or changed once they have been made. Their impact on the game is also absolute. That is why Eduardo Galeano goes so far as to call the referee "an abominable tyrant who runs his dictatorship without opposition" and a "pompous executioner" who "raises the color of doom" with a card: "yellow to punish the sinner and oblige him to repent, and red to force him into exile." The referee can even disqualify a goal, even after a crowd has erupted in exuberant celebration, by calling it offside or noting some other infraction that happened before it was made.[6]

While the referee is powerful, his subjectivity, and fallibility, is on constant display. There is only one referee on the pitch, patrolling a vast space. He has much more terrain to cover than officials in other sports. In basketball, three officials observe a space the size of the penalty box in soccer. In American football, there are seven or eight officials, with a careful division of labor between them. In soccer, while the assistant referees can help from the sidelines, they are often far away from where a foul has taken place. So a referee is in constant motion, trying to be as aware as possible of what is happening in different areas of the pitch. While the action might be focused around the ball, plenty of fouls can happen when the ball is far away.

Referees, furthermore, have to constantly make decisions based on unknowable things. In soccer, many actions that harm another player are only considered a foul if intentional. That means that referees are tasked with trying to determine what was going on in a player's head when, for instance, he stuck his foot out in front of another player. Was he just trying to reach the ball, or did he know he couldn't reach it, and stuck out his leg just so an opposing player would trip over it and fall? If the ball hits a player's hand, the referee has to decide whether this was intentional—whether the player moved his hand in order to touch the ball—or simply an accident in which the player could not avoid having the ball hit his hand. These decisions are particularly high stakes when they happen in the penalty box, in front of the goal, because if a referee determines a player intentionally hit the ball with his hand there, the referee has to give the other team a penalty kick.

Because referees are attempting to read intentions, of course, players work hard to hide their motives. This can create an infinite regression of interpretation and counterinterpretation. A player brutally kicks another player on purpose—but tries to do so in a way that looks completely accidental—and then jumps up in shocked surprise that anyone suspects he would ever intentionally have done something so terrible. Because it is key to draw a referee's eye, dramatically falling, flailing, or rolling about when fouled can be a useful tactic, notably because it can make a foul seem worse than it was, or even make it seem like something happened when it didn't. The Laws of the Game now include rules against "simulation," so in addition to punishing players who foul, a referee can punish a player for acting like he was fouled when he wasn't. In particularly egregious cases, a player can even receive a yellow or red card for this infraction.

Soccer becomes infinitely more fascinating once you accept and appreciate this theatrical dimension to the game. Among the many games being played on the pitch is a psychological one between players and referee. The players are always pushing at the boundaries of what is acceptable. This is not just about the individual performances by players feigning hurt or innocence, though they can be thoroughly entertaining. It is also about the absorbing form of psychic warfare that develops between the players and referee over the course of a match, and sometimes over many games, in cases where players and referees come to know each other. "Influencing the referee is a vital aspect of the game," writes Ruud Gullit, a Dutch player who was also a manager for Chelsea. Referees, he adds, "try to be objective robots, but of course they are only human." Many fans appreciate it when the players on their team successfully trick the referee. Nick Hornby recalls one player on the Cambridge team he supported during his college years, Tommy Finney, "whose dives and fouls were often followed by outrageous winks to the crowd." Such complicity between fans and players is not unusual. You hate it when the other team dives and gets a foul, or fouls and doesn't get a call, but you love it when your team does. In fact, you expect tricking the referee to be part of players' skill sets.[7]

Players try to influence the referees in countless ways. There are games where players argue constantly with the referee, about every decision, even if it is blatantly clear they did something wrong. When the ball goes out of bounds, both teams immediately, almost systematically, put their hands in the air to claim that it should be theirs. Such tactics only rarely impact the decisions of the referees in the moment. Yet the complaining is part of a game of attrition, aimed at sowing doubt in the referee's mind in the hopes that this will influence subsequent calls. If they believe they have made errors early in a game, referees might try to make things right later on, reestablishing balance and justice. The stakes for players are high in soccer, because if they can somehow pressure the referee into making a decision in their favor around a penalty kick or a red card given to an opposing team, that can often determine the outcome of the game. The persistent ambiguity surrounding many calls combined with the potentially dramatic consequences of one decision creates an incentive for players to constantly be working the referee.

In the midst of all this, the referee must somehow focus on getting calls right, without being influenced by the chattering or gesturing of players, in order to create a sense of justice about the game. Ideally, the referee wants to remain relatively unobtrusive, so that the game can unfold without too much intervention on her part. For this reason, many referees begin a game with a relatively open mind, allowing certain fouls to go unpunished at first so as not to stop the game too frequently. They don't want to overplay their hand, giving players yellow or red cards too early. Though there is no formal limit to how many cards can be given in a game, it is generally understood that they need to be used sparingly, in part because they can lead to the expulsion of players, which is understood as an extreme measure that shouldn't happen too often. Players know this and try to get away with early fouls. Gullit describes the "greatest first tackle of a game, *ever*" as being one committed by the Irish player Roy Keane during a men's World Cup qualifier against the Netherlands in 2001. In the first minute of the game, Gullit recalls, Keane sent a Dutch player "flying with a merciless tackle into his ankles from the back." The German referee blew the whistle, but with the game just beginning, he kept his cards in his pocket. For the Irish team, it was a victory. "The tone was set; the first blow struck," writes Gullit. "The intention was clear; the Irish had declared: you're getting nothing here today!"[8]

And yet the referee is also keeping score, and after a time, will often warn players that they have gotten away with something once or twice, but will not get away with more. Referees sometimes call fouls because of an accumulation of actions rather than just one incident. Watching a game, you can often see referees warning players about this, and players holding up a finger or two, arguing that they've only fouled a few times and should be given a break. The trick for players is to see precisely how much they can do without getting punished—to foul in a way that takes a toll on the opposing team while falling just short of a card from the referee. Gullit celebrates certain players, notably the Spanish star Xabi Alonso, because he "almost always gets away with fouls" in a way that crucially helps his teams.[9]

Referees also have to act as prophets or oracles at times, attempting to anticipate what might happen if they don't stop the game. When a player on an attacking team is fouled, for instance, the referee can decide not to stop play by calling the foul, in order to give an advantage to the attacking side. In such cases, the referee determines that the team has a better chance of scoring a goal if they continue to play than if the game is stopped and they are given a free kick. Once play has stopped naturally—after the ball goes out of bounds, for instance, or is caught by the goalie—the referee can still sanction the foul that was committed, if it is serious enough, by giving out a yellow or red card. Deciding when to give the advantage requires something of the uncanny: How, after all, can the referee predict the future? Generally, however, fans appreciate it when the referee allows play to continue in this way, because it fits the broader ethos that soccer should be flowing rather than stopping and starting.

In many respects, the best referees can hope for is relative invisibility, to be forgotten once a game is over. As for glory or praise, they can pretty much give up on that. Yet, while many fans content themselves with yelling at the referee, there can be a real pleasure in watching referees at work. They know and love the sport, and they have to be in extremely good shape, for they often run greater distances than many players. The vast majority of them are either volunteers or referee as a second career. When anthropologist Christian Bromberger interviewed French referees working in the first-division professional league in the 1980s, he found that they exuded satisfaction and commitment. They had worked hard to get to that level of refereeing, which required at least ten years of experience and a "multitude" of tests, both written and oral, on the rules of the game, along with extensive medical examinations. Though the referees were paid very little and had to deal with constant mistreatment and criticism from players who were paid vastly more, not to mention abuse by fans, they were driven by a mission to make sure rules were followed and order was maintained. Out of twenty-two referees who had been selected to referee French first-division matches, Bromberger found that seven were educators, and others were managers, policemen, or in the military. One of them explained he was inspired by his "conviction that, in life, the rules must be respected."[10]

It is fascinating and instructive to watch the different ways referees choose to approach a game. Sometimes referees seem intent on exerting their authority inflexibly, by making too many calls and handing out cards early in a match. This can sometimes work to control players, but in other cases it leads to a choppy, frustrating game. The best referees understand that the cards are really only a last resort, and that there are many other ways of exerting power. One of the things I like to watch for—in part because it allows my imagination to run free—is the conversations referees have with players. My favorite kind of referee is one that exudes a certain calm, perhaps a slight distance from (or perhaps disdain for) the shenanigans happening all around. With a little raised eyebrow, a tilt of the head, a smile and a pat—sometimes a bit patronizing—the referee says to players, "I see you. I know you." The wise referee, in the center of the chaos, knows that the players are aptly named: they are actors in a drama, performing to gain an advantage. The referee's goal is to understand the psychology of players, sympathizing with them and knowing them, but also reminding them that, though there are many gray areas, in the end there are lines not to be crossed and rules that must be followed. At their best, referees issue these reminders through words and gestures, rather than yellow and red cards. Otherwise, the referee becomes the focus of the game, and the punishments doled out to players end up shaping the outcome. When a referee has to make too many calls and gives out too many cards, there is a sense that she did not exert sufficient moral control by chiding and talking to players or through other small gestures of enforcement. To referee well, then, requires tremendous skills not only of observation but of persuasion.

The complexities of her role make the referee a central player in the game's symbolic and narrative dimensions. The referee, in fact, is a big part of what makes soccer such a rich source of emotion, debate, and conversation. Bromberger argues that every game of soccer can be seen as a "drama of fortune in this world." Soccer feels a lot like life, he suggests, not just because it is unpredictable, but also because it is so often unfair. In soccer, as well as in life, "success depends on a mixture of merit and luck." Being good isn't enough, because the system isn't set up simply to reward talent and virtue. More than other sports, he argues, soccer rewards "patience and deception" in dealing with the "devastatingly powerful referee." The only way for players to navigate what everyone can see is a "flawed system of justice," one in which decisions are inconsistent and sometimes arbitrary, is to "help yourself along with a little cheating." Throughout the game, the referee "counteracts the many forms of trickery with the strictures of the law." The process, however, is necessarily imperfect, and so inevitably "a match opens itself up to a debate of theatrical proportions." Those debates are precisely what constitute much of the activity of being a soccer fan. Talking about referees' decisions, often with great rage and passion, is an essential part of the bonding that creates community around the game. As we talk about and interpret the validity of the decisions made by referees, and the choices made by players, we are also sharing our broader visions of justice, virtue, and fate with one another. Soccer, Bromberger writes evocatively, "illustrates, in a relentless way, week after week, the uncertainty, fluctuation, and possible reversals offered by the present." The games keep coming, one after another, and in each of them destiny can be rewritten, again and again.[11]

That may be the secret to understanding why we put up with a game that is so often unfair, arbitrary, and cruel. During tournaments like the World Cup, the fates of national teams are frequently determined by controversial and ambiguous decisions made by referees. Millions and millions of fans watch this happen to their teams, powerless to do anything about it. At those moments, it becomes clear that soccer is one of the most effective tools for mass human torture ever devised.

In truth, however, we love the feeling of being wronged by the referee. It is one of the most powerful and cherished emotions a soccer fan can have. The rage that is directed at the referee is really just a condensed version of the rage that fans direct at the game. To truly love soccer, one probably has to love its fundamental perversity, the fact that theater and trickery—as much as people rail against them—are at the very heart of the spectacle. We tell ourselves that there *is* fairness in soccer, that on the whole the best teams win, that talent and virtue and hard work lead players and teams to victory. But our experiences of the sport constantly undermine that. One of the uncomfortable but fundamental truths about soccer is this: the fact that it is often so unfair is one of the reasons it is so endlessly absorbing. Without the all-powerful and endlessly fallible referee, we would have so much less to watch and to talk about.

Some refereeing decisions are as famous, or as infamous, as some of soccer's greatest goals. Fans of the French national team remember well a 1982 men's World Cup semifinal against Germany, during which the German goalie Harald Schumacher committed a brutal foul against French striker Patrick Battiston. Running out from his goal to challenge Battiston, Schumacher leaped up and struck him in the head with his elbow and knee. The French player fell to the ground, unconscious, twitching. The ball had passed Schumacher by the time the collision happened, so the tackle seemed particularly gratuitous. Standing over the prone Battiston, Schumacher—clearly knowing he had committed a foul—nervously handled the ball. But Dutch referee Charles Corver had not seen the incident and therefore made no call. After Battiston was carried off on a stretcher, the referee whistled for the game to continue. Because the red card Schumacher deserved would have left Germany down to ten players and without their first-choice goalie, the call was likely decisive in a match that ended in German victory. Schumacher was long vilified for the incident: calling someone a "Schumacher" became a nasty insult in France. As the referee who had failed to punish Schumacher, Corver was also long criticized. In 2016, decades later and long after his retirement, Corver was still being asked about this incident that in many ways defined his career.

Corver's memory of the episode speaks volumes about the curious perspective and position of the referee. "I never saw the incident," he recalls, because he was watching the ball, which he thought was about to go into the goal. (It went just wide of the goal post.) When Corver subsequently saw Battiston on the ground, he went and talked to his assistant, Scottish referee Bob Valentine, who told him "it was not intentional." The main camera filming the game also did not capture the incident, so those watching on television, including the Dutch match commentator, didn't see what had happened to leave Battiston unconscious on the ground. The game went on. While French fans and commentators were outraged about the decision, Dutch newspapers celebrated Corver's refereeing of the match, with one calling him "sublime." And FIFA's assessment of that year's World Cup referees gave Corver the highest mark among them all. Then, Dutch networks aired video footage that had been taken from behind the goal, clearly showing Schumacher striking Battiston twice in the head. Now, Corver was attacked for his mistake. Once he saw the footage, Corver recalls, he had to admit he had made the wrong call. But he hadn't seen it on the field—and he only has the one set of eyes. Among the characteristics Corver notes as being critical to being a referee is the good "fortune to see those things that matter." In this case, he wasn't so lucky. Though he had a long and successful career as a referee, he is most remembered for this one mistake.[12]

In 2009, another referee missed a call in another critical game involving France. Martin Hansson, from Sweden, was refereeing a decisive men's World Cup qualifying match between France and Ireland. The game was tied and went into overtime. In the 103rd minute, French forward Thierry Henry ran forward on the left wing and collected a pass in a way that was a blatant foul. He put his arm out so that the ball would hit and land just in front of his feet. Henry then passed the ball to his teammate, William Gallas, who scored a goal. Hansson allowed the goal to stand, as neither he nor the other referees had seen what became known, sardonically, as the "Hand of Henry," a reference to Maradona's famous Hand of God. For Irish fans, the stakes could not have been higher. They were kept out of the World Cup as the result of a clear foul. Henry afterward admitted what he had done and was criticized for not having confessed to the referee at the time that he had committed a foul. The idea that any player would admit guilt at such a moment, of course, is attractive but also naive. If he had done so, Henry could well have forfeited his team's qualification to the men's World Cup. As the referee who had failed to make the call, however, Hansson was also vilified. The Irish and international press heaped criticism on him. His promising career as a referee was, at least for a time, derailed. And though he lives in an isolated part of Sweden, some angry Irish fans went so far as to make the trek to harass him at his home.[13]

Cases like those of Corver and Hansson are outliers. Yet the fear of making this kind of error, one that will never be forgotten and will turn an entire nation against them, must weigh on many referees. That makes it all the more remarkable to see a referee at work calmly and decisively making one call after another, knowing that a single decision can lead to furious controversy, and even reshape a career.

International tournaments can be particularly complex to referee, not only because of the intense, global scrutiny that accompanies them, but also because they bring together players with different expectations and habits. Refereeing in England is not the same as refereeing in Brazil or the United States. There are varying national cultures of fouling, and of arguing. Some referees strictly censure dissent on the part of players. The eighty-year-old Corver, for instance, looks back fondly on the first time he refereed a match with Johan Cruyff. When Corver awarded a penalty against Ajax, Cruyff "waved his hand in a gesture of disapproval." As the team's reigning star, Cruyff had gotten into the "habit of doing that, and most of my colleagues tolerated it," Corver recalls. "Not me." Corver instead immediately pulled out a yellow card and this earned him Cruyff's respect. Later in his career, Cruyff twice came to see Corver after matches and gave him his match jerseys. "My son is still proud to own those," Corver said. For him, the key to refereeing is to communicate authority. "As a referee, you have to have the power to project a certain image and build a reputation for yourself." Players come to know referees within a league, and so it helps when they have built a reputation for fairness and strictness. This can also happen on the international stage, because referees who gain a good reputation in international competition will be brought back for subsequent tournaments. Some referees become well known among soccer fans, such as Howard Webb, an English referee who was consistently assigned both to important English Premier League games and international matches, including the hard-fought final of the 2010 men's World Cup between Spain and Holland.[14]

Today, Corver's account of the respect shown to him by Cruyff might seem a little quaint. Many contemporary referees endure an endless barrage of insults and back talk that would be considered insane in any other work setting. Imagine an office where, every time a superior made some decision, her employees crowded around, gesticulating, arguing, looking absolutely flabbergasted, and insulting the superior's mother. Or a courtroom in which, whenever the judge intervened on some point of procedure, a chorus of profanities echoed around the chamber, shouted by observers, while those on trial released a torrent of insults.

Galeano muses on the contradictory, and slightly tragic, lot of the referee, whose job seems always to be to make themselves hated. In fact, the "only universal sentiment in soccer," he writes, is that hatred. Yet everyone knows the game depends on the referee. Moreover, the effort a referee puts in on the field is, in a way, the ultimate expression of love for the game. He is "the only one obliged to run the entire game without pause." From "beginning to end," he chases around "the white ball that skips along back and forth between the feet of everyone else." Yet except when he holds it in his hands before the game begins, or sometimes when it stops, the referee isn't allowed to touch the ball. He is in the middle of everything, but excluded from the game he makes possible. There may, in fact, be no one who cherishes being on the pitch more than the referee: "Just to be there in that sacred green space where the ball floats and glides, he's willing to suffer insults, catcalls, stones and damnation."[15]

I remember well a day when, in East Lansing, Michigan, my club team composed of professors and graduate students from

Michigan State University ended up playing against a team of referees. It had been pouring rain, and the scheduled tournament had been called off, but we and the referees hadn't gotten the message. "Why don't we play a quick game against each other?" they suggested. It was a terrible mistake. Suddenly they had the ball, and they could play. Given that, even in this kind of club league, referees get their fair share of abuse game in and game out, these referees were seeking a bit of vengeance. We sensed this early on, and made sure to be extremely polite. The team of referees, wearing orange, went around us so fast, inexhaustible, laughing as they scored one goal after another. We managed only one against them, accomplished off a free kick that they graciously allowed us to take. In the end, they scored nine goals and walked away laughing, abuzz, almost relieved. Was this our gift to the referees? For once they could simply play, and score, without having to decide what was right and what was wrong.

In many other sports, technology has been readily incorporated into officiating. Referees can stop the game and watch a video replay before making a decision. Using this kind of technology in soccer has long been resisted by many fans, players, and managers, and by IFAB, with the idea that it would fundamentally alter the form and experience of the sport by introducing too many pauses. The flow so many cherish in soccer would, the argument goes, be interrupted too often. If technology promises more reasoned, scientific decisions, then, it also threatens to destroy the sport. There is something appealing, of course, about the idea that soccer can be made fairer through technology. Yet there is also something curious about this desire to improve the game. After all, soccer has conquered the world just as it is. Does it really need to be improved?

In recent years, however, boosters of technology have made important gains. During the 2014 men's World Cup in Brazil, FIFA allowed the use of something called goal-line technology for the first time in the tournament. Goal-line technology uses electronic sensors to determine whether the ball has crossed over the goal line and therefore whether a goal should be counted. Its introduction was a concession to the fact that referees had, with some frequency, made mistakes about this in the past, by giving a goal when the ball hadn't crossed the line or else claiming the ball hadn't crossed the line when it did. The latter was famously the case during the 2010 men's World Cup, when a goal scored by the US against Slovenia, which clearly went over the line, was disallowed by the Malian referee Koman Coulibaly. The decision was a lightning rod; suddenly all kinds of people who never seemed to care much about soccer before were enraged that this referee—who, some noted, didn't even speak English!—had stolen a goal from United States. As soccer journalist Paul Kennedy wryly puts it: Coulibaly's mistake had performed a miracle. "He accomplished what no one else could in more than 100 years. He made Americans care passionately about soccer."[16]

An even more dramatic change is in the works for the 2018 men's World Cup in Russia, which will incorporate something called Video Assistant Refereeing. The technology was used on a trial basis during the 2017 Confederations Cup, a tournament pitting the winners of various regional championships against one another in the venue that will host the men's World Cup the following year. A team of Video Assistant Referees sitting in a room full of television screens can watch replays in order to help the referee on the pitch make a decision. This recourse is not to be used often, or lightly. It is meant only for decisions involving goals, penalty kicks, and red cards.

So it is that soccer's rules are changing. After much lobbying, FIFA and IFAB also decided that, in the end, a hijab is not dangerous on the pitch. After the 2007 nondecision on the matter, national and local federations and individual referees continued to make their own decisions about whether a player could wear a hijab. Mansour could continue to play in a hijab, as she had long done, in Ottawa and other parts of Canada. In fact, as journalist Rosie DiManno wrote, even as IFAB was deliberating the question in England, Mansour was busy "scoring a couple of hummers in Ottawa" wearing a bright red hijab, color coordinated with "her team's red uniform." DiManno argued, "Only the most churlish, or pedantic, would claim that there is anything remotely provocative—or athletically unsafe—about the girl's head covering." She had interviewed Mansour and her mother, who was supportive of her daughter's decision. The girl, it turned out, had a particularly strong relationship to the hijab. "It's not something I would have chosen for her," her mother explained; she didn't herself wear a head scarf. "But she made that decision and I look at it as a blessing. She practices Islam, she prays five times a day. It makes her complete." In fact, the entire incident had made Mansour even more committed to wearing a hijab. The family was proud of all her teammates who had stood by her, in the process showing others "what it means to be Canadian." Mansour hoped that the officials wouldn't take too long to clear the way for her to play everywhere. After all, she planned to try out for the Canadian national soccer team in a few years.[17]

Mansour couldn't, however, play in Quebec, where the soccer federation had decided the hijab was "dangerous" and therefore outlawed by law number four. For a while, FIFA supported those who were against the hijab. It expanded on the IFAB decision, declaring that no players could wear a hijab in FIFA-organized games. A player who, like Mansour, wanted to compete internationally could not wear a hijab, even if the country she was playing for allowed it. In April 2010, FIFA banned an Iranian national girls' team from participating in the new Youth Olympic Games taking place in August of that year. The team's uniform included a covering of the neck and hair. In explaining their ban, FIFA not only argued that the hijab could pose a danger to players, but also cited another law which outlaws advertising on equipment. "Basic compulsory equipment must not have any political, religious or personal statement," declares this law. In 2007, IFAB had shied away from suggesting that the hijab ban had anything to do with religion. In 2010, however, this was exactly what FIFA was claiming. Although the youth team was eventually allowed to play in an adjusted uniform that included a tight hijab, FIFA was not willing to let the matter drop. In June 2011, the Iranian women's national team was prevented from playing in an Olympic qualifying match in Jordan. The decision was particularly heartbreaking for the players, because it came down only as they were about to go onto the pitch and effectively ended their hopes of playing in the Olympics. It stirred even more outrage than the previous decisions on the matter.[18]

These incidents launched a new round of debate about whether women should be allowed to play wearing a hijab. Prince Ali bin-al Hussein of Jordan, president of the Jordan Football Association, became a vice president of FIFA representing Asia in January 2011 and strongly advocated that FIFA formally declare that women could play in hijabs. Prince Ali and others pointed out that there were numerous contradictions in FIFA's policy. Many players sport religious tattoos, for instance, and make religious gestures before entering the pitch, before a penalty kick, or when celebrating a goal. Though these are not on the players' uniforms, they represent a kind of religious expression. As the writer Awista Ayub argued, FIFA's approach gave the impression of singling out Islam, since only the hijab was being banned formally. Indeed, the decision seemed to be "targeting one segment of the population—Muslim women."[19]

The lobbying of Prince Ali and others slowly succeeded in reversing the policy. In November 2011, the Asia Football Confederation approved a proposal to end the hijab ban, which Prince Ali was tasked with bringing to the FIFA executive committee. The committee, in turn, approved of the motion, and asked IFAB to reconsider its ruling. Finally, in 2012, IFAB allowed for a two-year trial period, during which an "athletic hijab"—specially designed by sportswear companies to cover the hair with a tight fabric—would be allowed in international competition. "There is no medical literature concerning injuries as the result of a headscarf," IFAB noted, agreeing that the athletic hijab could not be considered "dangerous." The decision guaranteed that national teams from Iran, Jordan, and elsewhere with players sporting hijabs would be allowed to play in international matches. The

French Football Federation, however, immediately implemented its own national ban against the hijab. In Quebec, too, girls and women wearing hijabs continued to be banned from playing. When a nine-year-old girl named Rayane Benatti went onto the pitch wearing a hijab just after the decision was announced, a referee told her that she had to take it off in order to play "for safety reasons." She refused, and was sent to the sidelines. "It made me feel very sad," Benatti later said. "I love soccer."[20]

In 2014, seven years after the original incident, FIFA ended the two-year trial period and formally declared that athletic hijabs would be allowed in international play. FIFA had, in the end, taken a stand on a question that has been at the center of political debate in a number of countries, most notably France. Those who lobbied FIFA successfully ultimately understood the powerful symbolism of what happens on the pitch. The presence of women in hijabs in international tournaments makes them visible in a way that, undoubtedly, will continue to stir up discussion and commentary. But, in a small way, the space of the pitch has been transformed, opening up new possibilities. Someday, a player on the Canadian national team may score the winning goal in an international tournament wearing a hijab—as Mansour had dreamed of doing—and in the process, offer a new way for people to envision and think about what it means to be Canadian.

The rules of soccer matter because the game matters so much, to so many. As the most visible embodiment of the Laws of the Game, and therefore of the institutions that govern global football, referees are both vital and vulnerable. They represent the institutions that govern global soccer, but are often left alone to figure out precisely how and when to apply the rules. The game depends on them entirely, for they are the ones who contain and control the action, the ones who shape the game by policing its limits. They are the focus of a level of rage, hatred, and accusation that is sometimes breathtaking to behold. They are attacked when they intervene too much and when they intervene too little. And yet, although it sometimes seems like everyone hates the referee, it also can often seem like everyone, both on and off the pitch, wants to *be* the referee. All fans think, at one point or another, that they are smarter and more observant than the referee in the game—that they would have seen the foul and made exactly the right call. It is common to see a player who has fallen to the ground holding up his hand as if it has a card in it, waving it about, insisting that the player responsible deserves a red card. The referee has to continually point out that she is the only one with yellow and red cards in her pockets. She alone holds this unique power. Sometimes referees hold up their whistles, a tiny symbol of control, and show them to players as a reminder that they are the only ones with the authority to start and stop the game.

Referees might get greater sympathy and understanding if someone developed a video game called "FIFA Referee," a companion to the extremely popular FIFA series of video games produced by EA Sports, where people get the thrill of taking to the pitch as virtual versions of their favorite players. These games are advertised as being particularly realistic, with the movements of players on-screen based on careful study of the movements of the players on which they're based. There is, however, one realm in which these games are deeply unrealistic: the referees always make the right call. Imagine what it would be like to play *as* the referee in such a game. You would never quite know where to look. Keeping your eye on the ball is critical, because you need to make the right call if someone is fouled as he advances. But focus only there, and players will know you aren't looking at them when they are away from the ball, which means they might be able to get away with something on the side. The sideline officials may see it—but then again, maybe their eyes are on the ball too. Imagine, too, a crowd of players rushing toward you, berating and insulting you. What do you say? How do you keep your composure? How many points would you get, in this imagined game, simply for not losing your cool under such pressure?

Every once in a while, fans and commentators conclude that the referee basically got it right. What doesn't happen enough— given that referees are, in a very real sense, the ones who make the game possible—is players or fans saying these simple words: thank you.

7

THE FAN

In September 2011, the Turkish Football Federation carried out a marvelous experiment. A few months earlier, a game in Istanbul involving the team Fenerbahçe had ended in violence, with fans attacking opposing fans and then invading the pitch. The game was canceled and the stadium evacuated, but many people were injured in the chaos. Police and soccer authorities have long struggled with how to stamp out such fan violence. One technique they have used is to punish the teams for the behavior of their fans, notably by forcing them to play in empty stadiums. Eliminating the crowd can clearly resolve security problems—no fans, no violence—but it also destroys the very spirit of the game. After all, what is a team playing for if not for the fans?

Struggling with how to respond, the Turkish soccer authorities came up with a novel idea. Instead of banning all fans from the stadium, why not just exclude the problem demographic: men? Fenerbahçe would be allowed to play in front of their fans, so long as those fans included only women and young children.[1]

It worked. Forty thousand women, along with a small number of children, attended the match. The only men in the packed stadium were the players and staff from the two teams, along with referees. Even the security forces in the stands and around the field that day were all women. As the game unfolded, there were some differences: the opposing team was greeted with applause, not boos, for instance, and the players threw flowers up toward the fans. Otherwise, everything was the same. There was a sea of yellow Fenerbahçe jerseys in the stands, and tens of thousands of voices singing songs and chants in support of their team.[2]

The experiment exposed a fundamental truth about being a soccer fan. It's not who you are that makes you a fan. It's what you do. You come to the stadium ready not just to watch but also to participate. You wear a jersey. You know the songs, and if you don't know them you learn them. You cheer even the smallest of victories—a header won, a beautiful dribble—and jeer with boundless rage when the referee makes a call against your team that you don't like. And what you do in the stadium is part of a larger story, of games from the past that you saw or heard about, and of hopes stretching forward. In the stadium, in the crowd, you are part of a web of meaning and action that spreads outward, uncontained and uncontainable.

Who is soccer for? What does it mean—or should it mean—to be a soccer fan? Naturally, in soccer fandom, as in seemingly every other realm of human life, there are self-appointed gatekeepers and judges who concern themselves with who is a "true" fan of one team or another and what that means. Yet soccer is welcoming, and there are many ways in which you can choose to be a fan and make the game yours. For some, fandom is part of a deep, ancestral tradition of rooting for a long-established local club. For others, it is as evanescent as can be, an affinity that lasts the course of a World Cup tournament, or even a single game. Soccer fans are as diverse as humanity. Fandom offers a spectrum of possibilities that is reshaped and reconstituted by those who decide to be fans at any one place and time.

What unites soccer fans of every affiliation and across the various degrees of affinity is the way in which they experience the sport as a source of joy and possibility, a way to be surprised, to revel in the unexpected. As Nick Hornby writes, being at a soccer game can make you feel that you are at the center of the world, offering "this powerful sensation of being exactly in the right place at the right time. . . . When else does that happen in life?"[3]

At the heart of fandom is a sense of possibility. Soccer never ends. It will always come up with some new surprise. That is, as scholar Grant Farred notes, what makes the game "life-sustaining." It is "the prospect and reality of pleasure—of utterly surrendering yourself to the experience of the game, of submerging yourself totally in an experience over which you have no control," that makes it a seemingly inexhaustible source of possibility. "The game becomes all, becomes pure pleasure: the prospect of infinite joy."[4]

The archetypal soccer fan is a man who, as a boy, was initiated into fandom by his father, whose fandom is a lifelong devotion to a single team and, through that team, a specific place. In *Fever Pitch*, his memoir about his years as a long-suffering Arsenal fan, Hornby offers a moving and humorous account of this kind of fandom. As he makes clear, for him, soccer was at first the only way he and his father connected in their otherwise difficult and strained relationship. Hornby shows how fandom and masculinity can become tightly intertwined, and how being linked to a team becomes a way of being a man in the world.

On his first trip to the stadium, Hornby writes, he was immediately struck by "the overwhelming *maleness* of it all." He also quickly noted something many fans know all too well: the game involves a striking amount of suffering. "What impressed me most," Hornby writes, "was just how much most of the men around me *hated*, really *hated*, being there. As far as I could tell, nobody seemed to enjoy, in a way that I understood the word, anything that happened during the entire afternoon." Hornby watched in wonder as men yelled in "real anger" at their own players—"You're a DISGRACE"—and, as time went on and the game went badly, "anger turned into outrage, and then seemed to curdle into sullen, silent discontent." "The natural state of the football fan is bitter disappointment, no matter what the score," Hornby opines. "Football teams are extraordinarily inventive in the ways they find to cause their supporters sorrow. . . . Always, when you think you have anticipated the worst that can happen they come up with something new." Hornby also recounts his early perplexity at the ways in which fans could recover rapidly from an awful defeat. After watching Arsenal lose horribly in a critical game at Wembley Stadium, Hornby attended another match not long after, still in a funk. Arsenal won this match, and he noted that for most fans, it was as if everything was just fine, even though the outcome of this game didn't matter nearly as much as the last one.[5]

In time Hornby came to understand that soccer fans take these rare moments of joy deadly seriously, and live them as deeply as possible. Indeed, fans feel they have earned them by suffering through so much disappointment and frustration along the way. As the literary theorist Hans Ulrich Gumbrecht notes, fans make a kind of deal when they enter a stadium. They have "invested their emotions" in the outcome of one game, "they have risked disappointment, perhaps even depression, in exchange for a chance to be present at a dramatic performance." A soccer season is a dramatic unfolding story, and fan culture is woven from its particular details, with songs and chants that make reference to prior games. Hornby writes about worrying over missing a single game; he fears that at the next one he "won't understand something that's going on, a chant or the crowd's antipathy to one of the players." It is by being there throughout, he argues, that one earns the kind of redemptive victory that comes along every once in a while. It is *because* you have seen so many tedious, frustrating games that "there is real joy to be had from those others that come once every six, seven, ten years."[6]

There was a time in his life, Hornby recalls, when "Saturdays were whole the point of my entire week, and whatever happened at school or at home was just so much fluff, the adverts in between the two halves of the Big Match. In that time football *was* life, and I am not speaking metaphorically." This level of devotion, as Hornby readily admits, can border on an unhealthy obsession. And certainly many a case of the flu has been caught during some awful, boring, rainy English Premier League game. The soccer fandom he depicts is not the kind you see in an advertisement for beer or chips, in which happy groups of friends are perpetually gathered around the screen, cheering a goal. Instead, Hornby suggests, it can be a lonely and rather weird pursuit. Soccer is "an alternative universe, as serious and stressful as work, with the same worries and hopes and disappointments and occasional elations." It "is not an escape, or a form of entertainment, but a different version of the world."[7]

Gumbrecht describes sports fandom as involving two connected sides: *analysis* and *communion*. Scholars Andrei Markovits and Emily Albertson similarly write that most fans combine *knowing* and *loving* a team or sport. When you watch a game as a fan of a team, you want to understand what is happening right in front of you, how a play can open the way for scoring, and therefore victory, for your team. Yet the flow of the game gains greater meaning when you know how it fits into a broader story. That story can be about the course of a given season or tournament, and what each game means within it. It can be about a beloved player whose moves and skills are riveting to watch, or who has faced and overcome significant challenges. Yet the circles of meaning can also stretch out much further, to the history of the team, to prior seasons or tournaments, to legacies of past victories and defeats. All of these infuse the specific moment of watching a game with significance and emotion, making what is happening in front of you part of a much larger story linking past, present, and potential futures. The feeling of being a fan is something you feel in your body, too, even outside of games. Gumbrecht, a professor of literature who is also a passionate sports fan, writes that every time he drives by the stadium at Stanford University, his heart beats a little faster.[8]

The meaning of fandom is also deeply social. It matters to you because it matters to other people, to fans you know because they are family or friends, or to those you don't know but nevertheless feel connected to thanks to the game. That is what makes sports

fandom a kind of ritual. You can describe the connections between fans—the way their chants and shouts and emotions link
up, the way they share in moments of remarkable intensity—as a
kind of communion. This is true for all sports, but it is especially
forceful in soccer simply because of its status as the most popular
and beloved game on the planet. The intensity reaches its peak
around men's World Cup matches, which are the most watched
events in human history. Victories in these competitions, not only
in the final but in earlier games as well, generate mass national
celebrations that are so intense that they can only be compared
to dramatic moments of political euphoria—such as the liberation of Paris in 1944 or the celebrations of Barack Obama's election in 2008—but they happen more frequently, and sometimes
last even longer. Most of those who participate in these celebrations are not devoted soccer fans, and often have only tuned in
for a part of the tournament. People remember these moments
for lifetimes, even across generations. Across the world, soccer
produces uniquely electric, beautifully convivial, and surprisingly
intense moments of celebration and communion.

What explains this depth of emotion experienced by soccer
fans? For those don't care about soccer, after all, it can seem
strange that people feel so strongly about something that is,
objectively, totally meaningless. As one philosopher writes in a
meditation on soccer fandom, the question of "whether a ball of
about 430 grams of weight and a circumference of sixty-nine cen-
timeters has passed through, with its full diameter, an absolutely
arbitrary surface defined by goals placed on a patch of lawn" can
hardly be considered a "world-shattering event." It is, objectively,
"of no more importance than a leaf dropping from some tree."

Goals, furthermore, are banal, happening "by the dozens every weekend," and the only thing winning a game leads to is playing another game, which also has to be won, and so on and so forth. As Christian Bromberger observes, it would be extremely difficult to explain to an alien coming to earth the intensity and passion with which human beings approach watching other people play the "futile" game of soccer.[9]

What seems like a contradiction, though, really isn't one. It is precisely the concrete meaninglessness of sports that allows fans to infuse them with such meaning. Being a fan is freedom to feel, and to share in feelings, in a way that you don't have to explain. "That is one of the things I like about football," writes the novelist Karl Ove Knausgaard. "You don't have to justify your opinions. You don't have to argue for anything at all. You can leave everything to feelings. Argentina plays shit football? I love them. Germany plays beautiful football? Who cares." You can support a team for many different reasons: how they play, what they symbolize, or just the fact that you happen to be attending one of their games. You can keep at it for decades, lifetimes, generations, or just for the space of a game. You can even change your mind during a game, as I have once or twice. If it weren't futile, it wouldn't be so fun, and therefore so important.[10]

The term "fan" comes from the word "fanatic," and it contains a tint of judgment: that there is something slightly irrational, or even dangerous, about the kind of attachment that ties individuals to a sports team. There have long been critics of the amount of energy and attention people put into sports. Some leftists have wondered, reasonably enough, whether all that energy among working-class fans could be better spent carrying out a revolution, or at least a strike. Some intellectuals pointedly distance themselves from what they see as the mania and distractions of fandom. Eduardo Galeano points out, for example, that the Argentinean writer Jorge Luis Borges "gave a lecture on the subject of immortality on the same day and at the same hour that Argentina was playing its first game in the '78 World Cup."[11]

Governments and police, meanwhile, are often most concerned about the unruliness of soccer fans, and the potential for violence that surrounds the game. During the 1980s, authorities—along with academics and journalists—in Europe, and particularly England, struggled to understand the root causes of the violent behavior of "hooligans." These groups of fans, mostly young men, often fought with opposing fans before, during, and after games, as well as turned their anger toward police and security forces that sought to contain them. Inside stadiums that had bleacher seating, groups of fans would sometimes charge at one another during the games, creating chaos in the stands. They threw bottles, coins, batteries, or even flares onto the pitch. In some cases, there were connections between far-right organizations and fan groups, many of whom used racist and anti-Semitic chants and symbols against opposing teams. The period saw a series of horrible footballing tragedies, including in 1985 at Heysel Stadium in Brussels and then 1989 at Hillsborough in England, in which a lethal combination of repressive policing tactics and crowd behavior led to people being crushed to death—thirty-nine in Heysel, and ninety-six in Hillsborough—and hundreds of others injured.[12]

In the past decades, the incidents of violence in European soccer have decreased, in part because most stadiums in England

and elsewhere eliminated bleachers and moved to assigned seating. Policing of violent fans has intensified, with the stadiums becoming spaces of increased surveillance. Under pressure from authorities and teams, fan organizations have worked to contain or exclude violent members of their groups.

Nevertheless, violence around soccer is far from gone, and many games are heavily policed. At a game I attended in 2007 at the Parc des Princes, where the team Paris Saint-Germain plays on the outskirts of Paris, fans of the opposing team were escorted into the stadium by police on horseback through a separate entrance. Inside the stadium, they were contained in an area surrounded by a very high orange metal fence. Outside the fence were lines of security, and the fans were covered by netting, to protect them from objects thrown at them from other parts of the stadium. As recently as the 2016 European Cup, there were fights between fans in the streets of Marseille and flares thrown onto the pitch during one of the games.

The problem is that the crowd is fundamental to the existence of soccer. Crowds can be unruly, and sometimes dangerous, but they are also what makes the game live. Crowds are also a constitutive part of the spectacle of soccer. No one really wants to attend or watch a game where eighty thousand people sit politely and occasionally clap, or spend the match checking their phones. The thousands of people jumping up and down in unison, intoning age-old songs, jeering or cheering together—that is what in many ways gives soccer its meaning. To police the boundaries of that, identifying what is acceptable and what is not, is a delicate and complicated operation.

In the late 1980s, at the height of the problem of the hooligans in England, the writer Bill Buford spent a year embedded
in various fan groups and wrote about his experience in a book
called *Among the Thugs*. He wanted to understand how the act of
being a fan, of attending a soccer game, can lead someone to participate actively, even joyously, in forms of violence most people
see as reprehensible. He describes how, after a frustrating game
against Chelsea, he joins a group of Manchester United fans who
are waiting, seeking, hoping for a clash with opposing fans, or
police, or anyone. "A crowd is forming," he writes, "and the effect
is of something coming alive." He stands with others, waiting,
"alive to the possibility that something is going to happen." Finally, it lets loose. The group begins to run, together. "I am enjoying this," writes Buford. "I am excited by it." Unable to catch
up to a group of Chelsea fans, the group turns its energy against
buildings, smashing windows. "And then they are gone. They
go over the crest. There is a roar, and then everyone flies—as
though beyond gravity—into violence. They are lawless." Buford
refuses to describe the details of the violence, instead trying to
capture the "sensual intensity" of that moment when the crowd
suddenly takes flight. In that instant, he finally understands what
all the people he has interviewed for his book have been trying
to explain about being part of the crowd. "They talk about being
sustained by it, telling and retelling what happened and what
it felt like," speaking about it "with the pride of the privileged,
of those who have had, seen, felt, been through something that
other people have not." He understands the attraction of the "ab-
soluteness" of violence, of the "state of adrenaline euphoria" it

can produce. "What was it like for me? An experience of absolute completeness."[13]

That search for completeness, of course, doesn't have to lead to the kind of violence Buford describes. It can be found in the more joyous, and comparatively peaceful, way that fans join together each week in soccer matches throughout the world. There is, as many have noted, something quasi-religious about soccer fandom. "Manchester United: The Religion" reads one banner hanging from the stands of that team's home stadium. A soccer match is a mass public ritual, complete with codes of dress and a kind of liturgy. Central to it is the faith that, by gathering together and cheering the team and jeering the referee and singing the songs, the crowd makes a difference. This belief in the crowd's power to affect the outcome is widespread enough that it is part of the structure of the game in many cases. In the European Champions League, where matchups in the final stages of the competition involve two games, one in the home stadium of each team, goals scored in the away stadium count more.

During the most intense moments of games, fans literally feel a kind of fusion with the players they are rooting for. It is a moment, writes Gumbrecht, when the "combined physical energy" of the crowd "connects with the players' energy and makes the players' energy grow," and "the separation between the crowd and the players seems to vanish." The crowd becomes one, as Hornby describes when retelling one particularly thrilling goal he witnessed: "The rows of people disappeared and were replaced by one shuddering heap of ecstatic humanity." Hornby insists that being a fan "is not a vicarious pleasure, despite all appearances to the contrary." Part of what makes being a fan so powerful is that you are a participant, with the capacity to change what happens in front of you. "Football is a context in which watching *becomes* doing," Hornby explains. In fact, he argues, it is even more than that: for fans, when their team wins, it is the expression of their power and devotion, the realization of all that they have put into the team over many years. At that moment, they celebrate their own "good fortune." In insisting how important fans are, Hornby reaches for a striking metaphor. "The players," he writes, "are merely our representatives, chosen by the manager rather than elected by us, but our representatives nonetheless, and sometimes if you look hard you can see the little poles that join them together, and the handles at the side that enable us to move them." Players, of course, might object to Hornby's characterization of them as parts of a foosball table being controlled by the fans. Yet he captures a truth about soccer: fans last longer than players and managers. While those on the pitch come and go, those in the stands often spend a lifetime there. "The only difference between me and them," Hornby writes provocatively, "is that I have put in more hours, more years, more decades than them."[14]

To be a fan is to go into a public space and perform a kind of belonging. You do it with your body. In England, fans are sometimes called supporters, and there is a way in which they feel that they are carrying the team with their bodies and voices and songs. In a study of the notorious fans of the English football club Millwall, Garry Robson describes how they learn to move, talk, and walk in certain ways that express their belonging as they go in and out of the stadium. Everything about them declares: "I am Millwall. I belong here. I know the ropes." While they spend much of the match caught in what Robson describes as "a kind of ballet of bad emotions and physical tension," when a goal comes they move together in raucous celebration—running onto the field, setting off fireworks, scuffling with police, unable to contain their "general hilarity." The entire section of the stadium occupied by the Millwall fans becomes "a pandemonious swirl of sound and movement, of screams and songs, shouts and dances, shakings and arms raised, as if in supplication, to the heavens."[15]

The Millwall supporters Robson studied largely live in the neighborhood their team is from, and their fandom is connected to the life and identity of their local working-class community. There and elsewhere in England, and throughout the world, people can be born into soccer fandom, with memories of players, victories, and defeats, along with repertoires of songs and chants, passed on from one generation to another.

Soccer, however, has been both local and global for a long time. Since the early twentieth century, journalists have had to find ways to share news of sporting events across long distances. Already in 1924, massive crowds gathered in a central plaza in Montevideo to cheer and follow the Uruguayan team as they played in the final of the Olympics. The technology was rudimentary: every few minutes, a reporter at the games in Paris sent a telegram with a few sparse details of the game. This was then read out to the crowd from a stage. When the final telegram came in, announcing a victory, the crowd burst into rapturous celebration. By the 1930s, radio had spread throughout Latin America, with inexpensive sets enabling more and more people to tune in from home. In 1938, when the Brazilian team traveled to Italy for the third World Cup, they were accompanied by a team of journalists, including a radio commentator named Gagliano Neto. His voice became the main medium through which Brazilians followed the news of their team's exploits, and they hung onto his every word as he narrated each moment in the match. The symbiosis between media and soccer was just beginning, but the basic relationship was in place: new technologies like radio, and later television and the Internet, enabled fans to follow games even when they couldn't be there in person. The global passion for soccer provided an eager audience for the new technologies.[16]

Although this media at first developed so that people could get news about their local or national teams playing far away, in time it created another possibility. Fandom no longer had to be local. You could read or hear or watch any team play, and fall in love. That is what happened to Farred as a boy in apartheid-era South Africa, when he read about a victory by a team called Liverpool, in England, in his local newspaper. This random encounter developed into a long-term and passionate connection to the team that over the years sedimented with new meaning. He didn't attend a Liverpool match until he was much older, and yet his fandom developed into one of the most important parts of who he is. He calls this kind of attachment "long distance love," and writes that it "teaches the fan to think, feel and be in entirely unexpected ways."[17]

When I teach my course on soccer at Duke University, I always come to know students who, without ever having left the United States, have become passionate fans of European soccer teams. Today, you can grow up in Ohio and become a die-hard Bayern Munich fan, owning jerseys and posters, and as deeply familiar with the team's history as any German. These connections are powerful, and they open fans up to new worlds of meaning, history, language, and geography. Soccer becomes a kind of pedagogy. For Farred, it was soccer that "engendered in me the need to know about other places, other histories, other forms of violence and oppression" than those he experienced firsthand. There was an irony in his Liverpool fandom, as he admits, for he was a black South African and the team did not have any black players, until a forward named John Barnes joined it in 1987. At Liverpool, as well as on the English national team, Barnes was repeatedly subjected to racial abuse, but the way he responded with a "deft, complicated awareness of race," inspired and taught Farred. Rooting for Barnes and for Liverpool at the same time, Farred felt his connection to the team deepen. "Any time I want, I can call up those loping, powerful runs," Farred writes lovingly, "shoulders dropped just a little, almost squared, like a boxer, cutting across the field, most often from his position wide of the left flank, feinting, picking up pace with an almost invisible burst of speed."[18]

Like many other black athletes, Barnes became a political symbol simply because he was challenging racial exclusion with his presence on the field. The beauty of his play, and his many goals, made fans adore him, and in the process challenged racism. Rooting for Barnes became a way of imagining a different kind of society. This has been true throughout the world, as fans have, at times, rooted for players or teams who challenged the social order in one way or another. In the British protectorate of Zanzibar in the early twentieth century, for instance, the men who worked as caddies on a golf course decided to form their own football team. These men were considered social inferiors by the European colonizers whose golf clubs they carried around. However, the colonial team turned the tables when, in front of thousands of spectators, they trounced a team of European men. The colonial authorities always did their best to suppress the political implications of soccer. Yet, over the subsequent decades, in Zanzibar and throughout the African continent, soccer fandom was often used to challenge and contest colonial power.[19]

The anticolonial dimensions of soccer were part of its appeal throughout Africa. Fans were also eager to see players move in particular ways that they felt represented their communities and their culture. Historian Peter Alegi writes that, as the game spread in colonies in Africa in the 1940s and 1950s, matches became "spectacles, feasts, and popular entertainment all wrapped into one." Fans came dressed in the colors of their clubs, of course, but they also brought music to the stands, and "drums and other percussion instruments provided the soundtrack to matches." In South Africa, drawing on a long cultural tradition of creating praise names for warriors, including the Zulu people who fought the English, fans developed names for successful players. In Brazzaville, Congo, meanwhile, as historian Laura Fair writes, fans "christened players according to their technical quality and styles, as in the case of a goalkeeper named 'Elastic,' and other stars named 'Dancer,' 'Phantom,' 'Magician,' 'Steamboat,' and 'the Law.'" Through their celebration of certain players, African fans communicated the kind of game they wanted to see. They often preferred the improvisational play that they were familiar with from their own informal play in streets and sandlots. With many games played without referees, it was the spectators themselves who determined who the real "winners" were "through their end-less analysis of players, strategy and style," argues Fair. "Good moves often made a bigger impression on fans than the actual score." As Alegi writes, there was a celebration, throughout the continent, of styles focused on "the cleverness, beauty and ex-citement of feinting and dribbling." Fans enjoyed such "delightful moves" for their virtuosity, but also because they saw in them an embodiment of cultural values that emphasized the importance of "creativity, deception and skill in getting around difficulties and dangerous situations in colonial societies."[20]

In the early 1950s, a Senegalese radio announcer known as Allou developed a style of match reporting on the radio that delved deep into West African storytelling traditions. He drew on the styles of the griot—hereditary musicians who for genera-tions have spoken the history of families and communities—to recount the exploits of these new heroes in real time. In one memorably tragic match, he recounted live as the player Iba Mar Diop scored a penalty kick at the last minute, winning the game for his team—only to collapse from a heart attack and die mo-ments afterward. Radio journalists such as Allou gave audiences a way to experience and understand such dramatic moments by connecting them to broader cultural narratives about heroism and sacrifice.[21]

Allou's full name was Alassane Ndiaye. He was part of a dis-tinguished Senegalese family. His uncle was Blaise Diagne, who had represented Senegal in the French National Assembly for decades, and was the father of the soccer star and later Senega-lese national team coach Raoul Diagne. Another of his relatives, Lamine Guèye, was mayor of Dakar and later the first president of the Senegalese National Assembly. Ndiaye grew up on Gorée, an island near Dakar. He attended university in Dakar and became a distinguished history teacher, and hosted a radio show about Senegalese history. Ndiaye had loved playing soccer as a child, and that is when he was given the nickname Allou, a shortened version of his first name, by his teammates.

Allou began his career as a sports commentator by accident. One day at the Parc Municipal des Sports in Dakar, he suddenly found the microphone thrust in front of him. It was just after World War II, and football was booming in Senegal. But there was only one journalist calling the games on the radio, a man named Pierre Véran. Perhaps he was tired, or perhaps he wanted to play a trick on Ndiaye. "I'm handing the microphone to my young colleague Allou," Véran declared suddenly. As he later remembered, Allou had hesitated for a minute or two, "as if drowning in an endless sea," and Véran looked at him expectantly. Somehow, though, Allou found his voice and began to narrate the match. Unexpectedly, he had found a new calling.[22]

From that moment on, he never stopped, and eventually became the most beloved soccer commentator of his generation in Senegal. Allou played a key role in the expanding popularity of the sport in his country. As was the case throughout the world during that period, media and soccer expanded together: the radio brought new fans, and the fans bought more radios. As historian Bocar Ly writes, Allou cut a striking figure along the side of the pitch with his microphone, always "elegantly dressed." He started each match the same way: "Thank you to the studio! Allou here, reporting from the Parc Municipal des Sports." Back home, people gathered around the radio, "ready to let themselves be seduced" by his electrifying voice. Allou had to help listeners visualize what was happening and, like other radio announcers, developed a rich and evocative language that brought together detailed description of plays and moves with a larger, poetic celebration of the meaning of the game. Fans were "transported into another world" as Allou turned the narration of games into an opportunity to reflect on almost all aspects of human life. He infused his accounts of matches with rich historical, cultural, and philosophical references. There was, Ly notes, no "lyric theme" that he hadn't at some point talked about in relation to soccer: "Love, death, human destiny, nature's charms and mysteries, the world and its abysses, grandeur, the beauty and nobility of sport, the power of God and his ineluctable decisions." Delving deep into Senegalese tradition, Allou created a universe of sound and reflection around each match.[23]

Though Allou was well versed in tactical questions, Ly argues that a game of soccer for him was always much more than "an abstract and narrow game of chess, a problem of applied tactics." It was an opportunity to create a work of verbal performance, a spectacle of vocal sound. He had an "ample and easy eloquence," and "an incomparable verbal richness and sumptuousness." He offered up a "spontaneous profusion of images," and used the rhythm of his voice to communicate the drama and emotion of the match to those who could not see it. "His voice, slow and suave when the game was calmly being played in the midfield," was "amplified and fired up when the action got closer to the penalty area or when danger became imminent," so that those who listened on their radios felt all the emotions that "constricted the hearts" of those in the stadium. Allou's live accounts of the games were "prose poems," a "poetry at once lyric and epic." In this, he was also teaching fans how to connect soccer to other aspects of their culture. His commentary gave fans new ways of thinking, and feeling, through a game.[24]

Allou also helped make certain players stars thanks to the way he talked about them. He lavished praise on a player named Mbaye Parka who was a forward for the Jeanne d'Arc team in the late 1940s. Allou called him a "prince of football," a "genius" in the attack whose playing was a "work of art." Allou effused, "Each of his plays is a delicious poem that brings value back to football by raising it to the level of the most exquisite of artistic representations." Allou described how Parka stepped out of his chauffeur-driven car, something then reserved only for the most important politicians and biggest celebrities. Parka was always somehow perfectly dressed: a towel thrown around his neck, his shoes, in Allou's words, "shining and lovingly tied." For those who gathered around to watch him walk into the stadium, Parka seemed "a god of the ball." As soon as the whistle blew, it "obeyed his most capricious moves," and he "manipulated it with a science, a dexterity, never seen in Senegal." More than any other player of his generation, Allou said, Parka had "penetrated" into the "very essence of football, its spirit, its magic spells, expressing its splendors with an ease and intelligence that no one will ever surpass."[25]

Given their prominence and following, soccer stars could also play a political role. During the struggles for independence in Africa, soccer was often mobilized for revolutionary purposes, most forcefully through the creation of the FLN team in Algeria in the late 1950s. Soccer also played an important role in struggles against apartheid, notably at Robben Island, where inmates including Nelson Mandela sustained their community and developed political skills by organizing a soccer league within the notorious prison. More recently, at the beginning of the Arab Spring uprising in Egypt, it was the fans of some of Cairo's oldest soccer teams, Al Ahly and Zamalek, who were often on the frontlines of the protests. There was a tradition of political organizing within the large, formal associations of fans tied to these teams. And the members of these groups had experience engaging in public conflicts with the police in soccer stadiums and before and after games. In these contexts, fandom has become explicitly political.[26]

Soccer and politics have also been intertwined in Latin America throughout much of the twentieth century. Amateur clubs in Chile, for instance, were often the place where Chileans began to practice politics as they organized their institutions and negotiated with local and national officials. During the years surrounding the election of the popular socialist Salvador Allende to the presidency in 1970, amateur soccer clubs in urban areas became important venues for political debate and mobilization. When the United States, intent on undermining and containing Allende's government, blockaded Chile and began supporting plots against the president, soccer clubs were part of a web of civic institutions that organized to provide necessities to communities and to defend the government.[27]

When Allende was overthrown on September 11, 1973, through a CIA-supported coup, the new military regime ruthlessly attacked civic organizations, including soccer clubs. The new junta banned elections within soccer clubs, seeing any form of democratic practice, no matter how small, as a threat. The military regime also used the soccer stadiums where Chileans had rooted for their national and professional teams to detain, torture, and execute the people they rounded up in the wake of the coup. Decades later, these stadiums became sites of mourning and commemoration. In 2003, Estadio Chile, where the popular folk singer Víctor Jara was executed in September 1973, was renamed Víctor Jara Stadium. And in the Estadio Nacional, a section of the stadium is now set aside as a memorial. The seats there remain empty during games—as many seats as there were prisoners killed in the stadium by the military regime.[28]

In the United States, politics infuses soccer as well. In the regional Gold Cup tournament, played every two years, immigrant communities in the United States get a rare chance to see their national teams play. The tournament is organized by the Confederation of North, Central American and Caribbean Association Football (CONCACAF), which also organizes the qualifying process for the World Cup. Gold Cup games take place throughout the United States, and Haitians, Salvadorans, Jamaicans, Trinidadians, Costa Ricans, and Hondurans pack into stadiums wearing their jerseys and waving national flags. During the 2011 Gold Cup, I traveled to watch a doubleheader—El Salvador versus Costa Rica and Mexico versus Cuba—in Charlotte's Bank of America Stadium, a place usually reserved for professional American football games. That day, most of the forty-six thousand fans were waving Mexican and Salvadoran flags. As their team scored one goal after another against Cuba—five in total—Mexican fans roared and jumped and tossed beer in the air. When the US faces off against other teams during the Gold Cup tournament, they often play in stadiums where their own supporters are outnumbered by those of the other team. This is especially true for games between the US and Mexico, the two teams that most often end up facing off in the final. But even teams from smaller nations attract massive numbers of fans. In a September 2017 World Cup qualifying match between the US and Costa Rica, it was supporters of the Ticos, as the Central American team is affectionately known, who were the majority in the stadium in New Jersey. And, in a defeat that contributed to undermining the US's chance to go to the 2018 World Cup, Costa Rica won 2–0.

This situation causes soul-searching, and occasional outbreaks of xenophobia, among some US fans. They ask, why does our national team have to play what amounts to an "away" game on US soil? And why don't immigrants, many of them US residents or citizens, root for this country's team instead of that of Mexico, Jamaica, or Costa Rica? In 2011, US goalkeeper Tim Howard—frustrated after a grueling 4–2 defeat at the hands of Mexico in the Gold Cup final—complained that the trophy ceremony was held in Spanish. The use of Spanish in the ceremony was a recognition that it is the most common language among the nations who compete in the tournament, and that much of the viewing audience in the US watched on Spanish-language television. Howard's comments, however, clearly called up broader tensions about immigration and language in the United States, stirring up debate among fans, many of whom criticized Howard. Players on the US men's team, which features many athletes of immigrant background, have since commented on political topics varying from protests of the national anthem to President Donald Trump's polices. As athletes become increasingly political across the US sporting world, the political stances and interventions of national team players will inevitably gain more and more attention.

There is a parallel debate in France, where French citizens of Algerian, Tunisian, and Moroccan background often pack into stadiums to root for the North African teams in games against the French national team. In 2001, a game at the Stade de France in Paris was even canceled after fans of the Algerian team invaded the pitch to prevent the French team from winning a much-anticipated "friendly" match between the two countries. In these contexts, the question of who people root for, and what it means, channels larger debates about immigration, identification, and national belonging. The tensions around this can ebb and flow, depending both on the broader political situation at the time and what happens in any given game. A tournament like the Gold Cup can also offer an opportunity for soccer fandom to be a positive, and convivial, space that represents the diversity of the United States and helps us embrace the fact that people can identify with multiple histories, places, and colors.[29]

Soccer in the United States has also been a crucial space for debates around gender and sexuality. In 2013, Robbie Rogers, a star forward on the LA Galaxy who had also played on the US international team, came out as gay. He was greeted warmly by fans and supported by coaches and players, as he recounted in his 2014 autobiography. At many MLS games, some fans and fan groups regularly wave rainbow flags and place them around the side of the pitch as a way of explicitly identifying soccer fandom with support of gay rights.[30]

Women's soccer in the United States is, in a sense, an inherently political space. The inequalities surrounding the women's game have led to consistent protests by players. The most recent was a lawsuit filed against the US Soccer Federation by a number of star players, including Hope Solo and Carli Lloyd, alleging that the fact that they are paid less than players on the men's national team is discriminatory. Although the US women's team has won three World Cups, and the men's team none, they are paid less and received far less prize money in 2015 than the men's team did for their appearance in the 2014 men's World Cup. Star players Megan Rapinoe and Abby Wambach have long been out as lesbians and vocal supporters of gay rights. After winning the 2015 Women's World Cup, an event which coincided with the Supreme Court's decision legalizing gay marriage, Wambach rushed to the sidelines and kissed her wife, surrounded by American flags draped from the stands by fans, creating a powerful image of openness and inclusion. The impressive expansion of women's soccer worldwide over the past decade offers encouraging examples of the possibility for political change. At the same time, it is clear that women's soccer—and women's sports more broadly—continues to represent a vital challenge both to many social attitudes and to structures of gender inequality. For many fans of women's soccer, that is part of the appeal of supporting women's professional and national teams. There is a connection and symbiosis between players and fans who share a common desire to create a different social reality.

In many parts of the world, there is still great resistance to the presence of women as players, and even as fans. This hostility takes its most extreme form in a practice depicted in the 2006 film *Offside*, by Iranian director Jafar Panahi. In Iran, women are not allowed into the stadium to watch soccer games. Some die-hard female fans try to sneak in, but they can be detained and even arrested and imprisoned for doing so. Panahi decided to represent, and critique, this practice by making a film depicting women who attempt to get into the stadium to see the Iranian national team playing in a men's World Cup qualifying match. He managed to get a permit from the government to film outside the stadium during an actual game between Iran and Bahrain, a pivotal match which would determine whether Iran would participate in the 2006 men's World Cup. The camera follows a group of women dressed like men—one wears a baseball cap with an Iranian flag tucked into it, draped around her neck—who one by one are caught and stopped by soldiers as they try to enter the stadium. Most of the film involves the group of women, detained in a pen outside the stadium, arguing with the young, rather feckless soldiers who are guarding them. What unites all of them is that they would rather be watching the game, though the women know far more about the match than any of the male soldiers.[31]

The outright exclusion of women from Iran's stadiums is extreme, but throughout the world men usually make up the vast majority of spectators in stadiums. As the experiment carried out in Turkey in 2011 suggests, that is not because women don't want to go, and probably has more to do with the fact that women feel uncomfortable, perhaps even unsafe, in the predominantly male space of the stadium. This is part of a much larger system of structures and habits that tend to exclude or marginalize women from many kinds of sports fandom. Throughout the world, notes one scholar, there is a deep relationship between "masculinity and sports," and usually male fans determine the codes and language surrounding fandom. In the United States, notably thanks to Title IX, which mandated equal access to sports opportunities for men and women at colleges and universities, this has changed in recent decades. Women are increasingly present as sports commentators and journalists, and women's soccer is gaining increasing recognition.[32]

Panahi's film *Offside* also hints at the possibility for something different. Throughout the film, some of the men help the women, understanding them as equals in the realm of fandom. At one point, one of the captive women manages to escape briefly and see the inside of the stadium. The contrast between the claustrophobic space of confinement and argument, which fills most of the film, and the open roar of the stadium and the sight of the green pitch in the middle is striking. Iran qualified for the men's World Cup that day, and at the end of the film, as the bus taking the women to prison winds through Tehran, crowds erupt into celebration in the streets. Some men eventually help the women escape into the crowd. Soccer, Panahi clearly shows, is for all Iranians.[33]

Today, fandom is global, with people rooting for teams far from their homes. Television, and live video streamed over the web, has become the dominant medium through which most people watch soccer, enabling new global connections while also teaching us to see and interpret the experience of the game in different ways. In the late 1980s, when Rupert Murdoch was pioneering the development of cable television in England, he quickly realized that soccer would be the key to getting people to do what they had never done before: pay for TV. Having failed to garner sufficient audiences by showing Hollywood movies, Murdoch began acquiring the rights to air English soccer matches.

The sport, he explained candidly, was the "battering ram" that got his cable boxes into people's living rooms.[34]

Now, most people who watch soccer the world over are sitting in front of televisions or computer screens. This shapes how they view and think about the game, for there is a profound difference between watching a game in a stadium and watching the same game through curated camera angles. While the camera sometimes offers, briefly, a broad view—and today you can often tune in to a "tactical cam" on some networks that allows you to see the whole picture—what we largely get is a finely crafted drama in which the ball is the star of the show. You rarely see the entire field, so the way a team is occupying the space, and the way players who are far from the ball are moving, is hard to understand. While the sounds of fans are transmitted over television, they are flattened, and the intricate relationship between the roars, chants, sighs, and chatter and what is happening on the field is lost, though of course it can be replaced by a similar experience in a sports bar or living room.

In this context, the voice of the commentator on television is an essential accompaniment to our experience of soccer, shaping what we see and how we think about it. The best commentators find a way not to be too present or insistent in their reading of the match, and they use a richness of vocabulary that makes listening to them interesting. English commentators, who are masters of the genre, might describe a long ball as "speculative" if it is not clear where it was meant to go, or they might refer to a clearance as "agricultural" if the ball is sent off into the stands, suggesting it was almost kicked into nearby fields. Commentators describe the mood of teams as well. They might be playing "with their tails up," for instance. Commentators have even been known to speculate about what is going on in the minds of players. Once I heard an announcer on Univision describe the arrival of Michael Bradley on the pitch for the US Men's National Team, when they were down against Mexico, by saying, "He runs onto the pitch, his bald head full of dreams!" At their best, commentators offer humor, even absurdity, as they try to capture the madness of the game. "Newcastle players might fear that when they get home tonight, [N'Golo] Kanté will be waiting for them on their doorstep," said Arlo White, the English commentator who frequently narrates Premier League matches aired in the United States on NBC Sports during a match between Leicester City and Newcastle United in March 2016. The comment humorously captured how relentless Kanté's defending is.

It is not only what the commentators say, of course, that matters, but also the energy and tone of their voice, the way it rises and falls with the action. You can listen to match commentary in a language you don't understand and still basically comprehend the ebb and flow of the game just from the changes in speed and intensity. In the United States, the long "Gooooooool!" celebrations of some of the great Spanish-language commentators have become a defining piece of soccer culture.

Commentators are supposed to be relatively objective, though of course sometimes their preference for a team comes through, especially when they are commenting on an international game. There are also some delightful moments when commentators effuse wildly about a goal or win. In 1982, when Norway defeated England in a men's World Cup qualifier, the radio commentator Bjorge Lillelien drifted into what Jonathan Wilson calls a "barely coherent delirium." He represented the victory in exaggerated terms as a win over a long string of English leaders, including Lord Nelson, Winston Churchill, and Princess Diana. "We have beaten them all, we have beaten them all!" he cried. "Maggie Thatcher, can you hear me? Maggie Thatcher . . . your boys took a hell of a beating! Your boys took a hell of a beating!" In the 2016 European Cup, an Icelandic commentator rivaled Lillelien in celebrating his team's defeat of England just days after the Brexit vote. He taunted them in an inimitable falsetto voice: "You can go home. You can go out of Europe. You can go wherever the hell you want. . . . England 1 Iceland 2 is the closing score here in Nice. And the fairy tale continues."[35]

The voice of commentators shapes the experiences of those who watch, and it can ultimately shape the game. In the film *Zidane: A 21st Century Portrait*, Zidane recalls himself as a child hearing the sound of the French television commentator Pierre Cangioni. Born in Corsica, Cangioni created the show *Téléfoot* in 1977 and offered news and commentary on matches on the show until 1982. "When I was a child," Zidane recalls, "I had a running commentary in my head when I was playing. . . . It wasn't really my own voice." It was Cangioni's. "Every time I heard his voice, I would run towards the TV, as close as I could get, for as long as I could. It wasn't that his words were so important. But the tone, the accent, the atmosphere was everything." The moment in the film is a powerful one, because you realize that Zidane is navigating a kind of time-spiral as he plays. As a child, he imagined himself on the pitch, his actions narrated by someone like Cangioni. In time, he actually made his way to the pitch and ultimately to the heights of the sport, his actions narrated by another generation of commentators. In a sense, as he is playing, he is always part of a script, an endless story that he writes and rewrites on the field.[36]

Part of being a fan is becoming slightly obsessed with certain players—with the way they move on the pitch, the way they look and dress, and their lives off the pitch as well. However we express it, there is a special sense of connection between fans and players that comes from the fact that we feel like they represent us—that, in a sense, they *are* us—as we watch them play. Social media now gives us new ways to express and share this feeling. Many of us now watch games as part of a virtual community, connected via Twitter or other social media platforms. When a player makes a great move, it instantly gets turned into a GIF and is circulated lovingly across the globe. In this way, we share our sense of delight about individual players and striking moments, often focusing not on a goal but on a delightful dribble—nutmegs, where the ball is passed between the legs of a defending player, are a particular favorite—or an expression of delight or despair. We can rapidly write about and share our enthusiasms, as literature scholar Jeff Nunokawa did on Facebook with an ode to Spanish striker Fernando Torres. Video games, meanwhile, have brought the link between player and fan to a whole new level. The immensely popular FIFA game enables players to actually feel like they are in the bodies of their favorite athletes, whose virtual selves are based on their real way of playing and moving. There are increasing numbers of people who may never play an actual game of soccer in their own bodies, but who play constantly through a video game. Additionally, the game is popular among players, and seems to even be changing the way real-life soccer is played, as they try moves out in the game that then migrate onto the pitch.[37]

Today the sight of soccer flashing across a television is a kind of universal visual language, something you can see almost anywhere. When it comes time for the World Cup, people across the globe are tuned in to the same games in a powerful moment of global communion. Several film directors have movingly, and humorously, captured this phenomenon, and the feeling that some games simply cannot be missed. In *The Cup*, the 1998 men's World Cup tournament is followed obsessively by young boys in a Tibetan monastery, who sneak off nightly to watch the game in a nearby village, ultimately discovering that the stern and ordinarily quite serious monks who are their teachers are just as enraptured by the tournament. *The Great Match*, set during the 2002 men's World Cup, follows three small groups—one on the steppes of Mongolia, another in the Amazonian rainforest, and a third traveling across the Sahara—as they desperately try to find a television in time to watch the final between Germany and Brazil.[38]

In his film about the devastating 1990 earthquake in Iran, *Life, and Nothing More*, director Abbas Kiarostami also captured the ways in which soccer can become all-important, as essential as life itself. Journeying through the disaster zone, Kiarostami searches for the actors from one of his previous films. Kiarostami eventually finds one of these actors, a young boy, and is relieved to discover he survived the earthquake. After they meet, Kiarostami asks the boy to recount what happened to him. Immediately, the boy starts talking about soccer. The earthquake hit a little after midnight, on an evening when four World Cup group matches had been played. For the boy, that was a crucial part of narrating the event, and in fact he begins the story by narrating the game and a goal scored. Kiarostami, clearly irritated, interrupts him to specify that he wants to hear how the boy survived the earthquake. The boy then recounts a terrifying tale, including the death of family members.[39]

Later, Kiarostami encounters a man who is setting up an antenna on a hilltop above a devastated village so that he can watch another World Cup match. Kiarostami asks the man if it might be a little bit inappropriate to watch soccer at a time like this. The man replies that he, like so many others, is in mourning, having lost many family members. Then again, the man says with a light smile and a small shrug, the World Cup only comes every four years. Kiarostami smiles too. He seems to understand, then, that the tournament is one of those things that has to be attended to, even in the midst of disaster. Perhaps that is precisely the point: even at the worst of moments, soccer can offer a kind of solace.

The men's World Cup takes place every four years. It is the most-watched soccer tournament and also the one that draws in and welcomes the largest group of fans. It is, in fact, the most-watched event on the planet. More people watched the 2014 World Cup final than had ever watched anything before in human history, and a new record will doubtless be set again in 2018. During the weeks of the World Cup, across most of the globe, everything seems to revolve around the tournament.

The World Cup was dreamed up in Europe in the years after World War I. But the man who created it, the Frenchman Jules Rimet, is surprisingly unknown. Like many of us, he didn't play soccer particularly well, but he believed in soccer with a quiet, quasi-religious fervor. He was of the generation that had gone through World War I, a conflict that left a monument in every French town with a list of the young men who died in the trenches. Rimet came home from war with a dream. Rather than sending their young to massacre each other with machine guns or stab one another with bayonets, nations might instead compete on the pitch. The idea was that national teams could celebrate their pride and difference through what he considered to be the most universal language on the planet: soccer. In 1920, Rimet became president of FIFA, which had been founded in 1904. Rimet immediately declared that his hope was that sport could help direct conflicts between nations in the modern world "towards peaceful contests in the stadium." There, he went on hopefully, "foundational violence is submitted to discipline and the rules of the game," and the only thing the victor takes home is "the joy of winning."[40]

Rimet's vision of the ways in which soccer can crystallize and channel nationalism was prophetic. The French sociologist Émile Durkheim, in his study of religious life, famously described what he called "collective representations" as being at the heart of social, political, and religious rituals in human society. A community, Durkheim argues, is something greater than the sum of its parts. When individual people come together to form a collective, they can do and be more than if they remain dispersed. Yet that sense of community can be relatively abstract unless it is represented in a concrete object—a collective representation. Durkheim focuses on the example of totems in Native American societies, but he points out that a flag does something similar. These objects serve as visible and tactile representations of the community. When you look at them, you see—and feel—the power of the collective.[41]

Soccer teams may be today's most powerful form of global collective representation. They are not, however, stationary objects like a totem or flag. A team is a collective representation in motion. The eleven players on the field stand for the nation, and through their individual and collective action determine its fate within the international competition. In the process, they vividly represent the broader community, which is connected to the collective through the actions and emotions of fans. The outcome of the game depends on the intricacies of individual choices by players, but those choices end up taking on symbolic meaning for entire nations.

Part of the draw of the World Cup is that many people who might rarely make a show of nationalism can, in the festival atmosphere, deck themselves out in flags and national symbols in a way that feels joyful and playful and creates connections across social and class barriers. In European countries such as France and Germany, where popular use of flags and other national symbols is ordinarily relatively rare, the World Cup and other major tournaments create a sudden explosion of public flag carrying, face painting, and anthem singing.

During a World Cup, national narratives take shape in the stories and actions of individual players. In fact, in a World Cup, it can often seem like a single player's entire life has been directed toward the instant when he scores a game-winning goal, bringing glory and fame to his nation. There is Diego Maradona's journey from a shantytown outside Buenos Aires to the moment when he used his hand, and then his foot, to defeat England in the

1986 men's World Cup. Or Zinedine Zidane's road from his parents' colonial-era migration to France, to the concrete plaza in the Marseille projects—where he played all day long but never liked to head the ball—to the moment when he scored two headers against Brazil to win France its first World Cup in 1998. In those instants, nations and individuals appear to merge. Maradona becomes Argentina, and all Argentineans are Maradona; Zidane is France, and all the French are Zidane. The crossroads between a player, his moment of glory, the fans, and the nation is what makes the World Cup into the unforgettable global spectacle it has become.

Most of those who watch the World Cup, however, are not rooting for their national teams. In 2018, only 32 nations will compete in the men's World Cup tournament out of 211 FIFA members. Even if your team makes it into the tournament, there is a fifty-fifty chance it won't make it past the group stage. So, you have to be open-minded, a little flexible. Many World Cup fans begin with vague allegiances, or sometimes multiple allegiances, and their fandom is shaped by the tale that unfolds in the course of the tournament. Part of the joy and allure of fandom in these contexts is precisely the freedom to choose any team you desire and later to change your mind. You can decide whom you want to stand with, for a time, based on any number of reasons. You might like how a team plays, or like the story of one or more of the players. You might just hate the opposing team. The connections may be ephemeral in many cases, but sometimes they grow into more. [42]

There is a great humanity to this. I personally watch many games in the World Cup rooting for both teams at the same time, feeling both happy and sad when someone scores a goal. I some-times feel delight for those celebrating alongside a nagging sor-row for the losing team. There are just too many good stories out there: every team, and perhaps every player, has one. The compo-sition of teams changes, too, and so as fans we need to always be ready to change with them. Many fans don't stand for a nation, but rather a way of playing and therefore a way of being. Those who rooted for the French national team of the 1990s, like me, were often drawn by the spectrum of backgrounds represented— Algerian, Armenian, Guadeloupean—a kind of global crossroads made up of many immigrant journeys, coming together on the pitch. The team became a potent political symbol in France, a re-sponse to the parochialism and xenophobia of the far right, espe-cially once the team secured the country's first World Cup victory in 1998. As a collective, they could serve as this kind of symbol only because they also played beautiful soccer. Though the team has had ups and downs since, for many fans outside the country it remains a favorite.

During the 1980s and 1990s, Germany was the team most Europeans loved to hate, mostly because of their infuriating habit of winning all the time with an effective, indeed often un-stoppable, style that many found boring to watch. The English player Gary Lineker famously and accurately once quipped: "Football is a simple game. Twenty-two men chase a ball for 90 minutes and at the end, the Germans always win." One of the most memorable of these victories was the 1982 semifinal against France, during which Harald Schumacher's foul against Patrick Battiston was not called by referee Charles Corver. A friend of mine, the French historian Jean Hébard, once vividly recounted to me the experience of listening to that game on the radio. He never forgot the anguish he felt at that moment. In 2016, we watched a European Cup game between France and Germany together in Paris, ruefully ready for another German victory. The last time France had beaten Germany in international competition was 1958, after all. When, instead, France won—thanks notably to brilliant playing by the ebullient star Paul Pogba, a child of immigrants from Guinea—we couldn't quite believe it. As we joined cheering crowds gathering to celebrate at the Place Saint-Michel, Jean told me he had been waiting for this moment since 1982, but had never expected it to come. The beatific smile on his face said it all.[43]

The Slovene writer Uroš Zupan movingly describes his own painful relationship to the German team. As someone who had grown up in post–World War II Europe playing games in which the Germans were always the bad guys, their endless victories on the soccer pitch left "scars, wounds on the soul, deep cracks on the face of beauty represented by the technical perfection and improvisational flair of the teams I loved." The Germans defeated the Dutch team, at the height of Total Football, in the 1974 men's World Cup final, and the French in the famously grueling 1982 men's World Cup semifinal. "With the Germans it was all tactics and power and, above all, a fanatical endurance that would not yield, that swept away all beauty and softness. . . . The Germans," laments Zupan, "did not outplay the teams they defeated; they simply ground them down with their endurance."[44]

These German teams included very few players of immigrant background, in contrast to the French team of the 1980s, for instance, which included a number of players with roots in the

Caribbean and Africa. Then, after France's 1998 men's World Cup victory and in the context of increasing debates about the place of immigrants in German society, the German national soccer federation increasingly emphasized training and recruiting players from a variety of different backgrounds. By 2006, the German team was pleasingly global, playing the kind of beautiful flowing soccer many fans claim to want to see. Many who at one time would have rooted against Germany now find themselves drawn to the team's flair and style, though of course some remain unpersuaded. Teams change, nations change, and our affinities and affiliations do too, thankfully. In this, soccer can sometimes offer a model of openness and freedom.[45]

In every tournament, there are teams from small countries, too, that become darlings simply because their presence and unexpected victories make us feel as if anything is possible. Even scoring one goal on the stage of the World Cup can turn a player into a legend. The Haitian national team has only been in the World Cup once in its history, in 1974. They faced Italy, which was one of the greatest teams in the world at the time, known for its impenetrable defense. After a scoreless first half, Haiti surprised the Italian team with three passes forward up the pitch. Philippe Vorbe slid the ball past Italian defenders to forward Manno Sanon, who rushed toward goal and scored against the legendary goalkeeper Dino Zoff. It was the first time any team had scored against Italy in nineteen games. As my Haitian friends who remember the moment tell me, the whole country seemed to shake as everyone jumped up and down in wild celebration. Italy came back and won the game 3–1, and Haiti lost its next two games as well. No matter: Sanon had, in that instant, become a national hero. Decades later, in 2009, a richly colorful mural in downtown Port-au-Prince celebrated the soccer player as part of a venerable pantheon of Caribbean national heroes. The Cuban revolutionaries Che Guevara and Fidel Castro were next to Jean-Jacques Dessalines, Haiti's venerated founder, and completing the group was Sanon, the goal scorer of 1974. To understand what the World Cup means to many people, you have to see how putting Sanon like this alongside major political leaders makes perfect sense. "Now and forever," noted the *New York Times* in 2010, "Manno is running, taking a pass from Philippe Vorbe, outrunning a defender, zipping past Zoff, shooting and—goal!"[46]

Other island nations have also surprised the world on the international stage. During the 2016 European Cup, the Icelandic team—managed by a man whose main career is as a dentist in a small town—defeated a series of supposedly superior teams, including England, playing in a crowd that included fully one tenth of the island's population of three hundred thousand. The Gold Cup tournament in the United States often features island territories that are not nations, notably the French Caribbean islands of Guadeloupe and Martinique. While they are not members of FIFA, they are part of the CONCACAF regional confederation, and so are able to send teams to this tournament. When Martinique competed in the 2017 tournament, the team was made up almost entirely of semiprofessional players from the island's small league. They played beautiful and riveting soccer, including a hard-fought match against the US team. Watching such games, learning the names of players you have never heard of before, and rooting for unlikely victories is part of the joy of watching international tournaments.

The reality, though, is that whomever you root for, they will al-most certainly end up losing at some point during a tournament. When a World Cup begins, anything seems possible, but that is ultimately a fleeting feeling. The trajectory, after all, is slow elim-ination of one team after another. If you are deeply committed to just one team, the fleeting moments of joy are inextricable from many more moments of disappointment and pain. Especially in a tournament like the World Cup, loss is the defining experience. Every team loses, in the end, except for one. As the games go on, one story after another ends. One absolutely brilliant goalie after another, each making a series of seemingly perfect saves, is beaten in the end. Resigned, sad beyond measure at the fact that one moment of defeat can erase all the other triumphs: that is the root of the feeling of melancholy that can set in as a tournament progresses.

It is for this reason that the climax of the tournament is often the end of the initial group phase and the move into the first elim-ination games. This is a time when there are still many teams, many possibilities, and when the games are often extremely ex-citing and open-ended. It is in this phase of the tournament that the most memorable games are played: Ghana's heartbreaking loss to Uruguay in 2010, for example, or the riveting matches be-tween Belgium and the US and between Algeria and Germany in 2014. The later games of the World Cup, while they are often global spectacles, often deliver up disappointing, even conserva-tive, soccer.

What makes participation in the World Cup so ebullient and addictive, nevertheless, is the potential to feel connected to so many places, the fact of knowing that you are part of a mass of humanity, perhaps billions strong, all watching exactly the same thing at exactly the same time. The experience of being at the tournament in person encourages a heightened version of this feeling. You, too, become a part of the spectacle, part of the team, part of the game, and its rituals. This is what makes the tournament humanity's greatest theater.[47]

When I went to the 2010 men's World Cup in South Africa, I learned to use and love a plastic horn known as the vuvuzela, which was commonly played by fans in the country. The vuvuzela became famous—and infamous—during the tournament, in part because many found the drone of the instrument, flattened through the sound on television, distracting and annoying. People at the tournament were annoyed too, and in fact on the way into the stadium the same merchants were often selling vuvuzelas and earplugs side by side.

Yet inside the stadium, the way this instrument accompanied the games was powerful, even spiritual. It infused the stadium with an indescribable energy. The vuvuzela, blown by tens of thousands, rises and falls in response to what is happening on the pitch. It reaches a climax when the teams walk out of the tunnel, calms down during the national anthems and picks up again during the first minutes of the match. Every moment from then on—every dangerous free, corner, or penalty kick—is punctuated by a shower of sound. This tsunami, humming throughout the stadium, can be hypnotic, especially during the celebration of a goal. When the game becomes boring, fans in one part of the stadium begin blowing the vuvuzela, and then it spreads like a breaking wave, pushing the players on the pitch toward the goal. It was the sound of the vuvuzela that offered the pilgrims from around the world, who shared neither language nor songs, a way of participating in creating the unique sonic geography of the stadium. Newcomers to South Africa for the World Cup understood this, and quickly acquired their vuvuzelas. During the different games, Mexicans, Japanese, Italians, Brazilians together created a choir that accompanied the players on the field. The vuvuzela became part of an act of communion that enabled fans from all over the world to share moments of a unique intensity.[48]

Events like this feel like a kind of miracle and an occasion for gratitude. That is the feeling that, Gumbrecht ultimately explains, most defines his relationship to the beauty of athletic events. For Gumbrecht, the answer to why people watch sports is ultimately simple. People are seeking beauty. And when they encounter it in a game, they are grateful for the gift. "Watching sports," he writes, "is a way of waiting for that which may occasionally happen but is never guaranteed to happen, because it lies beyond the pre-calculated limits of human performance." What is ultimately most fulfilling, even redemptive, in watching sports is this: "To see happen, occasionally, what we have no right to expect."[49]

"Years have gone by," writes Galeano in his "author's confession" at the beginning of his famous ode to soccer, "and I've finally come to accept myself for who I am: a beggar for good soccer. I go about the world, hand outstretched, and in the stadiums I plead: 'A pretty move, for the love of God.'" For Galeano, this allegiance to beauty is greater than loyalty to any team, or any specific country. "When good soccer happens, I give thanks for the miracle," he writes, "and I don't give a damn which country performs it."[50]

In the end, it is that search for beauty, for transcendence, for communion with others in moments of joy, that keeps people returning to this game. There is a mystery at the heart of soccer fandom, an unanswered question about precisely why this form of play can feel so powerful, even divine, again and again, to people in so many different parts of the world and in such different social circumstances. What is soccer? What makes this game what it is everywhere on the planet, a script endlessly repeating, with different players every time, altogether infuriating, unpredictable, and wondrous? The answer to that question lies in the experience each of us brings to it, to knowing and loving the sport, returning to it always, even when it disappoints us, seeking some form of redemption as yet unknown and unseen.

Soccer is yours. So take it. Make of it what you will: a symbol, a mirror, a story. Watch it. Talk about it endlessly. Speak it, this precious human language. Hold on to the delight it offers. For joy is a universal right. Play it. Find something, anything—a rock, a bicycle, a bag, a coconut—and make a goal. Put the ball down on grass, dirt, asphalt, sand. And then begin with a dribble, a pass, a kick. Everything lies ahead.

ACKNOWLEDGMENTS

My editor at Basic Books, Brian Distelberg, was the first to dream up this book and propose the idea to me. Of course I said "Yes!"—and working with him and the wonderful editorial and marketing team there, including Liz Dana and Melissa Veronesi, has made writing this book a pleasure. My agent, Wendy Strothman, was also enthusiastic from the first and helped me envision the work.

I wrote most of the chapters during a utopian 2016–2017 year at the National Humanities Center here in North Carolina, the perfect environment for musings on soccer and human nature. I am grateful to Marlene Daut, who happily was also a fellow at the NHC, and who kindly read early drafts of the chapters. Her keen editor's eye combined with her experience as a collegiate soccer player helped me find the right voice to tell these stories. Soccer historian Brenda Elsey provided me with useful comments on a later draft, as did my Duke colleague Negar Mottahedeh.

My thoughts here are rooted in many years of dialogue with fellow football scholars—including the wonderful network of the Football Scholars Forum led by Alex Galarza and Peter Alegi at

Michigan State University—as well as endless, often hilarious, conversations about Arsenal and African football with my friend Achille Mbembe. And they have been shaped by the insights and work of the Duke students in my Soccer Politics class, which I have taught since 2009, most recently with students reading and writing in multiple languages on our class blog.

Duke University has been a wonderful place to work on this topic over the years, allowing me to host events about soccer that have informed my work. A weeklong visit from Lilian Thuram in 2009 was without a doubt the coolest thing I've ever done as a professor, and ongoing conversations and visits with him since then have shaped my vision of the game. I learned a lot from the delightful crew that came together for a conference on "The Futures of Women's Soccer," co-organized with Joshua Nadel, in the spring of 2015: Shireen Ahmed, Jennifer Doyle, Brenda Elsey, Sarah Gerke, Mónica González, Jen Schaefer, and Jean Williams, along with local luminaries Carla Overbeck and Cindy Parlow Cone. And that summer, thanks to Grant Wahl and Avi Creditor at *Sports Illustrated*, a group of us from the con-ference—along with historian Lindsay Krasnoff—were able to bring feminist critical theory to that venerable magazine through the "Upfront and Onside" series of dispatches and analysis from the Women's World Cup.

That experience was one among a series of opportunities to write for magazines about soccer in recent years. I owe thanks to the editors and journalists who opened up these spaces for me. Sean Jacobs and Elliot Smith at *Africa Is a Country* were the first to reach out, and then *Roads & Kingdoms* and *Sports Illustrated* for their 2014 series on the men's World Cup. Franklin Foer had me join the remarkable crew penning reflections that summer for the *Goal Posts* blog, which also led to participation in what is probably the most literary fantasy sports league on the planet. In 2016, Josh Levin at *Slate* invited me to write about the European Cup. Writing for these venues helped me develop the voice for this book, and I thank them for the opportunities.

My son, Anton Dubois, offered crucial encouragement: accepting my curious obsession, he made me a customized Lionel Messi Lego figure with a speech bubble saying "Goal!," as well as a portrait of me with a soccer ball as a head. Katharine Dubois, also known as the novelist Katharine Ashe, offered crucial stylistic and interpretive guidance as I completed the final draft.

This work is meant to be an offering to the future of soccer, which I sense is in good hands thanks to the conversations I've had about tactics and free kicks with the young midfielder Zora Lentz, whom I look forward to cheering for on the US Women's National Team in about a decade.

NOTES

Introduction

1. Brenda Elsey, *Citizens and Sportsmen: Fútbol and Politics in 20th-Century Chile* (Austin: University of Texas Press, 2011), 257.

2. Gwendolyn Oxenham, *Finding the Game: Three Years, Twenty-Five Countries, and the Search for Pickup Soccer* (New York: St. Martin's Press, 2012), 52, 57.

3. Nick Hornby, *Fever Pitch* (New York: Riverhead Books, 1992), 191.

4. Diego Maradona, *El Diego: The Autobiography of the World's Greatest Footballer* (London: Yellow Jersey Press, 2005), 77.

5. Jean Eskenazi, "Eloge et universalité du football," in *Le Football*, by Jules Rimet (Monte Carlo, Monaco: Union Européenne d'Editions, 1954), 263–269; Fredrik Ekelund and Karl Ove Knausgaard, *Home and Away: Writing the Beautiful Game*, trans. Dan Bartlett and Seán Kinsella (New York: Farrar, Straus and Giroux, 2016), 328, 383.

6. Juan Villoro, *God Is Round: Tackling the Giants, Villains, Triumphs, and Scandals of the World's Favorite Game*, trans. Thomas Bunstead (Brooklyn, NY: Restless Publishers, 2016), 19; Ekelund and Knausgaard, *Home and Away*, 155; David Kilpatrick, *Obrigado: A Futebol Epic* (New York: Beadle Books, 2015), 8.

7. Jean-Paul Sartre, *Critique of Dialectical Reason, Volume 1*, trans. Alan Sheridan-Smith (London: Verso, 2004), 473.

8. Hans Ulrich Gumbrecht, *In Praise of Athletic Beauty* (Cambridge: Belknap Press, 2006), 190–191.

9. Eduardo Galeano, *Soccer in Sun and Shadow*, trans. Mark Fried (London: Verso, 1998), 9.

10. Villoro, *God Is Round*, 108–109.

11. Peter Alegi, *African Soccerscapes: How a Continent Changed the World's Game* (Athens, Ohio: Ohio University Press, 2010), 21–22; Gumbrecht, *Athletic Beauty*, 201.

12. Dave Zirin, "An Elite Soccer Team Protests ICE After Their Teammate Is Detained," *Nation*, August 7, 2017; Rachel Chason, "He Went to ICE to Tell Agents He Had Gotten into College. Now He and His Brother Have Been Deported," *Washington Post*, August 2, 2017.

13. Gwendolyn Oxenham, *Under the Lights and in the Dark: Untold Stories of Women's Soccer* (London: Icon Books, 2017), 87–107.

14. Geoffrey Douglas, *The Game of Their Lives: The Untold Story of the World Cup's Biggest Upset* (New York: Holt, 1996), 8, 18–20, 44–45; Alexander Wolff, "The Hero Who Vanished," *Sports Illustrated*, March 8, 2010.

15. Laurent Dubois, "The Making of Belgium's Golden Generation, and Imported Versus Cultivated Talent," *New Republic*, July 2, 2014; Laurent Dubois, "How Missing the Next World Cup Could Help the US in Future Ones," *Washington Post*, October 11, 2017.

16. *Once in a Lifetime: The Extraordinary Story of the New York Cosmos*, directed by Paul Crowder and John Dower (Miramax, 2006); on the recent history of the MLS see Grant Wahl, *The Beckham Experiment: How the World's Most Famous Athlete Tried to Conquer America* (New York: Three Rivers Press, 2010).

17. Aubrey Bloomfield and Sean Jacobs, "US Soccer: Not a Progressive Bastion," *Al Jazeera*, August 26, 2017; Matt Pentz, "Megan Rapinoe: 'God Forbid You Be a Gay Woman and a Person of Color in the US,'" *Guardian*, March 25, 2017.

18. Laurent Dubois, "The Stade de France—A History in Fragments," *Africa Is a Country*, November 15, 2015, http://africasacountry.com/2015/11/the-stade-de-france-a-history-in-fragments/.

19. Franklin Foer, *How Soccer Explains the World: An Unlikely Theory of Globalization* (New York: Harper Collins, 2004).

Chapter 1: The Goalkeeper

1. The letter was posted by Gianluigi Buffon on his Facebook page on March 21, 2016, and a translation posted that day by James Horncastle on Twitter @JamesHorncastle.

2. Edward Winters, "How to Appreciate the Fingertip Save," in *Soccer and Philosophy: Beautiful Thoughts on the Beautiful Game*, ed. Ted Richards (Chicago: Open Court, 2010), 149–160; Jonathan Wilson, *The Outsider: The History of the Goalkeeper* (London: Orion Books, 2012), 14–16.

3. Galeano, *Soccer in Sun and Shadow*, 4; Villoro, *God Is Round*, 109.

4. *Laws of the Game 2016/17* (Zurich: International Football Association Board, 2016).

5. On Bell in Marseille, see Christian Bromberger, "Football as World-View and as Ritual," *French Cultural Studies* 6 (1995): 293–311.

6. Winters, "How to Appreciate the Fingertip Save," 150–151.

7. Wilson, *The Outsider*, 111.

8. Ibid., 9–11.

9. James Walvin, *The People's Game: The History of Football Revisited* (London: Mainstream Publishing, 1994), 42–43; Bill Murray, *The World's Game: A History of Soccer* (Urbana: University of Illinois Press, 1998), 3–4.

10. Stefan Szymanski, "It's Football, Not Soccer" (unpublished paper, Ann Arbor, Michigan, 2014).

11. Wilson, *The Outsider*, 13.

12. Ibid.; Jonathan Wilson, *Inverting the Pyramid: The History of Soccer Tactics* (New York: Nation Books, 2013), 4.

13. David Goldblatt, *The Game of Our Lives: The English Premier League and the Making of Modern Britain* (New York: Nation Books, 2014), 35; Wilson, *The Outsider*, 119; Ruud Gullit, *How to Watch Soccer* (New York: Penguin, 2016), 22.

14. Wilson, *The Outsider*, 35, 40, 42.

15. Ibid., 99–100.

16. Ibid., 81–85; Galeano, *Soccer in Sun and Shadow*, 39–40, 61.

17. Vladimir Nabokov, *Speak, Memory: An Autobiography Revisited* (New York: Vintage Books, 1989), 185, 267–268; Wilson, *The Outsider*, 46.

18. Nabokov, *Speak, Memory*, 267; Wilson, *The Outsider*, 46.

19. Maher Mezahi, "Les Pieds-Noirs: Algeria's Forgotten Footballers," *French Football Weekly*, March 28, 2013, http://frenchfootballweekly.com/2013/03/28/les -pieds-noirs-algerias-forgotten-footballers/.

20. Mezahi, "Les Pieds-Noirs"; Galeano, *Soccer in Sun and Shadow*, 57.

21. Mezahi, "Les Pieds-Noirs"; Herman R. Lottman, *Albert Camus: A Biography* (New York: Doubleday, 1979), 39–40; Galeano, *Soccer in Sun and Shadow*, 57–58.

22. Albert Camus, *The Stranger*, trans. Stuart Gilbert (New York: Vintage, 1954), 70–71.

23. Galeano, *Soccer in Sun and Shadow*, 4–5.

24. Ibid., 117; Wilson, *The Outsider*, 60–65.

25. Hugh McIlvanney, *McIlvanney on Football* (London: Mainstream Publishing, 1997), 180–181.

26. Wilson, *The Outsider*, 16.

27. Hope Solo, *Solo: A Memoir of Hope* (New York: Harper, 2012), 33.

28. Ibid., 38–39.

29. Ibid., 20–21.

30. Ibid., 73–74.

31. Ibid., 101.

32. Carli Lloyd, *When Nobody Was Watching: My Hard-Fought Journey to the Top of the Soccer World* (New York: Houghton Mifflin Harcourt, 2016), 200.

33. Roger Kittleson, *The Country of Football: Soccer and the Making of Modern Brazil* (Berkeley: University of California Press, 2014), 12–13; Galeano, *Soccer in Sun and Shadow*, 87–90; Gumbrecht, *Athletic Beauty*, 217.

34. Kittleson, *Country of Football*, 12–13; Wilson, *The Outsider*, 137; Paulo Perdigão, *Anatomia de uma derrota* (Porto-Alegre: L & PM Editores, 1986); Antonio D. Angelo Junior Domingos, "Anatomia de uma derrota: adeus a Paulo Perdigão," *Universidade do futebol*, August 7, 2007, http://universidadedofutebol .com.br/anatomia-de-uma-derrota-adeus-a-paulo-perdigao/.

35. Wilson, *The Outsider*, 137.

36. Wilson, *The Outsider*, 137–139; Wilson, *Inverting the Pyramid*, 112; Kittleson, *Country of Football*, 13; Joshua H. Nadel, *Fútbol!: Why Soccer Matters in Latin America* (Gainesville: University Press of Florida, 2014), 73–74.

37. Wilson, *The Outsider*, 294–296, 304; Simon Kuper and Stefan Szymanski, *Soccernomics* (New York: Nation Books, 2009), 95–110.

38. Wilson, *The Outsider*, 294–296, 304.

39. The inimitable scene is here: https://youtu.be/BfEnYkK_ums.

40. "Here Are Our Africa Cup of Nations 2015 Awards," *Africa Is a Country*, February 9, 2015, http://africasacountry.com/2015/02/here-are-our-africa-cup -of-nations-2015-awards/.

Chapter 2: The Defender

1. Laurent Dubois, *Soccer Empire: The World Cup and the Future of France* (Berkeley: University of California Press, 2010), 22.

2. Wilson, *Inverting the Pyramid*, 290.

3. Dubois, *Soccer Empire*, 78–81.

4. Ibid., 83–89.

5. Ibid.

6. Ibid., 94, 122.

7. Ibid., 122.

8. Ibid., 124–130; Murray, *The World's Game*, 8.

9. Dubois, *Soccer Empire*, 130, 236–240; Lilian Thuram, *Mes étoiles noires: De Lucy à Barack Obama* (Paris: Philippe Rey, 2010).

10. Wilson, *Inverting the Pyramid*, 2; Murray, *World's Game*, 8.

11. Wilson, *Inverting the Pyramid*, 8; Murray, *World's Game*, 8.

12. Wilson, *Inverting the Pyramid*, 13–15. There is an intriguing parallel to the influence that the Carlisle Indian Industrial School had on the development of American football. The Carlisle team focused on aerial passing rather than carrying the ball in part to outmaneuver Ivy League opponents who were physically larger; see Sally Jenkins, *The Real All Americans: The Team That Changed a Game, a People, a Nation* (New York: Doubleday, 2007).

13. Wilson, *Inverting the Pyramid*, 13–15.

14. Ibid., 30.

15. Ibid., 30–31.

16. Kittleson, *Country of Football*, 38–39; Wilson, *The Outsider*, 135.

17. Wilson, *Inverting the Pyramid*, 67; on debates over style and national culture, see Nadel, *Fútbol!*

18. Wilson, *Inverting the Pyramid*, 31.

19. Ibid., 204, 330.

20. Julian Carosi, "The History of Offside," November 23, 2010, 1.

21. David Goldblatt, *The Ball Is Round: A Global History of Soccer* (New York: Riverhead Books, 2008), 36.

22. Carosi, "The History of Offside," 2.

23. Ibid., 2–4.

24. Ibid., 4–6; Paul Hoyningen-Huene, "Why Is Football So Fascinating?," in *Soccer and Philosophy: Beautiful Thoughts on the Beautiful Game*, ed. Ted Richards (Chicago: Open Court, 2010), 7–22.

25. Carosi, "The History of Offside," 4–6.

26. Ibid.

27. Wilson, *Inverting the Pyramid*, 36–37.

28. Ibid., 36–39.

29. Ibid., 39.

30. Ibid., 40–41.

31. Ibid., 45–47.

32. Ibid., 45–47, 51–52.

33. Bocar Ly, *Foot-Ball: Histoire de la coupe d'A.O.F.* (Dakar: Nouvelles Éditions Africaines du Sénégal, 1990), 14–17; Alegi, *African Soccerscapes*, 80–81.

34. Wilson, *Inverting the Pyramid*, 159–162.

35. Ibid., 163–166.

36. McIlvanney, *On Football*, 186, 190; Wilson, *Inverting the Pyramid*, 167.

37. Carosi, "The History of Offside," 8; Wilson, *Inverting the Pyramid*, 357.

38. Maradona, *El Diego*, 1, 6.

39. Goldblatt, *Game of Our Lives*, 70.

40. Kittleson, *Country of Football*, 38.

Chapter 3: The Midfielder

1. Aleksandar Hemon, "If God Existed, He'd Be a Solid Midfielder," *Granta*, no. 108 (2009): 10–11.

2. Hemon, "If God Existed," 15, 17.

3. Ekelund and Knausgaard, *Home and Away*, 59.

4. Oxenham, *Finding the Game: Three Years*, 56; Wilson, *Inverting the Pyramid*, 294.

5. The photograph was taken by Agence France-Presse. See http://www.gettyimages.fr/license/107866675.

6. Kittleson, *Country of Football*, 51, 60–61; Nadel, *Fútbol!*, 74–76.

7. Kittleson, *Country of Football*, 62–63; Galeano, *Soccer in Sun and Shadow*, 105–106.

8. Galeano, *Soccer in Sun and Shadow*, 66–67; Kittleson, *Country of Football*, 65.

9. Kittleson, *Country of Football*, 62–63; Galeano, *Soccer in Sun and Shadow*, 105.

10. Kittleson, *Country of Football*, 60–61; Wilson, *Inverting the Pyramid*, 118–119.

11. Wilson, *Inverting the Pyramid*, 118–119.

12. Kittleson, *Country of Football*, 63.

13. Wilson, *Inverting the Pyramid*, 235–236, 239.

14. Dubois, *Soccer Empire*, 95; Nadel, *Fútbol!*, 84; Wilson, *Inverting the Pyramid*, 236.

15. Kittleson, *Country of Football*, 53; Wilson, *Inverting the Pyramid*, 240–242.

16. McIlvanney, *On Football*, 176.

17. Ibid., 177.

18. Ibid., 178.

19. Ibid., 185; Laurent Dubois, "In the Theatre of the World Cup," in *Africa's World Cup: Critical Reflections on Play, Patriotism, Spectatorship, and Space*, ed. Peter Alegi and Chris Bolsmann (Ann Arbor: University of Michigan Press), 210–218.

20. McIlvanney, *On Football*, 180, 186, 188, 190.

21. Ibid., 191–192.

22. Ibid., 192–193.

23. Ibid., 194–196.

24. Ibid., 194.

25. Wilson, *Inverting the Pyramid*, 253.

26. Ibid., 205, 208–209; David Winner, *Brilliant Orange: The Neurotic Genius of Dutch Soccer* (New York: Overlook Press, 2008), 24, 26, 45; Víctor Durà-Vilà, "Why Playing Beautifully Is Morally Better," in *Soccer and Philosophy: Beautiful Thoughts on the Beautiful Game*, ed. Ted Richards (Chicago: Open Court, 2010), 141–148.

27. Wilson, *Inverting the Pyramid*, 209; Winner, *Brilliant Orange*, 28–29, 47.

28. Winner, *Brilliant Orange*, 37–38, 44.

29. Wilson, *Inverting the Pyramid*, 213; Winner, *Brilliant Orange*, 36, 46–47.

30. Wilson, *Inverting the Pyramid*, 211–212.

31. Winner, *Brilliant Orange*, 45.

32. Ibid., 135.

33. Wilson, *Inverting the Pyramid*, 216.

34. Gullit, *How to Watch Soccer*, 67.

35. Winner, *Brilliant Orange*, 58–59.

36. Ibid., 59, 132.

37. Ibid., 57–58.

38. Wilson, *Inverting the Pyramid*, 253.

39. On Zidane's career, see Dubois, *Soccer Empire*, especially chapter 6.

40. *Zidane: A 21st Century Portrait*, directed by Douglas Gordon and Philippe Parreno, (Universal International, 2006).

41. Javier Marías, "Fallen from the Sky," in *The Global Game: Writers on Soccer*, ed. John Turnbull, Thom Satterlee, and Alon Raab (Lincoln, Nebraska: University of Nebraska Press, 2008), 72–73.

42. Marías, "Fallen from the Sky."

43. The goal and interview can be seen here: http://www.dailymotion.com/video/x2ockb_but-de-zidane-contre-le-betis-sevil_sport.

44. Wilson, *The Outsider*, 117.

45. McIlvanney, *On Football*, 179.

46. Lloyd, *When Nobody Was Watching*, 27.

47. Ibid., 56, 63, 113, 137, 147, 189.

48. Ibid., 132.

49. Alicia Rodriguez, "An Ode to Rapinoe's Cross," *SB Nation: Angels on Parade*, July 10, 2011, http://www.angelsonparade.com//2011/7/10/2268925/an-ode-to-rapinoes-cross.

50. Lloyd, *When Nobody Was Watching*, 135, 148.

51. Ibid., 152–154.

52. Ibid., 201–202.

53. Ibid., 209.

54. Ibid., 210–211.

Chapter 4: The Forward

1. "Peamount United Player Scores Wonder Goal," RTÉ News video, 1:44, October 23, 2014, http://youtu.be/dyiI2jZTnhU; "Stephanie Roche Misses Out on FIFA Puskas Award as James Rodriguez Scoops Prize," RTÉ News, January 13, 2015, http://www.rte.ie/sport/soccer/2015/0112/672049-stephanie-roche/.

2. Gail J. Newsham, *In a League of Their Own! The Dick, Kerr Ladies Football Team* (London: Scarlet Press, 1997), 2; Jean Williams, *A Game for Rough Girls? A History of Women's Football in Britain* (London: Routledge, 2003), 26; Goldblatt, *The Ball Is Round*, 231; early sources on the history of women's football in Britain are collected by Patrick Brennan, "Women's Football" website, http://www.donmouth.co.uk/womens_football/womens_football.html.

3. Newsham, *League of Their Own*, 7–13; Williams, *Game for Rough Girls?*, 27.

4. Newsham, *League of Their Own*, 1–5, 18–19.

5. Newsham, *League of Their Own*, 7–13, 18–19; Williams, *Game for Rough Girls?*, 27; Robert Galvin, *The Football Hall of Fame: The Ultimate Guide to the Greatest Footballing Legends of All Time* (London: Portico, 2008), 11.

6. Newsham, *League of Their Own*, 19, 91–92; Williams, *Game for Rough Girls?*, 51.

7. Newsham, *League of Their Own*, 24–29, 32–39.

8. Ibid., 41–46; Williams, *Game for Rough Girls?*, 46.

9. Newsham, *League of Their Own*, 46–50.

10. Ibid., 51–54.

11. Ibid., 51, 55–58.

12. Ibid., 61–67.

13. Ibid., 66.

14. Ibid., 68; Andrei S. Markovits and Emily K. Albertson, *Sportista: Female Fandom in the United States* (Philadelphia: Temple University Press, 2012), 72–72; Oxenham, *Under the Lights*, 165.

15. Newsham, *League of Their Own*, 76.

16. Wilson, *Inverting the Pyramid*, 34.

17. Galeano, *Soccer in Sun and Shadow*, 140; Villoro, *God Is Round*, 171; *Maradona by Kusturica*, directed by Emir Kusturica (Telecinco Films, 2008); Nadel, *Fútbol!*, 48.

18. Maradona, *El Diego*, 1–6.

19. Ibid., 6; Galeano, *Soccer in Sun and Shadow*, 139–140.

20. Maradona, *El Diego*, 14–17.

21. Ibid., 70; Villoro, *God Is Round*, 193–194.

22. Nadel, *Fútbol!*, 46, 50–53; Galeano, *Soccer in Sun and Shadow*, 30–31.

23. Wilson, *Inverting the Pyramid*, 28–29; Nadel, *Fútbol!*, 53–55; Galeano, *Soccer in Sun and Shadow*, 30–31; Robert Farris Thompson, *Tango: The Art History of Love* (New York: Pantheon Books, 2005).

24. Wilson, *Inverting the Pyramid*, 34–35.

25. Ibid., 187.

26. Ibid., 245–246.

27. Ibid., 245–247; Grant Farred, *Long Distance Love: A Passion for Football* (Philadelphia: Temple University Press, 2008), 60–81.

28. McIlvanney, *On Football*, 257.

29. Villoro, *God Is Round*, 170; Maradona, *El Diego*, 87–88, 108.

30. Maradona, *El Diego*, 110–111; McIlvanney, *On Football*, 260–261.

31. Maradona, *El Diego*, 124, 127–128; McIlvanney, *On Football*, 260.

32. Maradona, *El Diego*, 130.

33. Ibid., 13, 130; McIlvanney, *On Football*, 265–266.

34. Maradona, *El Diego*, 128–129.

35. "Poesía de Victor Hugo Morales," *Taringa*, May 3, 2010, http://www.taringa.net/posts/videos/5380748/Poesia-de-Victor-Hugo-Morales.html; Gotan Project, "La Gloria," in *Tango 3.0*, (XL Recordings, 2010).

36. Maradona, *El Diego*, 131; McIlvanney, *On Football*, 262, 266.

37. Maradona, *El Diego*, 54–55.

38. Didier Drogba, *Commitment: My Autobiography* (London: Hodder & Stoughton, 2015), 3–9.

39. Drogba, *Commitment*, 15–18, 22.

40. Ibid., 39–40, 45–46, 141.

41. Goldblatt, *Game of Our Lives*, 70.

42. Drogba, *Commitment*, 59–60, 73–74; Christian Bromberger, *Le match de football: ethnologie d'une passion partisane à Marseille, Naples et Turin* (Paris: Editions de la Maison des Sciences de l'Homme, 1995).

43. Drogba, *Commitment*, 62–63, 188.

44. Ibid., 227, 230.

45. Ibid., 230–236.

46. Ibid., 236–237.

47. Ibid., 243–244.

48. Ibid., 244–245.

49. Goldblatt, *Game of Our Lives*, 70.

50. Todd Cleveland, "The Empire Strikes Back (or How Africa Won Euro 2016 for Portugal)," *Africa Is a Country*, July 14, 2016, http://africasacountry.com /2016/07/the-empire-strikes-back/.

51. Hornby, *Fever Pitch*, 191.

Chapter 5: The Manager

1. Alegi, *African Soccerscapes*, 46.

2. The most detailed study of the FLN team is Michel Nait-Challal, *Dribbleurs de l'indépendance: L'incroyable histoire de l'équipe de football du FLN Algérien* (Paris: Editions Prolongations, 2008); I draw here on a fuller analysis presented in Dubois, *Soccer Empire*, 180–197.

3. Dubois, *Soccer Empire*, 190–191.

4. Ibid., 190.

5. Nait-Challal, *Dribbleurs de l'indépendance*, 139; Dubois, *Soccer Empire*, 195–196.

6. Dubois, *Soccer Empire*, 196.

7. Sartre, *Critique of Dialectical Reason*, 450–452, 456–462.

8. Sartre, *Critique of Dialectical Reason*, 451.

9. Goldblatt, *The Game of Our Lives*, 277; Wilson, *Inverting the Pyramid*, 40–43, 49, 51–52.

10. Wilson, *Inverting the Pyramid*, 40–43, 49, 51–52.

11. Goldblatt, *Game of Our Lives*, 277–278; Goldblatt, *The Ball Is Round*, 447–448; Adam Powley and Robert Gillan, *Shankly's Village: The Extraordinary Life and Times of Glenbuck and Its Famous Sons* (Worthing, UK: Pitch Publishing, 2015); Farred, *Long Distance Love*, 9.

12. Goldblatt, *Game of Our Lives*, 278; James Corbett, "Bill Shankly: Life, Death and Football," *Guardian*, October 17, 2009.

13. Wilson, *Inverting the Pyramid*, 220.

14. Ibid., 220, 233.

15. Ibid., 224.

16. Ibid., 226–227.

17. Ibid., 229; Hornby, *Fever Pitch*, 125.

18. Wilson, *Inverting the Pyramid*, 307, 309, 319, 366.

19. Ibid., 313.

20. Ibid., 315–317.

21. Ibid., 328, 332.

22. Kittleson, *Country of Football*, 111–112.

23. Wilson, *Inverting the Pyramid*, 376.

24. Lloyd, *When Nobody Was Watching*, 157. Sundhage sang the Simon and Garfunkel song in a press conference two days before the 2011 World Cup final; the scene is captured here: http://youtu.be/TB1orJJX3dM.

25. Goldblatt, *Game of Our Lives*, 16.

26. Goldblatt, *Game of Our Lives*, 4–5.

27. "World Record Football Transfer Fees," BBC Sport, September 1, 2013, http://www.bbc.com/sport/football/23560273; Dubois, *Soccer Empire*, 95.

28. Alegi, *African Soccerscapes*, 97–103; Raffaele Poli, "Africans' Status in European Football Players' Labour Market," *Soccer & Society* 7, no. 1–2 (2006): 278–291.

29. Kuper and Szymanski, *Soccernomics*, 5, 84; David Kilpatrick, "Nietzsche's Arsenal," in *Soccer and Philosophy: Beautiful Thoughts on the Beautiful Game*, ed. Ted Richards (Chicago: Open Court, 2010), 41.

30. Kuper and Szymanski, *Soccernomics*, 57–58; Kilpatrick, "Nietzche's Arsenal," 42.

31. Kilpatrick, "Nietzche's Arsenal," 39–45.

32. Goldblatt, *Game of Our Lives*, 278–279.

33. Kuper and Szymanski, *Soccernomics*, 82, 84, 90; Wilson, *Inverting the Pyramid*, 307.

34. Goldblatt, *Game of Our Lives*, 279.

35. Ibid., 5, 68.

36. Amy Lawrence, "Arsène Wenger: I'd Tell God That Winning Is Not as Easy as It Looks," *Guardian*, October 21, 2016.

Chapter 6: The Referee

1. "Ontario, Quebec Differ over Soccer Head Scarf Ban," *CBC News*, February 26, 2007, http://www.cbc.ca/news/canada/ottawa/ontario-quebec-differ-over-soccer-head-scarf-ban-1.632266; Heather-Jane Robertson, "Bend It like Azzy," *The Phi Delta Kappan*, May 2007.

2. "Ontario, Quebec Differ over Soccer Head Scarf Ban"; Robertson, "Bend It like Azzy."

3. Murray, *The World's Game*, 37; Goldblatt, 184–185.

4. Elsey, *Citizens and Sportsmen*, 36; Paul Darby, *Africa, Football and FIFA: Politics, Colonialism and Resistance* (London: Frank Cass, 2002); John Sugden and Alan Tomlinson, *FIFA and the Contest for World Football: Who Rules the Peoples' Game?* (Cambridge, UK: Polity Press, 1998).

5. "Rule Against Hijab Stands: World Soccer Body," *CBC News*, March 3, 2007.

6. Galeano, *Soccer in Sun and Shadow*, 11.

7. Gullit, *How to Watch Soccer*, 49; Hornby, *Fever Pitch*, 91.

8. Gullit, *How to Watch Soccer*, 48.

9. Ibid., 48–49.

10. Bromberger, *Le match de football*, 178–179.

11. Bromberger, "Football as World-View and Ritual," 204.

12. Jan ter Harmsel, "Schumacher Battiston: Referee Corver Explains," *Dutch Referee Blog*, June 3, 2010, http://www.dutchreferee.com/charles-korver-about-battiston-and-schumacher/; Jan ter Harmsel, "Charles Corver: Dutch Referee of the Century," *Dutch Referee Blog*, November 29, 2016, http://www.dutchreferee.com/charles-corver-referee-century/.

13. *The Referee*, directed by Mattias Löw, (SVT Play, 2010), 28:31, http://vimeo.com/13425028.

14. Harmsel, "Charles Corver."

15. Galeano, *Soccer in Sun and Shadow*, 10–11.

16. Paul Kennedy, "Thank You, Koman Coulibaly," *Soccer America Daily*, June 19, 2010, https://www.socceramerica.com/article/38567/thank-you-koman-coulibaly.html.

17. Rosie DiManno, "Soccer Rulers Waffle on Hijab Issue," *Toronto Star*, March 5, 2007; Safia Lakhani, "Sporting the Veil: Representations of Asmahan Mansour in the Canadian Media," *Topia: Canadian Journal of Cultural Studies* 19 (Spring 2008): 85–98.

18. Curtis R. Ryan, "The Politics of FIFA and the Hijab," *Foreign Policy*, February 28, 2012.

19. Awista Ayub, "A Closer Look at FIFA's Hijab Ban: What It Means for Muslim Players and Lessons Learned," *SAIS Review of International Affairs* 31, no. 1 (2011): 43–45; Ryan, "The Politics of FIFA and the Hijab."

20. Andy Radia, "9 Year Old Quebec Girl Banned from Soccer Game for Wearing Hijab," *Yahoo News*, July 10, 2012, http://ca.news.yahoo.com/blogs/canada-politics/9-old-quebec-girl-banned-soccer-game-wearing-182157253.html.

Chapter 7: The Fan

1. "Fenerbahce Only Allowed to Admit Women and Children," BBC Sport, September 21, 2011, http://www.bbc.com/sport/football/14998237.

2. A video of the stands is here: http://youtu.be/1norC4txlTc.

3. Hornby, *Fever Pitch*, 192.

4. Farred, *Long Distance Love*, 15–16.

5. Hornby, *Fever Pitch*, 12, 20, 119.

6. Gumbrecht, *Athletic Beauty*, 207; Hornby, *Fever Pitch*, 175, 207.

7. Hornby, *Fever Pitch*, 76, 127–128, 156.

8. Gumbrecht, *Athletic Beauty*, 72, 205, 213–214; Markovits and Albertson, *Sportista*, 128–129.

9. Hoyningen-Huene, "Why Is Football So Fascinating?," 7, 9–11; Bromberger, "Football as World-View and Ritual," 293–311.

10. Ekelund and Knausgaard, *Home and Away*, 284.

11. Galeano, *Soccer in Sun and Shadow*, 33.

12. Goldblatt, *The Ball Is Round*, 543–545, 598–601.

13. Bill Buford, *Among the Thugs* (New York: Vintage, 1990), 198–205.

14. Gumbrecht, *Athletic Beauty*, 215–216; Hornby, *Fever Pitch*, 173, 178–179.

15. Garry Robson, *No One Likes Us, We Don't Care: The Myth and Reality of Millwall Fandom* (Oxford: Berg, 2000), 80–82, 87.

16. Nadel, *Fútbol!*, 82–83.

17. Farred, *Long Distance Love*, 15.

18. Ibid., 8–9, 15.

19. Laura Fair, *Pastimes and Politics: Culture, Community and Identity in Post-Abolition Urban Zanzibar, 1890–1945* (Athens, Ohio: Ohio University Press, 2001), 235–236, 242.

20. Fair, *Pastimes and Politics*, 236–237; Alegi, *African Soccerscapes*, 30–34.

21. Alegi, *African Soccerscapes*, 43.

22. Ly, *Foot-Ball*, 302–303.

23. Ibid.; Alegi, *African Soccerscapes*, 43, 59–60.

24. Ly, *Foot-Ball*, 303.

25. Ly, *Foot-Ball*, 19.

26. Peter Alegi, *Laduma!: Soccer, Politics and Society in South Africa* (Scottsville, South Africa: University of KwaZulu-Natal Press, 2004); Chuck Korr and Marvin Close, *More Than Just a Game: Soccer vs. Apartheid* (New York: St. Martin's Press, 2010); Anna Zacharias, "Only a Game? Not in Egypt," *The National*, June 24, 2014.

27. Elsey, *Citizens and Sportsmen*, 207–241.

28. Ibid., 242–243.

29. Dubois, *Soccer Empire*, 177–197.

30. Robbie Rogers, *Coming Out to Play* (New York: Penguin, 2014).

31. *Offside*, directed by Jafar Panahi (Sony Pictures, 2006).

32. Markovits and Albertson, *Sportista*, 155, 235–236, 242–243; J. Danielle, "Female Sports Fans and the Men Who Judge Them," *Jezebel*, February 4, 2011, http://jezebel.com/5752163/female-sports-fans-and-the-men-who-judge-them.

33. Panahi, *Offside*.

34. Goldblatt, *Game of Our Lives*, 17.

35. Wilson, *Inverting the Pyramid*, 280; "Watch This Soccer Announcer's Raucous Takedown of England After Iceland Victory," *PBS NewsHour*, June 28, 2016, http://www.pbs.org/newshour/rundown/manager-quits-after-english-soccer-iced-out-of-euro-2016/.

36. *Zidane: A 21st Century Portrait*.

37. Rory Smith, "How Video Games Are Changing the Way Soccer Is Played," *New York Times*, October 13, 2016.

38. *The Cup*, directed by Khyentse Norbu (Festival Media, 1999); *The Great Match*, directed by Gerardo Olivares (Film Movement, 2006).

39. *Life and Nothing More*, directed by Abbas Kiarostami (Farabi Film Foundation/Facets Video, 1996).

40. Dubois, *Soccer Empire*, 28.

41. Émile Durkheim, *The Elementary Forms of the Religious Life* (New York: Free Press, 1965).

42. Ekelund and Knausgaard, *Home and Away*, 284.

43. Ekelund and Knausgaard, *Home and Away*, 15; Laurent Dubois, "Paul Pogba's Joyful, Exuberant Moment of Brilliance Was the Play of Euro 2016," *Slate*, July 9, 2016.

44. Uroš Zupan, "Beauty Is Nothing but the Beginning of a Terror We Can Hardly Bear," in *The Global Game: Writers on Soccer*, ed. John Turnbull, Thom Satterlee, and Alon Raab (Lincoln, Nebraska: University of Nebraska Press, 2008), 177.

45. Ekelund and Knausgaard, *Home and Away*, 90–91.

46. "Haiti 1, Italy 0," *New York Times*, June 14, 2010.

47. Anne Delbée, *La 107e minute* (Paris: Quatre Chemins, 2006); Ekelund and Knausgaard, *Home and Away*, 244.

48. Laurent Dubois and Achille Mbembe, "Pourqoui nous aimons le vuvuzela," *Mediapart*, July 2, 2010, https://blogs.mediapart.fr/edition/la-balle-au-bond

/article/020710/pourquoi-nous-aimons-le-vuvuzela; Laurent Dubois, "In the Theatre of the World Cup," 210–218.

49. Gumbrecht, *Athletic Beauty*, 230–231.

50. Gumbrecht, *Athletic Beauty*, 32; Galeano, *Soccer in Sun and Shadow*, 1; Zupan, "Beauty Is Nothing," 181.

INDEX

Laurent Dubois is a professor of romance studies and history at Duke University, where he teaches the popular course Soccer Politics. The prize-winning author of five books, including *The Banjo*, *Haiti*, and *Soccer Empire*, he lives in Durham, North Carolina.

Photograph by Joel Elliot, National Humanities Center